Learning Disabilities Handbook
A Technical Guide to Program Development

Contributors

Robert F. Algozzine
The Pennsylvania State University
Assistant Professor

Sandra K. Alper
University of Iowa
Instructor at Northern Illinois University

Debora G. Boeck
Model Learning Disabilities Systems
Educational Specialist

David G. Carter
The Pennsylvania State University
Associate Professor

Glenn G. Foster
Model Learning Disabilities Systems
Co-director

Sidney R. Miller
Northern Illinois University
Assistant Professor

James H. Reese
Model Learning Disabilities Systems
Educational Specialist

David A. Sabatino
Northern Illinois University
Professor and Chairman
Model Learning Disabilities Systems
Co-director

Carl R. Schmidt
Model Learning Disabilities Systems
Educational Specialist

Edited
by
David A. Sabatino

LEARNING DISABILITIES HANDBOOK: A TECHNICAL GUIDE TO PROGRAM DEVELOPMENT

Northern Illinois
University Press

DeKalb   1976

Dedicated to:

Two educational administrators
who unselfishly serve learning-
disabled children in a school
district and an intermediate
administrative unit
    Mr. Earl Bonnett
    Dr. William Miller

      and

a very special friend and advocate of all handicapped
persons
    Dr. William Ohrtman

This manual was developed as part of Pennsylvania's
Service Demonstration Project—the Tyrone Model—
and is supported by a research grand under Title
VI-G from the United States Office of Education,
Bureau of Education of the Handicapped.

Contents

CONTENTS

Glen G. Foster and David A. Sabatino

6   INSTRUCTIONAL MATERIALS FOR LEARNING-DISABLED CHILDREN
James H. Reese and Carl R. Schmidt

CONTENTS

CONTENTS

Illustrations

Preface

You have in your hands an unusual book; neither textbook to be memorized nor handbook to be followed dutifully, this book is a crossbreed which integrates the knowledge gained from *operating* programs for children needing some additional educational assistance with that derived from research and applied literature. It is not strictly speaking a "how-to-do-it" manual; but it most certainly does present guidelines in many areas of program establishment and maintenance—instruction, instructional materials, inservice, parent participation, and evaluation among them—that will be found useful for the creation, operation, and effective survival of new child service programs. Covering, as it does, the whole temporal path from program initiation through evaluation, this book transmits specific advice from professionals who have operated programs (note that many worksheets and other data-logging devices are included).

Much of the professional experience distilled into this book represents the cooperative efforts of many individuals and agencies. Dr. Sabatino's immediate colleagues and their contributions are cited. Fiscal and substantive backing for the Tyrone, Pennsylvania, program represents, in my opinion, one of the most successful cooperative ventures in the history of federal learning disability funding. Operating under extremely deleterious budget conditions, the United States Office of Education, Bureau of Education for the Handicapped (BEH, USOE) provided funds for states presenting the most promising programs for learning-disabled children to establish model centers. The Pennsylvania State Department of Education had a well-established relationship with Pennsylvania State University, a relationship woefully infrequent between state departments of education and state universities. Dr. William Ohrtman, State Director of Special

Education, and Dr. David Sabatino, Professor of School Psychology at Penn State, worked together with BEH, USOE to develop one of the early model centers—the Tyrone Center, from which the ideas in this book were developed, tested, and forged into effective tools.

I was fortunate to visit the Pennsylvania Child Service Demonstration Project in 1973 and 1974 as the Research and Evaluation Director for the Leadership Training Institute in Learning Disabilities, itself a federally funded technical assistance program of BEH, USOE for the Model Centers based at the College of Education, Department of Special Education, University of Arizona. At Tyrone, I saw a unique phenomenon: University faculty and students, state personnel, and local administrators and teachers working together to produce a model program with federal monies for the children of Pennsylvania. No other state program in my experience hinged so heavily on state education department-university cooperation.

This book represents the intellectual power and its application that derives from the cooperative unit that was Tyrone, Pennsylvania State University, Pennsylvania State Department of Education, and BEH, USOE. That the small sum of money allotted to the Tyrone project was not lost in a budget as large as Pennsylvania's is a tribute to Dr. Sabatino and his colleagues. They have provided us a well-guided tour through their model learning disability center and given us words of advice, record-keeping forms as tools, and an integrating perspective as benchmarks for the establishment and continuation of other child service centers.

When again charged with the task of assisting new child-service programs, I will look upon this book as a tremendously useful companion. I think local programs can gain a wealth of detailed information from this book—more than any two-day federal consultant could even hope to provide. I hope you will allot the time to learn from the efforts of Sabatino and his colleagues.

Gerald M. Senf, Ph.D.
University of Illinois, Chicago
July 1975

Learning Disabilities Handbook
A Technical Guide to Program Development

1 A Continuum of Programs and Services

David A. Sabatino

FOLLOWING World War II, classes for so-called educable retarded children grew rapidly in this country. By the mid-1950s the number of special education classes in many states was doubling annually. It became obvious to most special educators and school psychologists that other groups of educationally handicapped children existed besides those with mental retardation. There was, in fact, a group of children who were normal in intelligence but who were not achieving academically. A report from the United States Health, Education, and Welfare Secretary's National Advisory Committee on Dyslexia and Related Reading Disorders (1969) stated that eight million children in America's schools will not learn to read adequately and that from three to five million of these children have average or above average intelligence. The question becomes one of definition: Are learning problems, learning disorders, learning disabilities, and minimal brain damage all one in the same? Or do they merely represent different problems of children from the same group? The answer is that a child who fails to learn may be minimally brain-damaged and have a measured perceptual/language problem. Another child may have exactly the same diagnosis and learn to read very well. "Learning disabilities" refers to a difficulty in academic achievement in at least one subject area, accompanied by a measured perceptual and/or language development problem. "Learning disabilities" differs from "learning disorders" in that a child with a learning disorder will not evidence a perceptual/language difficulty and will therefore not be categorized as a handicapped child. But most children who fail to learn to read (reading problem) do not happen to have measured perceptual-language impairments (learning disability) and are instead average or above intellectually, with academic reading problems (learning disorder). Minimal brain damage is characterized by overt behaviors, hyperactivity, distractability, etc., in the absence of any clinical signs or cerebral pathology or insults. What, then, is a learning disability? Before discussion can continue on the subject, the problem of definition should be reviewed.

Although the term *learning disabilities* is recent, professionals have been concerned with children who have problems in learning since the early part of the nineteenth century. Professionals in the medical field, psychologists, and educators have attempted to determine why children with normal intelligence (according to standardized psychometric tests) have difficulty learning and have hypothesized various reasons and causal factors.

Historically, the study of the learning disabled can be traced as proceeding through three major developmental phases: foundation, transition, and integration (Wiederholt, 1974). [See Figure 1.] These major phases are by no means rigid, as there is considerable overlapping in all of them. Each phase is characterized, however, by a differing general trend of emphasis which will be described. Throughout each phase, professionals tended to concern themselves with a specific type of learning disorder and work from a theoretical frame of reference accordingly. Thus, Wepman (1960) and Kirk (1963) concerned themselves with disorders of spoken language. Fernald (1943) investigated disorders of the written language. Perceptual and motor dysfunctions were the areas of study by Strauss and Werner (1942), Cruickshank (1961), and Frostig (1967).

The foundation phase existed from about 1800 to 1935. The medical professionals dominated this period, with major emphasis on the pathogenesis and causes (etiology) for specific learning disorders. Clinical studies on brain-damaged adults (before and after death) provided much of the information, the results of which were transferred to children exhibiting similar learning disorders. Serious disagreements among respected authorities over what part of the brain controlled what act of learning flourished, with classical arguments on localization and association of brain function.

Psychologists and educators provided the basis for most of the theories developed during the transition phase (1921-1960). While some professionals (mostly physicians) were still concerning themselves with etiology, the emphasis was shifted from the search for causes to instructional remediation and behavioral management. Educational interventions designed to assist children in overcoming learning disorders flourished. Theories offered during the foundation phase were utilized as the rationale for many of the remedial educational programs developed. Differences in the educational intervention used instructionally reflected the view of a particular authority working in the field at the time. Thus, Cruickshank (1961) developed an educational program to remedy learning problems stemming from perceptual and motor disorders, while Wepman (1960) was concerned with disorders of the spoken language and developed useful diagnostic tools and treatment methods in that area.

Now we are in the integration phase of the study of learning disabilities, according to Wiederholt (1974). In the last fifteen years the field has witnessed rapid growth, exhibiting a versatility to utilize a broad range of

Figure 1

Developmental-phase dimension	Type-of-disorder dimension		
	Disorders of spoken language	Disorders of written language	Disorders of perceptual and motor processes
Foundation phase	Gail 1802 Bouillaud 1825 Broca 1861 Jackson 1864 Bastien 1869 Wernicke 1881 Marie 1906 Head 1926	Hinshelwood 1917 Orton 1925	Goldstein 1927 Strauss and Werner 1933
Transition phase	Osgood 1953 Wepman 1960 Kirk 1961 Myklebust 1954 McGinnis 1963 Eisenson 1954	Monroe 1928 Fernald 1921 Kirk 1940 Gillingham 1946 Spalding 1957	Lehtinen 1941 Kephart 1955 Cruickshank 1961 Getman 1962 Frostig 1964 Barsch 1965
Integration phase	The field of learning disabilities 1963-		

A TWO-DIMENSIONAL FRAMEWORK IN THE STUDY AND REMEDIATION OF LEARNING DISABILITIES

J. Lee Wiederholt, *The Second Review of Special Education* (Pennsylvania: JSE Press, 1974), p. 105.

teaching materials and methods. An eclectic approach to learning disabilities has evolved. Diagnosis and an appropriate prescriptive program to remediate learning disabilities is now the accepted approach by most educators. The major problem is to establish the rules for formulating a teaching prescription based upon extant diagnostic evidence. Moreover, the field has not yet achieved any organized sense of direction, synthesis, or amalgamation of its theories, empirical data, methods, or beliefs into a usable integrated whole. Taxonomies, definitions, and the ordering process by which descriptive terminology is provided have not yet occurred. It is for that reason that the systems approach brings some degree of order to our confused state.

The Problem of Choosing a Definition

Obviously, one of the continuing debates within the field of learning disabilities is that of definition. Vaughan and Hodges (1973) reported collecting thirty-eight definitions of *learning disabilities.* The confusion over definition can be attributed to the fact that learning disabilities have not been the sole responsibility of special education. Several other disciplines such as psychology, medicine, and optometry have vested interests in the field of learning disabilities. As a result, a plethora of definitions has been posed, each attempting to satisfy the needs of the particular discipline it represents.

The Task Force I project (Clements, 1966) was concerned with terminology and definition. The task force recommended the use of the term *minimal brain dysfunction* rather than the term *learning disability* because the disturbances in learning behavior, attributable to a dysfunction of the nervous system, extend further than the classroom situation. This task force defined children with minimal brain dysfunction as "near average, average or above average general intelligence with certain learning or behavioral disabilities ranging from mild to severe which are associated with deviations of function of the central nervous system" (p. 9).

Two years later, in 1968, the National Advisory Committee on Handicapped Children reported to Congress that one of the critical areas of education for the handicapped was that of children with learning disabilities. The committee expressed the urgent need for more extensive research on etiology, diagnosis, and remediation in this field and the urgent need for trained teachers, particularly in special education.

The confusion over definition seemed to be ended when Congress included in Federal legislation (P.L. 91-230) the definition formulated by the National Advisory Committee on Handicapped Children (1968). The Federal definition reads as follows:

> Children with special learning disabilities exhibit a disorder in one or more of the basic psychological processes involved in understanding or using spoken or written language. These may be manifested in disorders of listening, talking, reading, writing, spelling or arithmetic. They include conditions which have been referred to as perceptual handicaps, brain injury, minimal brain dysfunction, dyslexia, developmental aphasia, etc. They do not include learning problems which are due primarily to visual, hearing or motor handicaps, to mental retardation, emotional disturbance, or to environmental disadvantage.

Unfortunately, the enactment of the National Advisory Committee's definition into Federal legislation has not provided consensus on definition. Hammill (1972) has contested the Federal definition on the grounds that it is impractical and insufficiently educational in focus for school use. While nebulous definitions may stimulate research in academic circles, the working special education administrator cannot afford the pleasures associated with academic rhetoric. His time is consumed by many duties, and a definition that cannot be anchored to policies and easily interpreted into procedural statements will invariably cause administrative confusion and inconsistency. The problem in using the Federal definition is that it more nearly states what a learning disability is not than what it is. McCarthy (1971) has quoted Gallagher as saying, "Whenever you start to define a horse, you first have to define a nonhorse (p. 14)." The nonhorse portion, or the exclusion clause, of the Federal definition is quite specific, i.e., whatever the learning disabled child is, he is not disabled due to a hearing, visual, or motor handicap, mental retardation, emotional disturbance, or environmental deprivation.

Beginning in the early 1960s and ending with the 1968 Federal definition, the definitions have made a distinction between minimal brain injury and learning disability. Learning disability appears to be closely associated with perceptual-language problems but generally cannot be diagnosed as clinical brain damage. The conventional, rigid classification of children (e.g., mentally retarded, brain-damaged, emotionally disturbed), based on categorization by IQ and other clinical determinants, has proven to be not only inflexible but dysfunctional, resulting in increased professional rule-bending. To avoid this problem, the Federal definition of *learning disabilities* may be adopted, since it is highly flexible.

The difficulty is in operationalizing that definition for practical use in the schools. Simply, the definition implies that the following four characteristics taken together are indicative of learning disability:

1. *Normal intelligence.* The child is able to perform at or above the normal range (IQ 85) on nonverbal language conceptual measures.

2. *Perceptual-language deficits.* Practically all learning disability theories hypothesize that when the perceptual reception of a stimulus is interfered with and the symbolic quality of that information is distorted (lost prematurely due to faulty retention function, or improperly sequenced and arranged), a deficit in perceptual performance is involved. A body of literature supports the supposition that both visual and auditory perceptual difficulties associated with the reception or expression of language relate (correlate statistically) to academic achievement deficits of children experiencing failure in school.

3. *Academic-achievement deficit.* An academic achievement deficit exists in a given subject (e.g., reading, quantitative skills, etc.). *Deficit* is defined as an inability to score above a given percentile on standardized achievement tests measuring proficiency in a subject area. This point could be adjusted to fall between the 20th and 30th percentiles for the normative population.

4.   *The absence of other primary handicapping conditions.*   Visual or
hearing impairment, mental retardation, severe cultural neglect, or
severe emotional disturbance might be examples of this.

The above characteristics enhance the identification of learning-disabled children on a broad spectrum of behavioral dysfunctions. It has become popular to regard the clinical categorical conditions only as labels and to include in the definition of learning disabilities all children, handicapped or not, who experience difficulty with academics or social adjustment to school. This diffuse interpretation of the term destroys its meaning, rendering it useless. In actuality, about 22 percent of the school population are learning disturbed (academically retarded), while about 2 percent to 4 percent are learning disabled.

To reiterate, it would appear that the concern for learning-disabled children has grown from work with the educable mentally retarded and brain-injured, and is related to programming for the emotionally disturbed. It is a recent area of interest and concern. The education of children with learning disabilities has overwhelming implications for both special and regular education, since these problems could be the most common of the so-called handicapping conditions.

CARE MUST BE TAKEN *NOT* TO CONSIDER EVERY CHILD WITH AN
EDUCATIONAL MISERY AS LEARNING DISABLED. ADDITIONAL CARE
AND CONCERN MUST BE SHOWN FOR AN OPERATIONAL DEFINITION OF
LEARNING DISABILITIES USABLE IN THE SCHOOLS.

Labels such as "perceptual handicaps," "brain injury," "minimal brain dysfunction," "dyslexia," and "developmental aphasia" are often interpreted synonomously with "learning disabilities." Hammill (1972) is correct in stating that these educationally meaningless terms fail to describe characteristics of measurable perceptual, language, or academic difficulties which, when diagnosed, can be treated with remediation programs.

Learning Disabilities—A Mosaic, Not an Entity

The field of learning disabilities is a mosaic, representing the efforts of many disciplines working from many points of view. Within the last decade, children with specific learning disabilities have become the focus of laboratory research, theoretical speculation, and numerous conferences and conventions. The problems associated with specific learning disabilities have been shared by a variety of professional fields, including medicine, psychology, neurology, general and special education, optometry, ophthalmology, audiology, and speech/language. The contributions made by these numerous disciplines are many. Yet the problems related to achieving a global theory that will promote an interdisciplinary attack on the problem of learning disabilities from many fronts simultaneously has not occurred. Consequently, the disciplines associated with learning disabilities tend to work in isolation, on a segment of the problem as each discipline sees it. The result has been piecemeal theorization on definitions that represent this or that point of view. Child identification (screening) procedures to verify those definitions and treatment approaches are too various to mention. The day-to-day clinical procedure, however, is somewhat brighter. Within the framework of farsighted multidisciplinary diagnostic-prognostic therapeutic settings, the disciplines have learned to communicate. Painful as this learning process has been, it has contributed greatly to the management of children with learning disabilities. Schools, communities, and parents have found that a broad spectrum service program including social work, medicine, psychology, special education, etc., contributes to their understanding and assistance in the development of programs for learning-disabled children.

Learning Disabilities—A Part of or Apart from Special Education ?

The critical crossroads in the field of special education have never been as well articulated as they are today. But special education administrators faced with the decision-making responsibility in providing programs for handicapped children can rarely use that clarity (e.g., for mainstreaming or against mainstreaming) in the task of developing beneficial programs.

What is special education, and how does it differ from regular education? Should learning disabilities resource teachers work only with known learning-disabled children, or should all underachievers receive the benefit of their knowledge and skill? What definition of learning disabilities is the right one? And more importantly, what are the components necessary to provide adequate services to learning-disabled children? These are all arguments that have been well stated. The question is how these arguments can be used to assist the working administrator.

Scagliotta (1969) provides a working definition of Special Education when he views it as an applied art that has a native character of its own:

Special Education cannot and should not exist as an accessory to the regular
educational program. It must exist as a separate entity unto itself, providing all the
facilities, services, and opportunities under one roof, and it should be administered
and served by a staff of learning-disability specialists—educational and psychological
(p. 8).

Reger (1972) confirms Scagliotta's concern but senses that the major contribution of special education
is to regular educators. He sees a maximally integrated program effort between regular and special educators.
He charges special educators to facilitate change in the schools, or else by their very presence they are
reinforcing complacency:

Special educators must plan a way around their function as agents who help
to prevent educational change. But it would not be enough simply to eliminate
special education programs; that is too simple a solution; further, it is an
administrative or legislative procedure that ignores what happens to children.
Instead, it is necessary for special educators to get more involved in "regular"
educational programs and to devise ways of effecting the very changes that their
services now discourage, i.e., services which allow regular education to drop its
problem. The special educator who ignores the mainstream of educational
programming, who attempts *only* to build a bigger and better special education
program, is helping to perpetuate a segregated special education empire (p. 355).

Ysseldyke and Sabatino (1972) reflect on a much too rigid special education system when they write:

Self-contained special education classes have failed to increase academic
achievement through the individualization of instruction tailored to "meet the

needs" of the children they serve (Elenbogen, 1957; Cassidy and Stanton, 1959; Thurstone, 1960; Johnson, 1962; Bennett, 1972; Sparks and Blackman, 1965). Special education classes, established primarily in an effort to relieve regular class teachers from the burden of teaching handicapped youngsters, were designed under the faulty assumption that categorically defined handicapped children are best served by homogeneous instructional techniques and materials. We in special education certainly realize by now that labels borrowed from medicine which we have converted into administratively convenient categories lend very little to the type of instruction we provide children. There is no instructional homogeneity in most classes of educable mentally retarded, emotionally disturbed, brain injured and learning disabled children. Special classes may be more aptly described as instructional nightmares in which a single teacher is expected to perform an impossible task.

Special educators have only recently begun to search for creative alternatives to self-contained special class placement (p. 59).

The alternatives to self-contained special classes should be expanded if the myriad of learning and behavioral disorders in the schools are to be properly served. It has been our experience that very few learning-disabled children need to be placed into self-contained classes. From a cost/benefit ratio, classes for learning-disabled children are expensive for the limited number of children contained in them. One such search for a system of creative alternatives is a continuum of services and programs described by Ysseldyke and Sabatino (1972) in a so-called step model (Figure 2).

Figure 2

SIX STEP SEQUENTIAL MODEL FOR N.R.R.C./P. RURAL UNIT

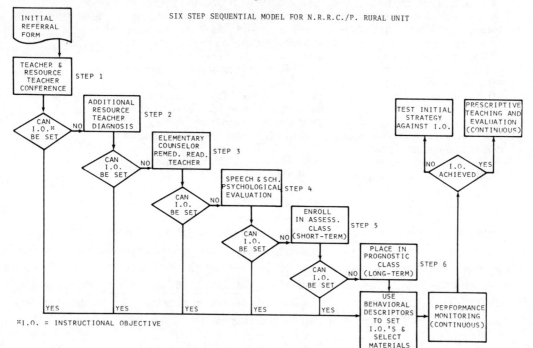

*I.O. = INSTRUCTIONAL OBJECTIVE

Step one begins with the teacher using a referral form similar to the one recommended in Chapter 3, requiring teachers to make a rather precise subjective judgment of a child's capability to perform in the instructional setting.

The referral form must be complete before the resource teachers can begin work in Step 1. Step 1 may lead directly to formulation of instructional objectives based on the behavioral descriptors ascertained from the teacher referral for children who can interact successfully with the regular curriculum and remain in regular classes (mainstreamed).

Step 2 requires the resource teacher to complete an informal diagnosis using instruments he selects. If an appropriate instructional objective can be established on the basis of assessment, then the resource teacher and referring teacher work to sequence and evaluate instructional objectives. Again, the child is mainstreamed.

Step 3 utilizes other personnel who are normally located in the school, such as the remedial reading teacher and elementary counselor. Special diagnostic test batteries which attempt to permit further identification or at least confirmation of the child's problems will be constructed for inclusion as a preplanned package to be tested on the demonstration site. The purpose is to bring together everyone in an elementary school building working on learning difficulties in order that they may (1) support the regular or special class teacher referring the child, (2) learn how to identify and prescribe at some level for learning disabled children, or (3) refer those for whom they cannot plan an instructional objective to the next level. One rather exact criticism of special educators is that they function too frequently in isolation. The system designed in this model eliminates such isolationism.

If an appropriate instructional objective cannot be established in Step 3, the resource person refers to other school personnel not normally assigned to the building but who operate in the district, such as school psychologists and speech therapists. This team, operating under the assumption that several heads are better than one, intensifies the search for those diagnostic keys that promise to open the door to the learning or behavioral disability.

If instructional objectives cannot be written in Step 4 which would allow the establishment of appropriate instructional objectives, the child may be referred to an assessment class structure on a short-term basis.

Step 6 is a long-term diagnostic class (prognostic class) where the children are seen by experienced diagnostic-prescriptive teachers. The size of the prognostic class is limited to five or six children. A child usually remains in the assessment class no longer than 6 weeks and in the prognostic class no longer than 6 months. The purpose in both cases is to return the child to the regular class with a working sequence of instructional objectives. The child's progress toward specific instructional objectives using these prescriptively assigned materials is continuously monitored by the resource teacher in that building (Ysseldyke and Sabatino, 1972, p. 61).

The Resource Concept

The primary thrust of the resource concept is the establishment of a center where specialists are available to provide unique instructional services to learning-disabled students and where such professional personnel can assist regular classroom teachers in servicing these students. Adelman (1972) criticized the resource-room terminology as being too restricted and overly structured. He advocated revising the resource room from a place to a concept, to include a much larger platform for services to handicapped children; hence, it would be "bigger than a room." He writes:

> . . . special education is at a point of critical transition. Current special education programs and categorically oriented educational practices are under attack. Various alternative (but not necessarily new) administrative structures and personnel roles and functions are being propounded as replacements for those practices which have fallen into disrepute. The resource room is a case in point.
>
> . . . the fact that he [Sabatino] focuses on the resource room and derivative approaches may tend to limit the potential impact of the "resource concept" and more generally, may limit the potential impact of special education personnel. Therefore, it is my intention to offer a broader conceptualization [than Sabatino's], first, of the contemporary task of special education and then, of the resource concept (p. 361).

It would appear that what Adelman is saying, in a very diplomatic manner, is that merely to position resource rooms squarely between a self-contained class for regular and handicapped children is to reduce significantly the power and robustness of such a program. That in fact, the responsibilities of resource room teachers are to plan orderly changes, preparing other teachers through daily contact and continuous inservice in the schools to receive handicapped children in their classes (attitudinally), while providing them materials to work with and demonstrating the use of those materials with the children in question. The dichotomy between regular education and special education is currently a critical deterrent to sound program development for learning-disabled children.

A conceptual transition is needed to bridge this formidable abyss. If regular and special educators are going to communicate meaningfully, that opportunity must be provided. Again, it is the desire of this program to keep the handicapped child as near the educational mainstream as possible. Thus, the mission of the resource room personnel must be more than that of performing a direct service to children.   The personnel in resource rooms must focus on obtaining attitudinal change and demonstrating a better way to do things within the structure of the school system, such as altering the view of teachers, parents, administrators, cooks, and custodians.   Reger (1973) emphasizes this mission when he writes:

> The mission of a resource-room program can be to change the schools. . . . First,
> a resource-room program has a teacher-in-action in the school building setting. This
> teacher is the primary agent of change; he or she can concretely demonstrate a
> better way, a new outlook, a different approach. The teacher can show positive
> results while working in concert with other teachers. The resource-room teacher
> can relate changes in a child in a classroom to altered methods and attitudes, and
> can suggest that any teacher could do the same –there is no magic, and there is no
> pathology. . . . Second, the resource-room teacher is not tied constantly to one
> classroom. . . . This teacher shares responsibility for children with all other teachers
> in the building who have children in the program. . . . (p. 16).

It is true that there is a change mission in the role of the clearly overburdened learning disabilities resource teacher. But the awesome and encompassing role places too much responsibility on any one person to bear if he is to continue to see children on a daily basis. Therefore, one alternative is to divide the role of resource teachers into at least two different major functions. The first is to work directly with individual and small groups of children in a direct habilitative and remedial structure.   The second is to work directly with teachers in the role of the strategist. In the discussion of the Tyrone Model continuum of services and programs, the distinction between learning disabilities resource room teachers and strategists will be clearly delineated.

What Are the Advantages of the Resource Room Concept?

The resource-room program attempts to show specific ways
in which all teachers can adapt to provide more effective
and appropriate instruction for more children.

Weiderholt

1.   Mildly handicapped pupils can benefit from specific resource-room training while remaining integrated with their friends and age-mates in school.

2.   Pupils have the advantages of a total remedial program which is prepared by the resource teacher but may be implemented in cooperation with the regular class teacher.

Reger

1.   There is no need to label children placed in the program as traditionally happens in special education programs. Nothing is gained by calling a child "emotionally disturbed" or "an MR." Such labels mean nothing when there is no administrative need to sort groups; they certainly add nothing to a teacher's fund of knowledge for instructional purposes. The focus in the program is upon specifically targeted behavior.

Weiderholt

3.   Resource rooms are less expensive because the teachers are able to serve a greater number of children than in special class programs.

4.   More children's needs can be served under the resource room arrangement than can be served by the present system.

5.   Since the resource teacher is assigned to a particular school (unlike some school psychologists, remedial reading therapists, speech correctionists, or other itinerant staff), he is less likely to be viewed as an "outsider" by the other teachers in the school.   In addition, he probably better understands the programming problems in a particular school.

Reger

2.   Children can be kept in the mainstream of the school. There is no stigma attached to going to the resource room for assistance.

3.   Children have the dual advantages of receiving both large-group instruction and individual or very small-group instruction.

4.   There is greater leeway for flexibility in instructional techniques, for trying alternatives, for varying approaches. The classroom teacher is a major beneficiary of flexibility because of the available feedback.

5.   As fewer children with moderate problems need to be placed into special self-contained classes, many children who have mild problems who would not have been

Weiderholt

6.   Because young children with mild, though developing, problems can be accomodated, later severe disorders may be prevented.

7.   Because disability diagnoses are not necessary for placement purposes, pupils are not labeled in any way as handicapped.

8.   Because the labeling and segregation are avoided, the stigma invariably associated with receiving special attention is minimized

9.   Since most schools are large enough to accomodate one or more resource rooms, pupils can receive help in their neighborhood school.

10.   Pupils are the recipients of flexible

Reger

placed into special classes can receive assistance. This can become very critical for the child who is just beginning his downward spiral which in a few years would send him into a special class. The preventive aspects of the program are enormous.

6.   For schools that tabulate "numbers of special children served," for the same amount of money more children can be served in resource-room programs than in special classes.

7.   For schools that utilize "diagnostic centers," the need for such service is greatly reduced; the resource-room teacher can provide most such services right in the building. An important feature of such on-the-spot service is that it is directly connected in an

Weiderholt

scheduling in that remediation can be applied entirely in their classrooms by the regular teacher with some resource teacher support or in the resource room itself when necessary; also the schedule can be quickly altered to meet the children's changing situations and needs.

11. Because placement in the resource room is an individual school matter involving the principal, the teachers, and the parents, no appreciable time lapse need occur between the teacher's referral and the initiation of special services for the child.

12. Under this alternative, medical and psychological work-ups are done only at the school's request rather than on a screening

Reger

ongoing manner with the child's instructional program, and the evaluation performed is relevant to the problem(s) involved. "Diagnostic centers" that primarily perform a labeling function are assets to administrative placement procedures, but are of little or no use to the child or teacher.

8. Generally, there is much greater parental and community support for a resource-room program than for some other options existing in the typical school. A parent with a child who displays moderate problems is going to be much happier about resource-room placement than about a special class placement.

The major disadvantage for the resource-

Weiderholt

for placement basis; thus, the school psychologist is freed to do the work he was trained to do instead of being relegated to the role of psychometrist.

13.   Since the resource room will absorb most of the "handicapped" children in the schools, the special classes will increasingly become instructional settings for the "truly" handicapped pupils, i.e., the children for whom the classes were originally intended. (1974, p.6)

Reger

room program already has been cited: that it can become subjected to whimsical change. Other problems are related to underfunding, expecting miracles of the program, listless or negative leadership, territorial conflicts with other specialists or nonschool agencies, working from a roving cart, lack of time for discussions with other teachers, etc. However, these problems have been touched upon earlier and will not occur if guidelines are established—and followed.

A final note: No mention has been made about the types of children who could be served in a resource-room program although this was alluded to when it was mentioned that labeling is not necessary. This omission has been deliberate. Every school has its own

definition of "handicap," with so-called objective measures notwithstanding. The resource-
room program allows each school to act upon
its own definition of handicap or disability
and try to resolve its own ecological
educational problems. (1973, pp. 19-21)

The Model Learning Disabilities Continuum

One of the themes hopefully conveyed in this chapter is the necessity of developing the administrative
structures for a total learning disabilities program. It is important that each component be clearly understood
and that alternatives to existing program aspects be permitted to develop, if not encouraged. The whole of
the program must be larger than the sum of its parts. If local school district special education directors seek
only to offer education classes to their constituents, then children will have to be bent to fit programs. The
school psychologist will have to fit children to accomodate the program's faulty and limited dimensions.
Planned program reentry and planned program entry (mainstreaming) of handicapped children into regular
education will not occur. The opportunity for a child to recycle through a regular program for a period of
time, supported by a learning disabilities resource teacher will never be attempted. If a child is to find help
in a resource room or through a learning disabilities strategist, and if the gravity of the child's learning disability

warrants an assessment class placement, then a fully developed continuum of services and programs should be spelled out in detail from the inception of the program.

Before describing the three service alternatives for learning-disabled children as implemented by the model program, it is necessary to clarify the role of the program supervisor. The program supervisor is responsible for the coordination of learning disabilities programs and services with district programs and with other agencies and professional services as needed. This includes:

1)   describing and explaining the program's operational procedures and responsibilities to elementary school faculty and auxiliary personnel, and

2)   coordinating the program's services with those existing in the district, e.g., elementary guidance counselor, reading specialist, speech therapist, and elementary supervisor. The program supervisor is responsible for organizing and implementing screening procedures for identifying children and for assisting the program's teaching staff in diagnosing individual problems of these children and in implementing appropriate intervention strategies. Other responsibilities are:

a)   to coordinate data collection activities for the purpose of program monitoring,

b)   to coordinate the selection and requisition of instructional materials and teaching supplies,

c)   to assist in the development and implementation of curriculum,

d)   to assist in planning and presenting inservice workshops for the base elementary school teachers,

e)   to assist in dissemination of information concerning efforts with local parent-teacher groups and other interested community service organizations.

The program supervisor acts as an ambassador or liaison bewteen the district and program personnel and a supervisor or monitor of activities and progress. A discussion of the supervisor's role in teacher, program, and class evaluation schemes will be covered in detail in the tenth chapter.

Assessment Class Teacher

The assessment class teachers are responsible for diagnosing individual problems of children assigned to them and for providing comprehensive educational programs for each child. The latter includes the implementation of motor training, perceptual training, language activities, development of academic skills (reading, arithmetic, spelling, writing), academic remedial activities, and modification of inappropriate classroom behavior patterns. They are responsible for keeping the regular classroom teachers informed of the progress of the children in the assessment class. This can be accomplished through informal talks, regularly scheduled conferences, and progress reports. They are also responsible for preparing both the child and the regular class teacher for the child's reentry into the regular classroom. It is important that the assessment class teacher and regular class teacher cooperate in this effort so that the transition is smooth and that specific instructional or management strategies began in the resource room will continue in the regular classes.

Assessment Class

The operational aspects of the assessment class are:

1.   *Population:*   Those elementary pupils who have been identified by the screening program and whose problems are of such a nature that they warrant intensive educational intervention.

2.   *Curriculum:*   Provides individualized informal assessment using direct remedial materials from reading, arithmetic, spelling, and writing. Appropriate supplemental activities in the areas of visual and auditory perception, language, and motor training are also important. Emphasis is placed on the modification of inappropriate classroom behaviors and the development of positive self-concepts.

3.   *Enrollment:*   Six pupils maximum enrollment depending upon the number of teachers and aides—and the role of the aides.

4.   *Length of enrollment:*   This class is not a permanent placement for any child. The child is re-evaluated on a schedule of six-week instructional blocks, and it is decided whether the child remains in the class for another six-week block of instruction or returns to his regular class with resource room support.

5.   *Staffing:*   At least one learning disabilities teacher and one teacher aide; two teachers are ideal.

6.   *Ancillary services:*   The assessment class teacher has supportive services from the program's school psychologist and program supervisor and the district's guidance counselor and speech therapist. The delivery of these services is of prime importance and, therefore, receives priority over other requests.

Although the assessment class services a smaller number of children than the typical special class, it should be housed in a classroom with 450 square feet of space so that the teacher can implement learning and skill centers for both small group and individual instruction, a "time-out" area, and a free-play area.   The teacher and aide should not have to lose valuable time setting up and putting away materials and equipment as activities change, as they would have to do in a smaller room without work stations.   The classroom should have work tables for each learning center, pupil desks for individual work, and folding screens and carrells to provide privacy for the children as they require it.

The basic furniture for implementing the ideal assessment class would be as follows:

2	rectangular tables
4	round tables
24	chairs
1	storage cabinet
1	filing cabinet
2	storage shelves with rollers
4	folding screens
2	mobile A-V carts

Special Education Resource Teacher

The special education resource teacher provides direct services to individuals and small groups of children, and strategist services to classroom teachers. In the first role, the resource teacher is responsible for the instructional assessment of the children assigned to him and the preparation and delivery of individualized developmental and/or remedial programs. In this capacity, he teaches six or seven instructional periods per day (9:00 to 12:00, 1:00 to 3:00). During the remainder of the school day, he fulfills his strategist role. In this role he assists regular teachers in establishing instructional objectives for referred children, in obtaining suitable teaching methods and instructional materials to augment these objectives, in demonstrating materials and curriculum frequently used in regular or special classes with groups or total classes for short blocks of time, and in establishing behavior management programs when necessary. The resource teacher serves one building and is available to the teachers the entire school day. He also assists the assessment teacher when a child from his building is returning from the assessment to his regular class. We strongly recommend that the resource teacher provide a direct service schedule to the children on a four-day basis. The fifth day should be coordination day, providing opportunity to prepare inservices, see parents, organize paraprofessional activities, etc.

Resource Room

The operational aspects of the resource room are:

1.   *Population:* The resource room serves pupils in all grades who are identified by the screening procedures but whose problems are not severe enough to warrant placement in a full-time self-contained class or the assessment class. In the high school we recommend a learning center with equipment to provide reader service, time-recorded lessons, and other types of programmed self-help lessons.

2.   *Curriculum:*   The resource room teacher provides individualized instruction in perceptual training, language development, motor training, and academic skill development and implements activities for social and emotional development.

3.   *Enrollment:*   For any given eight-week instructional block, the minimum enrollment seen is no less than sixteen children a day; that is, the resource teacher should service at least sixteen different children a day. For the school year, the resource teacher should serve a minimum of thirty children. She can do this by working two-day schedules for some groups and four-day schedules for others. Children should progress through individualized work into group activities. Generally, the more rapidly this change occurs the better.

4.   *Length of enrollment:*   The length of enrollment is dependent upon individual progress. Pre-post evaluations are conducted following each eight-week instructional block. These evaluations determine whether a child continues in the resource room for another eight-week instructional block, returns full-time to his regular class, or perhaps is referred for enrollment in the assessment class or other special setting. Daily criterion-referenced evaluations serve to validate the instruction void.

5.   *Instructional Periods:*   Children receive instruction in either one-to-one situations or in groups not exceeding three pupils for any given instructional session.   Instructional sessions are for a minimum of 20 minutes and a maximum of 45 minutes.   Children should be seen, whether on an individual basis or in group sessions, for at least three instructional periods per week.   Massed daily practice is recommended for short periods with some children.

6.   *Staffing:*   Each resource room is staffed by a certified special education teacher who is trained as a learning disabilities resource teacher (not just a self-contained class teacher).

A resource room should not be located in full-sized classrooms. There is no ideal setting, but broom closets and the corner of the stage are not good places. However, a room with at least 140 square feet of space to store material for the year is excellent. The room should have all the comfort characteristics of a regular classroom—adequate lighting, ventilation, temperature control—and should receive as much consideration and maintenance as a regular classroom. But it should not look like a regular classroom. It should provide the child with a break from that atmosphere. A resource teacher should not have to share the nurses' rooms or the library or work in a "castoff" room located in the basement of the school. The resource room should be easily accessible to the children and teachers. A resource room teacher is in a school to help children and support the regular classroom teachers; his/her facilities should help promote such activities.

Basic furniture for each resource room is as follows:

1	rectangular table
4	chairs
1	filing cabinet
1	storage cabinet (wood)
1	portable chalkboard
1	bulletin board
2	pupil desks

Special Education Strategist

The special education strategist is both an extension of and an alternative to the resource teacher. The operational difference between the resource teacher and the strategist is that the strategist spends very little time providing direct services to individuals or groups of children, and works in support of the regular class teachers providing them with instructional and behavioral management techniques. The resource teacher usually works with a limited number of children in just a few buildings, providing direct services to children as a primary function. The strategist is responsible for the diagnostic work-ups of the children assigned to him and generally works in several schools. In this case the diagnostic work-up includes classroom observation, instructional assessment, and several instructional periods. Once the strategist has obtained sufficient information for programming the child, he discusses this information with the classroom teacher, and they come to a mutual agreement about how the classroom teacher can provide for the child in the classroom. The strategist monitors the child's progress and the teacher's implementation of the program by scheduling two visitations per week. Once the teacher has the program operating smoothly and on a regular basis, the strategist can reduce the conferences to one per week. If the initial program proves unsuccessful, the stratigist and teacher have the option of altering the program and recommending or requesting additional services from district and program personnel.

The purpose of the observational periods is to give the strategist more definitive information concerning what the child has been taught and how the material was presented. Once he has completed the classroom observation and instructional assessment, he establishes an instructional objective for the child. He then initiates a search for an appropriate match between the child's learning characteristics and an instructional material and/or strategy to achieve success through an initial teaching prescription. Thus the strategist can make fairly specific recommendations to the classroom teacher.

The strategist, unlike the resource teacher, does not have a specific teaching room, and he retrieves needed materials from the program's Instructional Materials Center or borrows from the resource teacher. Although the strategist's major role is assisting and supporting the classroom teacher, he may also provide instructional assistance beyond diagnosis to the resource teacher or the self-contained class teacher.

Special Education Instructional Materials Center

It would be desirable, although financially unrealistic, for each teacher to have all the instructional materials necessary to provide a full range of teaching strategies to learning-disabled children. Since it is impossible to supply each teacher with every possible existing material useful to learning-disabled children, a program should establish a central (or beyond in a large city) Instructional Materials Center to support the roving resource teachers and strategists. The Center supplies the teachers with duplicates of those materials occasionally used with some children. In this way, the program is able to:

1)   provide each teacher with basic equipment and materials necessary for day-to-day operation of services, and

2)   provide a support system for retrieval of additional materials.

The Materials Center also permits the learning disabilities teachers to supplement regular classroom activities by providing materials to the regular classroom teacher.

A simple library system can be used to classify and catalog the materials in the Materials Center. Thus, the teachers are able to retrieve materials with ease as they need them. It is highly desirable, however, to employ a librarian/secretary to catalog and index the materials and to facilitate the use of the Materials Center by the teachers.

    The cost of implementing a Materials Center would be:

Furniture	$ 500.00
(work table, chairs, filing cabinets, storage cabinet, shelves)	
Instructional materials	$4,000.00
(programs, kits, workbooks, etc.)	
Audio-visual equipment	$ 500.00
	$5,000.00

    Following the initial year of operation, the cost of maintaining the Center would be approximately $2,000 to $3,000 for the replacement of consumable supplies and the purchase of additional materials. In developing a budget for implementing a learning disabilities program, additional funds (approximately $1500) should be included to cover personal travel expenses for the resource teachers and particularly for the strategist.

Preparing Learning Disabilities Professional Personnel

    The worth of any program is reflected in the personnel that contributes the human effort to that program. In short, strong personnel will succeed in spite of a poorly designed program. Poorly trained personnel, or those with limited energy to achieve a goal, can scuttle the best designed program. Therefore, a practical question is: Where does one find qualified resource-room teachers?

The most common reason for failure of resource-room programs is poor teaching. Reger (1972) writes:

> The resource-room teacher must be an expert, and the expertise must be created and developed in administrators and supervisors. Most classroom teachers are not prepared to become resource-room teachers, whether they have a background in regular elementary or special education teaching. To transfer a teacher to a resource-room program of the kind suggested here without preparation or training is to establish a high-risk failure situation. Previous teaching experience is necessary for resource-room teachers because they must become a part of the teaching staff; they must know at least as much about teaching as the average teacher they serve, but in addition they must be far more knowledgeable than the average teacher about materials, child behavior, strategies, techniques, management, and "public relations." They must be aware of their mission and have the technical skills to meet immediate problems without losing sight of the larger perspective. It is time for teacher-training programs to develop the resource-room teacher as an expert in dealing with these tasks. The current practice of training "MR teachers," and similar label-laden characters, if it is to continue (as it undoubtedly will for a long time), should at least make room for advanced training of a "generalist in special education—the resource-room teacher." (pp. 357-58)

Weiderholt (1974) describes the major characteristics of the resource-room teacher:

> Regardless of how the resource-room teacher is selected, he must possess several competencies and have at least one important "personality characteristic." This

characteristic is the ability to work effectively with colleagues. In the past, we have
noted some of the difficulties in communication that arise between the resource teacher
and the regular education teachers concerning children who are shared.

    Because of the shared responsibility in some content areas, the resource teacher
must be able to efficiently communicate the need for and facilitate change in programming in the regular classroom. As a result the resource-room teacher will have
to be highly skilled in public relations, as the success of his program depends in no
small part on the support of the regular classroom teachers. In addition to the ability to work effectively with colleagues, the resource teacher needs to be competent
in at least two other areas. First, he must be able to do most of his own educational
and behavioral assessment. Second, he must be able to successfully develop and
implement individualized programs.   (p. 4)

One of the most devastating circumstances in the field of learning disabilities has been the inability of
our colleagues and universities to train personnel adequately. Under the provisions of special education
certification in most states, professional personnel in learning disabilities have been trained to work in self-
contained classes. This writer seriously doubts that the number of resource-room or strategist training sites
has reached a total of ten in the United States. Even more serious, however, is the ineptness of our present
training efforts. Professional personnel in the area of learning disabilities are frequently taught and supervised
by professors who lack qualifications. In short, few—if any—trainers have ever designed a program or
functioned as a resource teacher.

    Seldom do students in learning disabilities receive practical placement where ample population exists
and university supervision is adequate. It is our opinion that learning disabilities teachers should not be

trained at the baccalaureate level. A very specialized Master's degree program (probably a two-year devotion) is necessary which sharply differentiates, through training, those students who desire self-contained class positions from those seeking positions as special education resource teachers. Special education strategists and school psychologists working on multi-disciplinary support teams also necessitate specific training in how to relate to the community and provide instructional support to other educators. Currently, public or private school administrators hiring learning disabilities teachers must prepare them (or retrain them) on the job through well-structured inservice activities. That situation seems unforgiveable, since there is not a serious lack (quantity) of learning disabilities teachers; obviously, attention should be paid to the quality of their training.

> There is a desperate need for those responsible for university training programs and the practitioners in special education to work more closely together. In 7 years of observing the local as well as the statewide scene in New York, I have observed this as a continuing, basic, and severe need. It is common practice for training programs to be established without discussing them with those who will be expected to use the products of the training systems. In my years as the third largest employer of teachers of children with severe learning difficulties in New York State, I have yet to be asked by directors of university training programs what our needs are or whether their products are effective; this lack of communication is true of other administrators in the state. The result is that training-program graduates emerge with irrelevant knowledge and minimal competence; the burden then falls on employers to establish training programs to do what should have been done in the university. It is all very wasteful and un-necessary.   (Reger, 1972, p. 359)

Coordination of Services

The ultimate goal of any educational program is to provide needed services and programs. It should not be necessary to adjust and readjust the child to the program. Instead, the program should fit the child. To accomplish this end, a coordinated effort among all program components and personnel is highly necessary. In cases of specialized programs for children with handicaps, school services and other agencies act cooperatively in their attempts to eradicate the adverse effects of handicapping conditions and in implementing an effective program on a day-to-day basis. The teacher serves as one member of a team working along with psychologists, guidance personnel, medical specialists, speech therapists, administrators, and parents, as well as with specialists from outside agencies. A major problem which faces the coordination of services is "how to organize" a team which works well. When an interdisciplinary team concept prevails in screening, diagnosis, and planning, the overall program for the child takes on direction and increased meaning.

Responsibility for coordination and implementation of services in a learning disabilities program is a basic concern of leadership. The efforts of all the persons who provide services to each child must be organized and integrated with the regular class teacher as well as the learning disabilities specialist. Team concepts and a balanced, effective schedule seem to be realistic aims of the administration in regards to instructional services for children with learning disabilities. Unfortunately, there is no simple formula for organizing, coordinating, and implementing these services. Each district must analyze its services in order to implement them in an organized and effective manner.

Each child's instruction should be carefully blended with other developmental activities wherever possible. This will help insure a consistent approach and concentrated, remedial efforts. The coordination of services must strengthen and support the total educational effort in order to meet the many diverse needs of children with learning disabilities. The teacher is primarily concerned with educational prescriptions which treat the child's learning disabilities. The success of these treatments depends largely upon coordination with related disciplines. It must be kept in mind that the ultimate growth of a learning-disabled child is largely dependent upon the nature, the extent, and the quality of coordinated efforts, as well as the amount of additional support, provided at each stage of the child's development.

Summary

This chapter has attempted to describe the necessity of multiple program components to provide adequate alternatives for the mosaic of unique learning and behavioral problems. The choice of restricting alternative program arrangements leads to one simple decision. That is, children must be structured to fit the dimensions of a given program. That decision, as a direct response to a limited service and program offering, or an absence of a continuum, inhibits the flow of instructional delivery. Obviously, there are realistic constraints to how big a program can be. Bigness should not be misconstrued as a substitute for a continuum of programs and services. That common assumption has already been disproven by a multitude of small, rural, and financially restricted districts such as the ones where the MLDS is administered in Pennsylvania. Two reasons for failure to develop a full range of programs and services are (1) poorly understood and articulated goals, and (2) the inability to conceptualize the full dimensions of a learning disability program. If that is the case, then read on; Chapter 2 offers the reader a planning-evaluation program guide.

LEARNING OBJECTIVES
Chapter 1

Cognitive Objectives

After carefully reading this chapter, you will be able to:

1) Identify and describe the three major developmental phases in the evolution of learning disabilities.

2) Recall the characteristics the MLDS has drawn from the federal definition of "learning disabilities" in order to make it workable within a school environment.

3) Distinguish between the areas of responsibility for remedial reading teachers and learning disabilities specialists.

4) Recognize the field of learning disabilities as being represented by many disciplines.

5) Describe the approaches to remediation of the learning disabled.

6) Identify the basic functions of the "step model."

7) Determine and list the advantages of the "Resource Room Concept."

8) Define the role of the "program supervisor."

9) State the responsibilities of the "Resource Room Teacher" and list the operational aspects of the resource room.

10) State the responsibilities of the "Assessment Class Teacher" and list the operational aspects of the assessment class.

11) Define the role of "Special Education Strategist."

LEARNING   OBJECTIVES
Chapter 1

Affective   Objectives

After reading this chapter, the author intends that you will:

1)   Be aware of the problem in operationalizing many present-day definitions of learning disabilities.

2)   Accept the fact that care must be given not to consider every child with an educational misery as learning disabled.

3)   Value the principle of a gestalt approach in working towards the field of learning disabilities.

4)   Judge the importance of an instructional materials center.

5)   Associate the worth of an educational program with the quality of personnel contributing to it.

6)   Value the principle that educational programs should be tailored to fit the child.

7)   Value the principle of developing the administrative structure for a total learning disabilities program.

READER'S NOTES

A PROGRAM & SERVICES PRIMER

Historically, the study of the learning-disabled child can be traced as proceeding through three major developmental phases:

1_____

2_____

3_____

These major phases are by no means rigid, as there is considerable overlapping in all of them. However, each phase is characterized by a differing general trend of emphasis. Throughout each phase, professionals tended to concern themselves with a specific type of learning disorder.

[Refer to p._____in the manual.]

[Refer to p._____.]

The _____**Phase** (approximately 1800-1835) characteristics:

_____

_____

_____

_____

READER'S NOTES   **A PROGRAM & SERVICES PRIMER**

                               _____

                               _____

                               _____

[Refer to p._____]   The_____Phase (approximately 1921-1960) characteristics:

                               _____

                               _____

                               _____

                               _____

[Refer to p. _____.]   The_____Phase (approximately 1960-   ) characteristics:

                               _____

                               _____

                               _____

A PROGRAM & SERVICES PRIMER

The alternatives to self-contained classes in special education should be expanded if the myriad of learning and behavioral disorders in the schools are to be properly served. From a cost/benefit ratio, classes for learning-disabled children are expensive for the limited number of children contained in them. One such search for a system of creative alternatives is a continuum of services and programs described by Ysseldyke and Sabatino (1972) in a so-called:

[Refer to p._____ in the manual.]

_____

This approach utilizes the talents of a school's professional staff and places each staff member into a unique position, as part of a team effort.

To clarify this approach, fill in the following steps in the order they appear in this chapter.

[Refer to p. _____.]   Step 1

_____

_____

_____

READER'S NOTES   A PROGRAM & SERVICES PRIMER

[Refer to p._____.]   Step 2   _____

_____

_____

_____

[Refer to p. _____.]   Step 3   _____

_____

_____

_____

[Refer to p._____.]   Step 4   _____

_____

_____

_____

[Refer to p. _____.]   Step 5   _____

_____

_____

_____

READER'S NOTES   **A PROGRAM & SERVICES PRIMER**

[Refer to p. _____.]   Step 6

_____

_____

_____

_____

_____

The resource room plays a vital role in offering services to
the learning-disabled children. List below some of the advantages in utilizing the resource room concept:

[Refer to p._____]

_____

_____

_____

_____

_____

_____

_____

_____

_____

READER'S NOTES

A PROGRAM & SERVICES PRIMER

The whole of the program must be larger than the sum of its parts. If local school district special education directors seek only to offer special education classes depending upon school psychologists to fit children to accomodate that program's faulty and limited dimensions, then planned program entry (mainstreaming) into regular education, or the opportunity for a child to recycle through a regular program for a period of time supported by a learning disabilities resource teacher, will not work.

It is important to understand the responsibilities of the program supervisor when discussing the three service alternatives provided by the MLDS in working with learning-disabled children. In the space provided, place suggested areas of responsibility for the program supervisor.

_____

_____

_____

A PROGRAM & SERVICES PRIMER

_____

_____

_____

_____

_____

The ultimate goal of any educational program is to provide needed services and programs. It should not be necessary to adjust and readjust the child to the program. Instead, the program should fit the child. To accomplish this end, a coordinated effort among all program components and personnel is highly necessary. Responsibility for coordination and implementation of services in a learning disabilities program is a basic concern of leadership. The efforts of all the persons who provide services to each child must be organized and integrated with the regular class teacher as well as the learning

READER'S NOTES

A PROGRAM & SERVICES PRIMER

disabilities specialist. Team concepts and a balanced, effective schedule seem to be realistic aims of the administrator in regards to instructional services for children with learning disabilities.

In discussing variations in strategies for approaching remediation of the learning disabled, several general trends surface:

I.   PERCEPTUAL TRAINING
Some characteristics

[Refer to p. _____ in the manual.]

_____

_____

_____

_____

II.   MOTOR, TACTILE, AND KINESTHETIC TRAINING
Some characteristics

[Refer to p. _____.]

_____

_____

_____

_____

A PROGRAM & SERVICES PRIMER

III.   LANGUAGE TRAINING
Some characteristics

[Refer to p.＿＿＿ in the manual .]

_____

_____

_____

_____

IV.   PSYCHOTHERAPY AND BEHAVIORAL MODIFICATION
Some characteristics

[Refer to p.＿＿＿ .]

_____

_____

_____

_____

V.   DIAGNOSTIC-PRESCRIPTIVE TEACHING
Some characteristics

[Refer to p.＿＿＿ .]

_____

_____

_____

2 A Systems Approach to Learning Disabilities: A Program Planning Guide

David A. Sabatino

I T IS NOT the intent of this chapter to popularize the administration of a learning disabilities program merely by linking it to management systems terminology. Public education is nearly a century removed from the one-room schoolhouse, and yet most administrative decisions are made from the seat of someone's chair on the basis of little information, frequently far removed from the action related to that decision. In fact, most decision makers in the public schools are those least familiar with the critical aspects (task areas) of a learning disabilities program. The results of such seat-of-the-pants decision making are programs that reflect a lack of preplanning and that are frequently inefficient in the use of financial or personnel resources. It is recommended that a school system not enter into a learning disabilities program with less than one year of preplanning time in which the goals and objectives for the program are clearly stated.

This chapter will attempt to outline those component areas critical to a learning disabilities program that should be considered in developing and evaluating a program.

The first step in developing a systematic procedure for administering a learning disabilities program is to define program goals. When program goals are not clearly defined, the alternatives to established goals are vague and hard to formulate, making system synthesis and organization either too rigid or too fluid. Unquestionably, two different options are available to school systems attempting to develop and maintain a learning disability program. One is to be concerned with brick and mortar, staff relationships, number of children served, opinion of the community, and the ability to "sell" a program on some basis—probably that of greatest appeal. The question of who determines what a program should be is irrelevant and must not be raised if one is to administer this option. The other option is to adopt a Program Evaluation and Review Technique (PERT), or Critical Path Method (CPM), or other techniques referred to under the heading of systems analysis, which request that the staff involved specify its goals and objectives and develop a procedure for evaluating them.

The most difficult aspect of the second option is to specify the goals and objectives for a program, in order that an evaluation process which will serve as a comprehensive screen or backdrop can be initiated. Evaluation data are the only valid means a school district has to assess and account for its objectives, state alternatives, and conceptualize a total program by seeing each component aspect in relation to overall program goals. Option two is still not a panacea. A program management scheme provides the direction to be utilized in the establishment of a planning/evaluation process, but it does not supply the substantive content for a program. Process and content are two different sides of the same coin. A learning disabilities program may have great objectives and a wonderful evaluation format, yet the instructional content may be utterly disastrous. The opposite is more generally true, however; that is, good things happen instructionally with children, and no one is quite sure why.

What Is a Systems Approach?

> The term *systems* carries the connotation of analysis and development....No comprehensive system development can take place without prior systems analysis. Systems... denotes all activities involved from the original analysis of the problem through the final implementation of recommendations....[it involves] utilization of scientific mathematical techniques applied to organizational operations as part of management's decision-making activities. (Banghart, p. 20)

Lerner (1973) defines a system as:

> a set of objectives, together with relationships between the objects and between the characteristics of these objects. System analysis deals with the selection of elements, relationships, and procedures to achieve specific objectives and purposes....A systems approach is extolled as a technique to prevent splintering and fragmentation of a field by bringing component parts, subsystems, or elements into a total relationship with each other....One goal of systems analysis is, in fact, to provide a means of crossing boundaries and of bringing diverse elements and operations and specialists toward a definite systems purpose. (p. 16)

A learning disabilities program certainly fits the above description. To activate such a program successfully, people from all disciplines are needed. Since viewpoints are frequently quite different, some commonalities are needed to bring their views to a focal point. When special educators were isolated in self-contained classes to serve most areas of exceptionality, special educators and regular educators needed only to acknowledge one another's existence. The serious problems in implementing mainstreaming strategies are certainly a case in point. The articulation of common goals, regardless of variance in historic philosophies about children (particularly handicapped children), has revealed more differences between regular (basic) and special education than some of us would have thought existed. Certainly, because of the absence of any nationally acceptable definition of learning disabilities, a learning disabilities program might just as easily be administered by a regular education group as by a special education team. It just so happens that state legislators have offered excess cost support to "handicapped" children and that "learning disabilities" is a "soft" category of the groups of children labeled as minimally brain-injured or neurologically impaired. The difficulty with the softness of this label is that *learning disabilities* is also frequently used synonymously with *learning disorders* (underachievment with normal intelligence and without perceptual-central language impairment). Learning-disabled children may be operationally defined as underachievers with normal intelligence, having measurable perceptual-central language impairment. It is true that even though a distinction in definition between learning disorders and learning disabilities may exist, a difference in the nature of the problem in the classroom may not exist. The difference then may be what is needed (and the projected expense) to correct the learning disability as opposed to the learning disorder. It is our belief that most differences in viewpoint are mere rhetoric (academic exercises) if they do not focus on the issue of the prognostic time required to correct the problem. Therefore, the real problem is how to operationalize a program for those children who will not progress unless other services beyond remedial reading ore offered to them. It does not make sense to say that we can cross each bridge in program development as we come to it. The predictable problems must be outlined in advance and dealt with before they occur as a crisis that must then be quelled at the expense of a great deal of administrative and teacher time and effort.

   A learning disabilities program is identifiable by the sum of its parts. Its character is its contributing aspects, the personalities and skills of its members, and the view maintained by those who use its services in an attempt to satisfy its reasons for existence (credibility). The roles of resource teachers must be clearly delineated by all the teaching members of a school system, or confusion will result. The role differences between learning disabilities resource room teachers and psychologists or speech therapists must be clearly specified. When a regular class teacher refers a child, to whom does she direct the referral and what does she expect in return? These and other issues are the aspects that contribute to a total learning disabilities program, and they must be understood in the light of coordinated program efforts.

The sharp distinction between curricular content and educational process must be kept in mind. In review of these two concepts, content is the substance, or what actually happens in the classroom, or makes the wheels of an organization run. The process is the administrative or instructional structure which guides the operations; it is the frame, axle, and hubs upon which the wheels turn. A systems design is not to be misconstrued as providing substantive considerations or instructional content for a program.

Kipfer (1973) has noted in her description of systems management that the application of analysis is educational process and not curricular content. Although she uses the term *therapy* to describe the important function, it appears that *therapy* is used synonymously with *instruction*. Her basic postulates are:

a)   instruction is the major function of special education;

b)   instruction is only effective when it accomplishes the basic purposes of the specific program in which children are placed;

c)   not all benefits of instructional content are measurable with handicapped children;

d)   administrative, supervisory, and diagnostic functions provide important supportive services to the major function of motivation;

e)   these supportive services must relate directly or indirectly to instructional services because if they do not they are difficult to justify;

f)   a comprehensive paradigm of the instructional process should relate to its supportive services, with a diagnostic-prescriptive program continuum, such as the step model demonstrated in Chapter 1.

The Model Learning Disabilities Systems

The Model Learning Disabilities Systems evolved from the Tyrone Model Program, which was initially housed in the Tyrone Area School District, Tyrone, Pennsylvania. The initial mission of the Tyrone Model Program as a federally funded Title VI-G Child Demonstration Program was to develop a comprehensive i-dentification process, instructional procedure, and program planning-evaluation process within a school dis-trict as a model program for other school districts to adopt and adapt to their program goals. Then, through technical assistance, the program aspects of the model were delivered to other school districts through an out-reach, referred to as the Model Learning Disabilities System. It was felt that a comprehensive prototype could be used to help other school districts develop similar programs. The reason this idea was abandoned as an extension of technical assistance was that most school districts do not have goals, objectives, and eval-uation procedures for their learning disabilities programs. It became obvious that to transport a program from one district to another provides program content without the process or structures to make it indige-nous to the receiving district. That type of technical assistance is poorly defined because it lacks a planning/

evaluation procedure. Stufflebeam (1971) defines *evaluation* as "the process of delineating, obtaining, and providing useful information for judging decision alternatives" (p. xxv). He adds, "the major reason evaluation is in difficulty is that knowledge of the decision-making process and of the methodologies for relating evaluation to decision making is woefully inadequate" (p. 16).

To enter into a school district with a set of preplanned recommendations not designed for and by that school is analogous to leaving a person dying of thirst with only a small thermos of water. To provide a school district with a planning-evaluation systems design from which its personnel can plan, develop, and evaluate their goals and objectives for a learning disabilities program is the equivalent of leaving a thirsty person with the drilling tools to obtain a steady, lasting source of water.

In Perspective

The Model Learning Disabilities Systems, as currently designed, has four major missions. These are to:
1.   develop an identification process that will provide a systematic means for diagnostically operationalizing the federal definition;
2.   explore alternatives to the current delivery of services and programs (primarily self-contained classes) in an effort to determine the necessary components to achieve a behavioral program that would be administratively effective and efficient;
3.   demonstrate sound educational practices to other practitioners;
4.   offer technical assistance to school districts within the Commonwealth of Pennsylvania on

program planning, development, and evaluation within a systems context.

Two major concerns confronted the MLDS staff in offering technical assistance to school districts. It was obvious that a model learning disabilities program could not be transported from one district to another without confusion in the effort to duplicate a program in a geographic location other than the one it was originally developed to serve. The variance in personnel, geography, ideology, and previous program development for any given school system makes the transporting of a so-called model program from one district to another a high-risk venture. But it was also obvious that in the absence of transporting a total program, certain critical features related to program success must be viewed as necessary ingredients by a district if decisions are to be made on how a total learning disabilities program will materialize.

In essence, a consolidated plan of attack which includes the critical aspects necessary for achieving stated objectives of the program is important for program survival.

The responsibilities assigned a given person and the timelines established for the products and processes representative of the school district's efforts must be clearly delineated before the program is initiated. The overriding central purpose of a systems approach is to see that the many and varied aspects necessary to a learning disabilities program are organized and structured into an integrated whole. If learning-disabled children are to succeed academically and socially, it is necessary that the program not only survive but also provide continuous comprehensive instructional and behavioral management support needed for children in both regular and special education classes.

The Whole Must Be More Than the Sum of Its Parts

It will be reiterated several times in the course of this document that one of the major philosophic beliefs of our group has been that any program representing less than a total effort is tokenism. The risk involved in a piecemeal learning disabilities program is the chance that (1) it may not meet the expectations placed on it by the users, or (2) it may destroy the professional spirit of overburdened personnel attempting to do too much for too many. In either case, the results are disastrous to the children being served.

Every administrator, regular class teacher, or special educator has learned the importance of a balanced program versus isolated program aspects. The difficulty lies in achieving a balance in knowing what resources exist, what the problems are (predictably) that will constrain program development, and how to make things happen in a planned, evaluated, and orderly fashion to achieve what should be occurring in keeping with the goals and objectives of a given program. Delivering long-term plans in the form of goal statements and then evaluating that planning at specified short-term intervals is a far cry from just letting something happen. The analogy might be the circus juggler who must account for the balls that are in the air, while recognizing that both hands may also be full. Scheduling three rooms in a building for 40 itinerant personnel in a given week is an example of having balls in the air while one's hands are busy doing other things. Some type of organization is needed to accomplish that task, or crisis will prevail on a weekly basis. The organizational structure that we have decided upon to guide planning and evaluative efforts is a systems approach, simply because it permits us to:

1.   identify the vital aspects of a learning disabilities program;
2.   arrange with a given school system those aspects in which it is interested and which it can afford and decide how it will order (in a sense of priorities) those that it will have now and those it will add later until a comprehensive, balanced program is achieved;
3.   establish the goals and objectives of a well-defined learning disabilities program;
4.   obtain evaluative data on what is happening, while increasing the information upon which future decisions can be reached in relation to the program objectives.

Accountability

In a recent report of the Council of Exceptional Children Interagency Committee, the Executive Director of the Association for the Education of the Visually Handicapped summarized his concern for accountability:

All of special education, and categorical programs such as those for the visually handicapped especially, must provide proof of their worth. The few people with responsibility for funds tend to ask why special children are "special" and, even more, whether special education is doing more for these children than the regular classroom could do. If we are to defend our programs we must have facts. (Association for Education of the Visually Handicapped, 1973, p. 8)

Increasing pressure is being placed on special educators to provide evidence that efforts with exceptional children are beneficial (Lessenger, 1971). If charged to communicate the effectiveness of their programs, they must (1) state precisely what outcomes the program is designed to facilitate and (2) present evidence that the outcomes have, in fact, been produced. These demands on classroom teachers for accountability necessitate the use of an evaluation process; but the principles of evaluation may well be one area where preservice academic preparation is limited or nonexistent for most teachers.

The special educator in the classroom or resource room, faced with the day-to-day reality of teaching children, does not need to learn another obtuse theoretical model or be overwhelmed by the academic prose in which most evaluation articles are written. Nor does he need what Ohrtman (1972) has aptly described: "the in and out researcher...[who] gets two sets of kids, does A to one group and B to another, compares them and [shows] one group does better than the other at the .01 level—then off to the next project "(p. 377). Vergason (1973) and Jones (1973) have delineated many of the problems associated with the evaluation process. Jones (1973) writes that before any school district should presume to devise a system of accountability for special education, the following questions should be answered:

1.   What are the common and specific goals to which the teacher and school are striving?

2.   What student, community, or societal need inventories are available, on paper, to indicate change strategies which should be undertaken?

3.   What specific and measurable performance objectives have been written down that would enable parents, students, and teachers to understand the minimum expectations of the unstructured programs?

4.   What analysis of the existing delivery system is available to indicate that the
      current educational input approach is manageable as compared to the
      alternatives?

Vergason (1973) states that one area in which special educators can be more definitive about their
programs is that of standardized terminology. Stufflebeam (1972) has recently assumed a position similar
to that of Scriven (1967), who states that the fundamental goal of evaluation determines the value of a
program or instructional activity. Originally, Stufflebeam (1968) saw evaluation as a systematic process
of "delineating, obtaining, and providing useful information for judging decision alternatives" (p. 129). The
CIPP (Context, Input, Process, and Product) Model he developed represents a frame of reference for presenting alternatives to decision makers and can provide a classroom teacher with information about his program;
but this evaluation is too complex for daily use in the classroom.

Other evaluators have discussed plans for curriculum and course evaluation (Cronbach, 1963; Krathwohl, 1965; Lindvall et al., 1964; Michael and Metfessel, 1967; and Popham, 1969), while still others have
presented theoretical evaluation models (Aikin, 1969; Hammond, 1969; and Provus, 1969). These plans
generally represent similar processes for conducting educational evaluations, but they do not offer a simplified procedure for the already overburdened classroom teacher to use.

The term *evaluation* is not a good one because it increases anxiety without having a particular universal meaning. All sorts of atrocities have been accomplished in the name of evaluation. To reduce the ambiguity associated with the term, we are concerned with evaluation of context and not of personnel. In Chap-

ter 10 of this text, evaluation procedures for learning disabilities personnel are discussed.   Personnel evaluation is not done by an outside review (external to the school district); personnel policies and the evaluation
of people hired by a district must be established in line with that individual and that district's expectations
for career development.   Proger, Carfioli, and Kalapos (1973), in a discussion on evaluating instructional
materials, have made some very fitting remarks:

> The careless use of the term "evaluation" has led to misconceptualized models....An
> exhaustive description of characteristics of the learner, the material, the setting of instruc-
> tion, and so on does not constitute evaluation, although it is useful in delimiting the gen-
> eralizability of evaluation results.   Evaluation refers to the actual judgments that are made
> with regard to the quality of the material, its success in use with students, and other strengths
> or weaknesses.   True materials evaluation implies that a definite position (favorable or un-
> favorable) is taken concerning the materials evaluated; neutrality is not a virtue.   It is un-
> fortunate that some evaluation models for materials have relied almost entirely upon de-
> scriptive analyses of materials and have disregarded judgmental evaluations.   Items on a
> materials-evaluation form that deal with description should be clearly labeled as such. The
> same should be done for items that concern judgmental evaluations.   When this distinction
> is made, it is apparent how little (and that of poor quality) is being done in the genuine
> sense of materials evaluation (p. 272).

The above quote was not added to elicit support for subjective or qualitative judgments. The point is
that judgments will always be necessary, even when a criterion or standard is established.   The crucial question
is: what is the standard or criterion and who is doing the evaluation.   In answer to the question of where to
begin, begin by evaluating the context of the school district.   The context is what that district *says* it is doing,
what, in fact, it *is* doing, and what its goals are.

Goals and Objectives

There are several goals (unmeasurable aims) and objectives (measurable) inherent to a learning disabilities program.   The main goal is to provide equal opportunity for each child to learn at his optimum level
and rate, with as little segregation as possible by ability, race, sex, and socio-economic level from the context
of the educational mainstream.   The secondary goals are to provide a continuum of services and programs
that will support learning-disabled children and their teachers with diagnosis, curriculum, and direct remediation and evaluation, whether the child is in regular or special education. Some other possible goal statements for a learning disabilities program are to:
1.   isolate, segregate, or label as *few* children from the educational mainstream as possible;
2.   have the school and community citizens informed about the learning disabilities program;
3.   provide additional support services to the learning-disabled child who is experiencing diffi-
       culty in a learning disabilities program;
4.   provide demonstration and resource teacher assistance to teachers of students who show a
       particular skill deficiency which may be related to learning disabilities;
5.   provide continuous diagnosis and monitoring of children who have a serious enough learning
       disability that they must be taught in a self-contained class;
6.   provide continuous feedback to children and their parents on progress as children participate
       in any program or service aspect of a learning disabilities intervention;

7.   provide evaluation of the total learning disabilities program according to criteria established with a systematic procedure which services the district;

8.   develop a systematic screening procedure that will permit screening, identification, and initial diagnosis;

9.   promote preschool programs;

10.   develop secondary career programs.

Objectives are measurable aspects that reflect the process and product of a given goal. An objective should state *what* is to occur, in what time frame (*when*) or order it is to occur, and *how* it is to occur. Objectives must be specific to each factor or function listed in the task areas.   This idea of specific objectives for each function, under a general program goal for a given task area, is self-explanatory when one studies the Program Planning Guide which appears later in this chapter.

Context Evaluation

The first phase in evaluating a program is to listen carefully to what the administrators, teachers, and students say a program should accomplish. Two things should be carefully noted, as the information will later be compared to what the district's goals are.   First, the attitude or commitment to the program must be determined.   It should be understood that the people associated with the program must also believe in it personally. The absence of such belief generates clichés and an air of triteness. Second, program constraints must be determined. The constraints of implementing a learning disabilities program are generally financial limitations, staff (level of training, type of training, abilities), and the physical facilities that are currently available. The most important constraints are the attitudes within the system as well as those outside it, primarily those of the community.

All programs have to be developed within the budgetary framework and facilities available. It is possible, however, to make internal changes that could alter constraints. An example of a change of this nature might be the use of limited funds to employ a resource teacher for the entire district. The resource teacher's energies are then channeled into one school in the district by providing an intensive program at that one school for one year. As the program sells itself, the budget will be provided (or, if necessary, the teacher would be moved to another building the next year) until every school in the district has an equal opportunity to benefit, as opposed to spreading one person too thin.

Achieving Desired Goals

The management-by-objective(s) worksheet was developed to determine what is happening, what should happen (goals), and why it is or is not happening (constraints). In an initial meeting between a district's school administrators, agreement is reached about which aspects of the evaluation will be the district's responsibility and which will belong to the learning disabilities staff. District administrators, other teachers, or support staff can provide peer and third-party evaluations. In the latter case, the amount of involvement that the MLDS staff is to provide is critical.   The decision reached could be made on the school's previous evaluations of its learning disabilities program. It is the goal of the MLDS staff to put as much of the responsibility for the evaluation directly into the hands of the teaching administrative staff as possible. Obviously, having the district evaluate itself is preferred to using an outside resource or another outside agency to provide the evaluation.   Nonetheless, the point is that some type of decision is necessary; and the more comprehensive a screen upon which a program can be exposed, the better are the decisions that will guide the future development of the program.

A Learning Disabilities Program Planning Guide

The framework or process within which learning disabilities programs are built can be called *Task Areas*.   There are seven task areas identified as crucial to a realistic effort in initiating and maintaining a well-developed learning disabilities program.   These are:

Task Area 1   Inservice
Task Area 2   Personnel Management
Task Area 3   Referral Process
Task Area 4   Pupil Identification and Placement Process
Task Area 5   Instructional Systems
Task Area 6   Program Coordination
Task Area 7   School and Community Participation

Each task area is composed of functions that are of critical importance to the overall workability of a given process. The order of these functions has a general but not an absolute flow, and it is frequently necessary to rearrange the order from time to time. In some school districts not all of the task areas will apply. In fact, in some school districts none of the stated functions will be applicable.   The predominant feature of a systems approach is that the sum of the parts do not overpower the whole; but in keeping the gestalt of what constitutes the major goals of a good program, it is possible to identify individual parts. In fact, from a qualitative point of view, it is possible to identify strong ones, weak ones, and ones that should be strengthened in addition to ones that should not be included at all.   From this baseline data it is then possible to strengthen individual functions so that they become more effective or possibly curtail them because of their ineffectiveness or lack of necessity.   In short, when each function has a stated objective and the process, product, timeline, evaluation criteria, and constraints are stated, then planned decision-making can commence.   The evolution of a decision frequently is based on evaluative data, not whimsical decisions generated because "they say so."

The program planning guide used by the MLDS staff provides space for the objectives, processes, product, timeline, evaluation criteria, and constraints for each function.   To facilitate ease of reading, a glossary describing each task area and components is presented (or has been prepared).

Inservice Task Area

Inservice is used to denote some type of formalized professional preparation beyond a bachelor's degree program. It is usually contrasted to preservice training, which generally occurs on a college campus. *Inservice* is a hazy concept because it ranges from creating a state of awareness, to brief information exchanges, to one or two-day workshops or several week-long institutes. The short-sightedness and limited applicability of most preservice college courses has caused many states to use total on-school sites, allowing inservice hours to carry a professional who is just beginning from entry-level to permanent certification. School districts and intermediate units or regionally based cooperatives are developing budgetary capabilities to provide inservice education for teachers based on the fact that most teachers have minimal entry level skills when they leave the preservice preparation program.

1.   *Administrative Inservice*

Far too frequently, administrators are overlooked in information exchange efforts. Yet it is obvious how important it is to get good information to them. In the inservice chapter (Chapter 8) outlines are given for the stages of inservice work, beginning with a working meeting with chief administrators and/or one-day workshops for supervisors. The purpose of an administrative inservice program is to: (1) detail how a learning disabilities program can be facilitated to run smoothly and (2) set the goals for the program. Frequently, programs are oversold, and if realistic goals are not established, then expectations become unrealistic and disenchantment follows.

2.   *School Board Inservice*

Schedule meetings with the school board, hopefully not at the time of a regular meeting but at some other time when the central focus is the cost, goals, objectives, and organizational structure of a learning disabilities program.

3.   *Teacher Inservice*

This component should be a continuous effort which occurs at two levels.   First, each building (at the building level) should receive a short work session on "who is learning disabled" (see referral inservice) and "what are the expectations and organization of the program."   Second, a continuing inservice should occur between learning disabilities teachers and basic education teachers over actual children.   Consultants can be used, but they are used most effectively at the case conference level.

4.   *Supervisor Inservice*

The role of a supervisor has been a confusing one, especially to the supervisor. There is little consistency as to what supervisor (regular or special education) will be assigned the task of supervising the learning disabilities program.   More frequently than not, the supervisor knows less about learning-disabled children and programs than does the learning disabilities teacher.   To provide supervision, usable information (especially the sort found in Chapter 10 on personnel and program evaluation) is critical.   Supervisors should be included in the principal's workshops, exchanging information at these meetings.   There are times when supervisors and learning disability teachers need to work at role relationships and establish decision-making points.

5.   *Paraprofessional Inservice*

Another group of often overlooked personnel, especially in terms of speciality information, are paraprofessionals and aides.   Aides frequently receive a general orientation to the school. Such a program is inadequate if they are to respond to hyperactive, low self-concept children as part of a treatment team, working under the teacher's directions and not against an educational milieu of which they must be a part. The objectives that guide an aide's function are widely divergent from school system to school system and from class to class. Another area of coordination is that of employing aides and parent volunteers as tutors. The role relationships seem to generate quite a bit of conflict.

6.   *Support Team Inservice*

The diagnostic-educational support team, comprised of a psychologist, physician, speech-language person, an audiologist, ophthalmologist-optometrist, and a social worker, needs special small conference meetings to discuss referral processes, placement decisions, the role of the learning disabilities teacher, etc. One of the major discussion points should be how the learning disabilities teachers obtain the service of the support team, how long they must wait for such service, and how the information will be reported.

7.   *Community Inservice*

Community awareness of a learning disabilities program is also critical to the success of that program. Newspaper and radio releases, public forums at PTO and PTA meetings, and special issue seminars are good; but the key to community inservice is to initiate a chain of informed people. If teachers are informed, they inform parents, who, in turn, offer goal information to other community members. Such a chain is based on presenting the goals of the program clearly and consistently.

Figure 3

MODEL LEARNING DISABILITIES SYSTEMS: PROGRAM PLANNING GUIDE

PROGRAM GOAL:				Code:	
	Date:	Administrator Responsible	MLDS Team	MLDS	: 1 2 3 4 5
	District:	Intermediate Unit	District/ I.U. Team	District/ I.U.	: 1 2 3 4 5

I. INSERVICE TASK AREA	OBJECTIVES specific measurable aim for each task designated	PROCESS	Time Line	PRODUCT	Time Line	EVALUATION CRITERIA	CONSTRAINTS	KEY
1. Administration								
2. School Board								
3. Teachers								
4. Supervisors								
5. Paraprofessionals								
6. Support Team								
7. Community								
8. Other								
Academic Year _____								
1. Administration								
2. School Board								
3. Teachers								
4. Supervisors								
5. Paraprofessional								
6. Support Team								
7. Community								
8. Other								
Academic Year _____								

Personnel Management Task Area

1. *Immediate Supervisor*
    Identify the immediate supervisor of the program with primary role function statements.
2. *Number and Type of Personnel*
    List the number of learning disabilities personnel to be employed and their function (special class, assessment class, resource, strategists, etc.).
3. *Personnel Qualifications*
    List the qualifications for the personnel listed in 2, e.g., Bachelor's or Master's degree, years of experience, etc.
4. *Teacher/Building Ratio*
    Decide the number of buildings that will be represented, and transportation for a self-contained class.
5. *Teacher/Children Ratio*
    Determine the number of children to whom each learning disabilities teacher will provide services.
6. *Personnel/Management Procedure*
    Establish any objectives that provide for career development, program development, or major thrusts for the year's efforts that learning disabilities teachers should accomplish, e.g., mainstream a specific number of children, hold a specified number of building inservice meetings, etc.

A SYSTEMS APPROACH

Figure 4

MODEL LEARNING DISABILITIES SYSTEMS: PROGRAM PLANNING GUIDE

PROGRAM GOAL:	Date:	Administrator Responsible	MLDS Team		Code:		
	District:	Intermediate Unit	District/ I.U. Team	MLDS : 1 2 3 4 5			
				District/ I.U. : 1 2 3 4 5			

11. PERSONNEL MANAGEMENT TASK AREA	OBJECTIVES specific measurable aim for each task designated	PROCESS	Time Line	PRODUCT	Time Line	EVALUATION CRITERIA	CONSTRAINTS	KEY
1. Immediate Supervisor								
2. Number & Type of Personnel								
3. Personnel Qualifications								
4. Teacher/Building Ratio								
5. Teacher/Child Ratio								
6. Personnel Management Procedure								
7. Other								

Academic Year _____

1. Immediate Supervisor								
2. Number & Type of Personnel								
3. Personnel Qualifications								
4. Teacher/Building Ratio								
5. Teacher/Child Ratio								
6. Personnel Management Procedure								
7. Other								

Academic Year _____

Referral Process Task Area

It may seem peculiar to separate referral process from identification process, but too frequently the very important process—that is, who gets referred and who receives the referral and for what disposition—is lost in a busy fall schedule.

1. *Referral Inservice*

    Hold a building-by-building discussion of (a) the criteria for selecting children for referral, and (b) the procedures for referring them to a specific person in that building who coordinates the efforts of the referral process.

2. *Referral Criteria*

    Determine those dimensions (scores on group tests, observations, previous history, failure lists, etc.) that key a referral decision. Referral criteria should be written for the system and fed into the district's nervous systems through the referral inservice.

3. *Referral Process*

    Decide: (a) who receives the completed referral, and whose signature specifies that the child is, in fact, referred; (b) what person or team reviews the completed referrals.

4. *Referral Follow-up*

    Decide who coordinates the post-referral process and makes certain the child receives appropriate program placement.

Figure 5

MODEL LEARNING DISABILITIES SYSTEMS: PROGRAM PLANNING GUIDE

PROGRAM GOAL:				Code:	
	Date:	Administrator Responsible	MLDS Team	MLDS : 1 2 3 4 5	
	District:	Intermediate Unit	District/ I.U. Team	District/ I.U. : 1 2 3 4 5	

III. REFERRAL PROCESS TASK AREA	OBJECTIVES specific measurable aim for each task designated	PROCESS	Time Line	PRODUCT	Time Line	EVALUATION CRITERIA	CONSTRAINTS	KEY
1. Referral Inservice								
2. Referral Criteria								
3. Referral Process								
A. Receiving								
B. Reviewing								
4. Referral Follow-Up								
Academic Year _____								
1. Referral Inservice								
2. Referral Criteria								
3. Referral Process								
A. Receiving								
B. Reviewing								
4. Referral Follow-Up								
Academic Year _____								

Pupil Identification and Placement Task Area

1. *Identification Process*

Decide which person coordinates the specific activities that will be reflected in establishing whether or not a child meets program criteria.

2. *Identification Criteria*

Establish those criteria that identify the presence or absence of skill level in: (a) academic areas, (b) intellectual levels, and (c) perceptual-language behaviors that establish admission into a learning disabilities program.

3. *Support Team Involvement*

Describe the role and coordination of the diagnostic support team for: (a) learning-disabled children and (b) other children referred as learning disabled who failed to meet identification criteria. The objectives should be specified for all members of the support team.

4. *Identification Reporting Process*

Decide the form of any written or oral reports and the person to whom they are to be sent.

5. *Diagnostic Process*

Establish the minimum level of diagnostic procedure to support the initiation of curriculum decisions.

6. *Placement Decisions*

Follow the program specified for each child seen in the identification and/or diagnostic pro-

Figure 6

ACADEMIC YEAR_____

IV. PUPIL IDENTIFICATION & PLACEMENT PROCESS TASK AREA	OBJECTIVES specific measurable aim for each task designated	PROCESS	Time Line	PRODUCT	Time Line	EVALUATION CRITERIA	CONSTRAINTS	KEY
1. Identification Criteria								
A. Academic								
B. Intelligence								
C. Perceptual-Language								
2. L.D. Teacher								
3. Support Team								
A. Psychologist								
B. Speech Therapist								
C. Physician								
D. Audiologist								
E. Ophthamologist								
F. Case Worker								
G. Other								
4. Reporting Process								
5. Diagnostic Process								
6. Placement Decision								
7. Parent Conference								

cess.   One of the ways to destroy a learning disabilities program is to go through an elaborate re-ferral-screening process to identify children, both learning disabled and those who are not, only to permit children to continue the same program they had before they were referred.   The person or team responsible for placement decision must be spelled out.

7.   *Parent Conference*

The last official act of any identification and/or diagnostic procedures is to inform parents of: (a) outcome or results; (b) necessary programs; and (c) their roles in home and school management.

Instructional System Task Area

The act of establishing and regulating an instructional flow is referred to as an instructional system. Its functional components are to:

1.   *Determine Instructional Time per Child*

Set the minimum and maximum time permitted for each instructional activity per day, week, and year, and possibly how much time is left before the child leaves the school environment for the adult world.

2.   *Establish Instructional Priorities*

Set instructional goals to obtain a reasonable modification in academic skills or behavior.

Figure 7

MODEL LEARNING DISABILITIES SYSTEMS: PROGRAM PLANNING GUIDE

PROGRAM GOAL:						Code:	
	Date:	Administrator Responsible		MLDS Team		MLDS : 1 2 3 4 5	
	District:	Intermediate Unit		District/ I.U. Team		District/ I.U. : 1 2 3 4 5	

V. INSTRUCTIONAL SYSTEM TASK AREA	OBJECTIVES specific measurable aim for each task designated	PROCESS	Time Line	PRODUCT	Time Line	EVALUATION CRITERIA	CONSTRAINTS	KEY
1. Instructional Time Per Child								
2. Establish Instructional Priorities								
3. Establish Instructional Objectives								
4. Select Instructional Methods								
5. Instructional Evaluation								
6. Progress Reports								
Academic Year _____								
1. Instructional Time Per Child								
2. Establish Instructional Priorities								
3. Establish Instructional Objectives								
4. Select Instructional Methods								
5. Instructional Evaluation								
6. Progress Reports								
Academic Year _____								

3.   *Establish Instructional Objectives*
       Formalize the specific, three-part objectives specified in Chapter 5.
4.   *Select Instructional Methods*
       List the enabling steps representing methods and materials selected, where available, for each prescription.
5.   *Make Instructional Evaluation*
       Outline the manner in which each objective-prescription will be evaluated for its effectiveness and efficiency.
6.   *Finalize Progress Reports*
       Determine the type of written and oral report prepared, when it is to be prepared (how often), and to whom it is to be delivered. Reports to parents, teachers, support team, principal, and supervisors are critical.

Program Coordination Task Area

This task area primarily represents the management scheme for a learning disabilities program and includes the following questions which must be answered:
1.   *Program Placement*
       Who is responsible for program objectives?

Figure 8

MODEL LEARNING DISABILITIES SYSTEMS: PROGRAM PLANNING GUIDE

PROGRAM GOAL:		Date:	Administrator Responsible		MLDS Team			Code: MLDS : 1 2 3 4 5
		District:	Intermediate Unit		District/ I.U. Team			District/ I.U. : 1 2 3 4 5

VI. PROGRAM COORDINATION TASK AREA	OBJECTIVES specific measurable aim for each task designated	PROCESS	Time Line	PRODUCT	Time Line	EVALUATION CRITERIA	CONSTRAINTS	KEY
1. Program Placement								
2. Instructional Decision								
3. Program Decision								
A. Inservice								
B. Referral Process								
C. Identification Process								
D. Placement Decision								
E. Instructional Systems								
F. Instructional Evaluation								
4. Support Team Coordination								
5. Community Awareness/ Participation								
6. Program Evaluation								
7. Other								

Academic Year _____

2, *Instructional Decision*
What person, within a staff and line level, makes decisions?

3. *Program Decision*
Who has the responsibility for:
- (a) inservice—when, where, and who
- (b) referral process
- (c) identification process
- (d) placement decision
- (e) instructional systems
- (f) instructional evaluation

4. *Support Team Coordination*
How do they receive referrals, who coordinates the team efforts, what are the primary objectives of the team's efforts?

5. *Community Awareness and Participation*
What procedures and coordination of those procedures bring the program to the community and the community volunteers of all types to the program?

6. *Program Evaluation*
What are the procedures for evaluating the program, its personnel, and the decision-making objectives?

Figure 9

ACADEMIC YEAR_____

VII. SCHOOL & COMMUNITY PARTICIPATION TASK AREA	OBJECTIVES specific measurable aim for each task designated	PROCESS	Time Line	PRODUCT	Time Line	EVALUATION CRITERIA	CONSTRAINTS	KEY
1. School Participation								
A. Program								
B. Diagnostic/ Support Service								
C. Instructional Intervention								
D. Information Dispersion								
E. Peer Evaluation								
2. Community Participation								
A. Information Dispersion								
B. Community/Parent Involvement								
C. Sibling/Peer Tutoring Involvement								
D. Community/Parent Student Evaluation								

School and Community Participation Task Area

This task area requests the objectives for a preplanned program to guarantee school and community awareness, information to them, discussion in return, and evaluation.

1. *School Participation*

Essentially places demands on the learning disabilities program to keep regular and vocational educators, administrators, and other staff fully informed and feeling a part of this program; and asks that school personnel (especially regular educators) evaluate the learning disabilities program through a planned evaluation program. We regard this as a two-way street; that is, the learning disabilities personnel evaluate the regular program format, and the regular teaching staff evaluate the value of the learning disabilities service delivery.

2. *Community Participation*

Can be guaranteed only when the components are clearly spelled out, e.g., peer tutoring and teacher-mom tutoring, and when a parental and consumer (student) evaluation procedure has been identified.

Summary

The purpose of this chapter was to identify the major aspects, or components, of a learning disability program, then develop a planning-evaluation guide for each of the program aspects by delineating the objective(s), process, product, time line, evaluation criteria, and constraints for those components that were identified.   The rationale was that the administrative, supervisory, and supportive services and the instructional delivery aspects of a program must be communicated as components attempting to fulfill objectives of the same program.   Program objectives must therefore be well articulated and in synchronization with one another.   If they are not well articulated aspects of the same program, then they may well represent distinct departments with even more distinct departmental missions.   Therefore, programmatic boundaries can definitely mediate against the good of any effort if they do not share its goals.   To prohibit or at least reduce this occurrence, it is strongly recommended that objectives and goals be established by the working membership of any program which will provide a direct course of action for all those contributing.

Before any committee or working group can agree on specifically stated objectives, it may be necessary for them to develop a program model reflected in the chapters on the systematic screening process to identify learning-disabled children utilizing an operational definition of learning disabilities: Chapter 5—a chapter on instructional systems; Chapter 6—useful instructional materials; Chapter 7—secondary program aspects; Chapter 8—in-service activities; Chapter 9—a chapter on parent and community involvement, and on mobilizing community resources; and Chapter 10—program and personnel evaluation.

The second point of this chapter is the need to have a process for developing and coordinating the critical aspects of the program content.   It is likely that many teachers will view this chapter as an administrative one.   It is true that the process of an organization will flow administratively in the direction and at the rate at which administrators provide responsible and responsive decision making.   Hopefully, most special education administrators will find this chapter a helpful review, general administrators will find it a good orientation, and principals may see it as assisting them to anticipate or plan at the building level.   But the major overriding purpose of this chapter was to acquaint teachers and support team members (counselors, school psychologists, and speech therapists) with the components of a total program.   It was the intention of this chapter to provide all the learning disabilities team members with a program gestalt, at least as we see it, based on our four years of work in the Pennsylvania Project.

LEARNING   OBJECTIVES
Chapter   2

Cognitive   Objectives

After carefully reading this chapter, you will be able to:
1)   State the reasons for "systems approach" when implementing a learning disabilities program;
2)   Recognize the initial options open to the MLDS staff in developing a learning disabilities program in the absence of clearly defined program goals;
3)   Identify and justify the role of the MLDS in providing technical assistance to a school system;
4)   Define "systems approach";
5)   Identify the values of the systems approach in the planning and evaluating utilized by the MLDS staff;
6)   Assess "context evaluation."

L E A R N I N G   O B J E C T I V E S
Chapter   2

Affective Objectives

After reading this chapter, the author intends that you will:

1)   Distinguish between "content" and "process";

2)   Be aware of the questions asked of special educators in the area of accountability;

3)   Accept the main goal of a learning disabilities program;

4)   Associate the constants of implementing a learning disabilities program in this manual with constraints of program implementation in your district;

5)   Be aware of the MLDS practice in the area of evaluation responsibility;

6)   Demonstrate competencies in using the MLDS Program Planning Guide in initiating and maintaining a well-developed learning disabilities program;

7)   Value the principle of the MLDS systems approach.

SYSTEMS APPROACH PRIMER

The initial problem in developing a systematic procedure to administer a learning disabilities program is the absence of clearly defined program goals.   When the MLDS was confronted with this problem, the staff had two options open to it:

OPTION I	OPTION II

[Refer to p._____in the manual.]

The role of a model program (e.g., Tyrone Model Program Learning Disabilities Systems) is to provide an evaluation process which serves as a comprehensive screen or backdrop which a school can use to compare and contrast its

READER'S NOTES

SYSTEMS APPROACH PRIMER

objectives and stated alternatives and to conceptualize a
total program by seeing each component aspect in relation
to overall program goals.

In order to clarify the systems approach, analyze the two
definitions (Banghard, p._____, and Lerner, p._____)
and place brief summaries of their definitions in the blanks
provided.

Banghard	Lerner

[Refer to p._____.]

READER'S NOTES

SYSTEMS APPROACH PRIMER

Now, in your own words, place the definition of systems
approach in the blank provided below and then compare it
to the previous definitions.

_____

_____

An important aspect of systematic approaches is to realize
the difference between "process" and "content." The
distinction between the two in the initial phase of a system
approach is vital to the effectiveness of program success.

READER'S NOTES

[Refer to p._____in the manual.]

[Refer to p._____]

SYSTEMS APPROACH PRIMER

The content is the _____,
or what actually happens in the classroom, while the process
is the _____
which guides the operation.

The focus of a systems approach centers in the process. The
central purpose of the systems approach is to see that many
and varied aspects necessary to a learning disabilities program
are organized and structured into an integrated whole. Every
administrator, regular class teacher, or special educator
knows the importance of a balanced program versus isolated
program aspects. The responsibility in achieving a balance
is knowing what resources exist, what the problems are
(predictably) which will constrain program development,
and how to make things happen in a planned, evaluated, and
orderly fashion to achieve what should be occurring in keeping with goals and objectives of a given program. Delivering

SYSTEMS APPROACH PRIMER

long-term plans in the form of goal statements and then evaluating that planning at specified short-term intervals is a far
cry from just letting something happen.

In order to understand clearly the mechanics of the systems
approach, the following activity has been designed to aid
the reader.

List aspects of a program most familiar to the reader (e.g.,
social studies, math, extra-curricular, etc.) under the
systems approach presented:

Checklist

Determined

Yes [   ]   No [   ]

Determined

Yes [   ]   No [   ]

Program Goal(s)_____

_____

_____

Objective(s)_____

_____

_____

READER'S NOTES   SYSTEMS APPROACH PRIMER

Process_____

_____

_____

Determined   Timeline dates_____
Yes [ ] No [ ]   Product_____

_____

Determined   _____
Yes [ ] No [ ]   Timeline dates_____

                                 Evaluation_____

Determined   _____
Yes [ ] No [ ]

                                 Constraints_____
Determined
Yes [ ] No [ ]   _____

                                 _____

                                 _____

SYSTEMS APPROACH PRIMER

This makeshift chart should give the reader the basic concepts involved in developing a systems approach, in relation to a program most familiar to him/her.

As stated by the MLDS, the systems approach allows you to:

1_____

_____

2_____

_____

3_____

_____

4_____

_____

In achieving desired goals of a program the MLDS staff has developed the Management by Objectives Worksheets which aid in actualizing the systems approach.

READER'S NOTES

SYSTEMS APPROACH PRIMER

These worksheets help in determining what is happening in the program, what should happen in the program, and why it is or is not happening. The process by which the learning disabilities program is formulated and implemented focuses on seven critical Task Areas. These are:

1_____

2_____

3_____

4_____

5_____

6_____

7_____

[Refer to p._____ in the Manual.]

Each area is composed of functions that are of critical importance to the overall workability of a given process. The order of these functions has a general, but not an absolute,

READER'S NOTES

SYSTEMS APPROACH PRIMER

flow, and it is frequently necessary to rearrange the order
from time to time. In some school districts not all task
areas will apply.

The predominant feature of the systems approach is that the
sum of the parts does not overpower the whole; but in keeping the gestalt of what constitutes the major goals of a good
program, it is possible to identify individual parts, weak
parts, and parts that should not be included at all.

In short, when each function has a stated objective and the
process, product, timeline, evaluation criteria, and constraints
are stated, then planned decision-making can commence.

In order to understand the "how," MLDS staff members
have utilized the systematic approach in planning/evaluating
a learning disabilities program.

INFORMATION DISPERSION

		Time Line
OBJECTIVE	80 percent of the parents at Jones High School will be informed of the purpose and substance of the Learning Disabilities Program	2/1
PROCESS	Radio spots	1/15
	Newsletter	1/17
	Seminar	1/19
		1/25
PRODUCT	Parents knowledgeable in purpose and substance of LD program	1/19
		1/25
EVALUATION CRITERIA	Survey to be sent home every day after seminar	
CONSTRAINTS	Money for radio spots; speakers for seminars; parental attitude	

READER'S NOTES

SYSTEMS APPROACH PRIMER

Although highly simplified, this brief extraction of a function under the Task Area of School and Community Participation gives the reader some insight into the preplanning stage which eventually leads to the development of a learning disabilities program beneficial to child, community, and society.

OVERVIEW REVIEW

It is recommended that a school system not enter-into a learning disabilities program with less than_____

_____.

Technical assistance, as utilized by MLDS is the supportive direction used in the establishment of a planned evaluative process and is not the_____

_____

_____

[Refer to p._____in the Manual.]

[Refer to p._____]

READER'S NOTES

SYSTEMS APPROACH PRIMER

The institution of education has moved into an era of accountability. The special educator in the classroom or resource room, faced with the day-to-day reality of teaching children, does not need to learn another obtuse theoretical model or be overwhelmed by the academic prose in which most evaluation articles are written. Jones (1973) writes that before any school district should presume to devise a system of accountability for special education, the following questions should be answered:

1 _____

_____

2 _____

_____

[Refer to p._____]

Most evaluation procedures developed thus are far too complex for the already overburdened classroom teacher to use. However, the term *evaluation* has come to have a "ring" of ambiguity, and for this reason, clarification on the type

SYSTEMS APPROACH PRIMER

of evaluation being discussed in a systems approach for developing/evaluating LD programs is necessary.   We are concerned with _____

_____

[Refer to p._____]

evaluation and not that of personnel.   The task of personnel evaluation is not the prerogative of an_____

_____.

[Refer to p._____]

Context evaluation is what a district says_____

_____;

[Refer to p._____]

what in fact, it is_____,
and what_____are.

There are several goals and objectives which are inherent to a learning disabilities program.   The main goal is to:

[Refer to p._____]

_____

_____

_____

READER'S NOTES

SYSTEMS APPROACH PRIMER

Some secondary goals that you would perceive to be important are:_____

_____

_____

_____

_____

Objectives are measurable aspects that reflect the process and product of a given goal. The effective objective is specific in nature and answers the criteria of: (1)_____

_____ (2)_____

_____ (3)_____

Initiating context-evaluation involves several phases. The first phase is that of observing the goals of the learning disabilities program. In order to accomplish this phase, one must listen carefully to what administrators, teachers, and students say the program should accomplish. This can be maximized by

READER'S NOTES   **SYSTEMS APPROACH PRIMER**

determining the attitude of the people involved. Secondly, looking at the constraints of the program, both within and outside the program, constraints can include such things as:

_____

_____

_____

As each function under each task area is developed (goals, objectives, etc.) in the planning guides, context evaluation is utilized to provide for effective parts which flow into a successful whole (learning disabilities program).

DEFINITIONS

Task Area:_____

Context Evaluation:_____

Process:_____

Systems Approach:_____

_____

3 Screening Children for a Learning Disabilities Program: The MLDS Screening Procedure

Glen G. Foster and David A. Sabatino

Overview

THIS chapter deals briefly with the definition of learning disabilities and the operations necessary to render an educational decision regarding learning disabilities. The screening system developed by the Model Learning Disabilities Systems (MLDS) is described in detail and its characteristics are noted.

Toward a Definition of Learning Disabilities

The Council of Exceptional Children's State and Federal Information Clearinghouse devoted their first publication (1968) to the variations among the states in the identification of and development of programs for children with learning disabilities. Their conclusion was that "the child with learning disabilities is the newest and perhaps the most ill-defined newcomer to the generic category of the handicapped."

It should be obvious from reading Chapter 1 that widespread agreement has yet to be achieved concerning the criteria to be used in assigning a label to the learning-disabled child. Therefore, the prevalence of this problem within the educational setting cannot be determined. The components indigenous to this disability category are not operationally defined, but incidence figures have been suggested, ranging from one percent of the school population to thirty percent (Lerner, 1971).

The federal definition of learning disabilities (see Chapter 1) is essentially a definition by exclusion and differentiates learning-disabled children from those with mental retardation, sensory impairments, social-emotional problems, and cultural differences. It implies a relationship between learning disabilities and conditions referred to in the past as perceptual handicaps, developmental aphasia, dyslexia, brain injury, or minimal brain dysfunction.

Confusion exists between the concepts of exogenous brain injury and learning disabilities. Many authorities stress the commonality between brain dysfunction and learning disabilities to the extent that the terms are used synonymously. This is not the stance taken by the staff of the Model Learning Disabilities Systems. We feel that cases of verifiable central nervous system involvement (e.g., cerebral palsy) should stand alone as a disability category requiring assessment and remedial procedures not necessarily appropriate for the learning-disabled child. In addition, children with so-called "minimal involvement" cannot justifiably be labeled as brain damaged. It is our opinion that the medical profession has been kind and considerate in signing the papers necessary to facilitate educational service for children needing a brain damaged label to be admitted into remedial programs. Such a practice indicates that clinical signs of neurological involvement are not demonstrable but that the child in question may have observable perceptual and/or language impairment associated with neurological involvement (Taylor, 1961).

Such practice is inappropriate, however, because it emphasizes a causal relationship between academic achievement and brain injury that has not been supported in the literature (Kaufmann, 1973). By divorcing the learning disabilities category from the minimal brain damage syndrome, emphasis can be placed on the educational procedures that will aid such children. The removal of the cause-effect parameter of the learning disabilities definition also opens the door for an operational description of the components necessary to render an educationally usable description (diagnosis if one prefers).

Operationalization of the Term Learning Disability

While the federal definition of learning disabilities is based largely on the exclusion of other disability categories, inherent in the definition are three components that can be operationally measured. These include normal intelligence, a learning problem as evidenced by academic difficulties, and some evidence of a perceptual/language handicap.

Academic Achievement

Academic achievement deficits may be found in any of the skill areas of reading, writing, spelling, or arithmetic. An easily identifiable feature of learning disabilities is poor performance on any of the following: word recognition, reading vocabulary, reading comprehension, writing, spelling, or arithmetic reasoning or computation. These areas of difficulty frequently result in poor performance in other academic areas and cause personal-social discomfort in the classroom setting. The MLDS has found readily available norm-referenced, standardized measures to be adequate for screening purposes in the areas of academic achievement.

Percentile scores serve as a basis for deciding on the presence of an academic difficulty. Percentile cutoff points can be manipulated as appropriate for a given area and extent of services available. This system generally operates on the assumption that a score below the 20th percentile on any achievement subtest, in the presence of normal intelligence, is indicative of an academic dysfunction. It should be noted that the proposed screening system does not make use of discrepancy scores between academic performance and measured intelligence, as the lowered reliabilities of such scores make their usage problematic (Salvia et al., 1974). The system, instead, operates on the assumption that (1) limited academic performance on an achievement measure represents a learning problem and (2) any child capable of demonstrating normal intelligence is capable of evidencing success in school (Kagan, 1969; Keough, 1971).

Intelligence and Language

Intelligence is defined as cognitive ability that reflects the formation, association, and mediation of language concepts. Effective measurement of this basic psychological process requires the administration of nonverbal and verbal tests to aid in the initial differentiation among receptive, central, and expressive language deficits, contributing cultural factors (e.g., bilingualism, etc.), and other factors that inhibit normal language development.

The MLDS suggests a verbal or nonverbal IQ of 85 as the lower limit for accepting a child as having demonstrated the ability to develop language concepts at a rate comparable to normally developing children of the same age. If a child does not obtain an IQ of 85 or above, it is suggested that the child receive remedial services different from those appropriate for a learning-disabled child. Very often learning-disabled children show a marked contrast between verbal and nonverbal measured intelligence. A difference of 16 or more IQ points on two different measures is considered as a significant indicator of a language difficulty. Such a difference may enable a child to obtain eligibility for services, whether or not a perceptual handicap can be demonstrated.

Perception

The measurement of perception has long been hampered by both semantic and philosophical problems (Sabatino and Foster, 1974). Confusion exists both as to the nature of the perceptual processes and as to the way they are to be evaluated.

An analysis of the views put forth by a number of researchers and educators has led to the generation and adoption of the following definition of perception:

> Perception is the process of interpreting neurally coded information, e.g., attaching meaning to information received by the senses. It is realized that perception does not operate independently of the processes of sensation and cognition, but it does seem to have measurable qualities that permit ascertaining the level of skill performance within and between separate modalities (Sabatino and Foster, 1974).

In assessing a child's level of perceptual development, it is important to measure both the auditory and the visual components of the perceptual processes. Considerable energy has been expended in the past on the measurement of visual-motor perception, often to the exclusion of visual discrimination, visual memory, and/or auditory perceptual abilities.

Recent literature in the fields of visual and auditory perception, however, indicate that these areas are now receiving increased attention (Chalfant and Schefflin, 1969; Wolfe, 1968). It would appear that most currently available measures of visual and auditory perceptual skills are unsatisfactory even for screening purposes. Available measures often rely on unsatisfactory normative samples, unstandardized administration procedures, and nebulous conceptual bases. In response to this need and in accordance with the definition of perception noted, Sabatino and Foster have developed and standardized two instruments designed as measures of perception. These are the Test of Auditory Perception (TAP) and the Test of Visual Perceptual Discrimination and Memory (VPDM), a motor-free test of visual perception. The MLDS's screening system incorporates these two devices as both a means of assessing skills in the auditory and visual modalities and a basis for comparison of relative modality strengths. These instruments may be purchased by writing to the authors of this chapter.

Thus, the three components (stated below) of the MLDS's definition of learning disabilities have been operationally defined in keeping with the federal definition. It seems that while most authorities may have different ideas concerning the content of the diagnostic process to render a diagnosis of learning disabilities, they are agreed on the major components. These components include: (1) balance between receptive-expressive language skills and the ability to formulate and express symbolic language concepts; (2) the presence of specific academic achievement skill weaknesses; and (3) balance between test performance of the perceptual modalities, perceptual integration, and central conceptual language skills.

Overview of Screening Model

The MLDS screening model is an attempt to operationalize the federal definition of learning disabilities; it provides an effective means of screening large numbers of potential candidates for learning disabilities services. The system is the product of three years of development and continuous change.

To meet this end, the process incorporates a combination of inservice, teacher observation and referral, and individualized testing. Children who meet the criteria necessary for inclusion in the learning disabilities program are determined as eligible by progressing through various referral stages.

Classroom teachers receive inservice training that allows them to make appropriate choices as to which children to refer. A classroom teacher-learning disabilities specialist conference allows some of these referrals to be eliminated before formalized testing is begun. Individualized testing is composed of three stages as eligible children proceed through tests of academic achievement, verbal and non-verbal intelligence, and perceptual skills. Children not meeting the evaluation criteria are eliminated at each stage of the screening process and are referred to other agencies if appropriate.

The screening process allows for the efficient screening of a large number of children. The testing time for eligible children averages 80 minutes.

MLDS Screening System

In operationalizing the definition of learning disabilities, the MLDS has developed a screening system that can be used effectively to differentiate large numbers of children in order to identify those appropriate for inclusion in a learning disabilities program.

Such a system must assess the child's level of performance in each of the component areas previously described. To meet this end, a multistep screening system has been developed and revised over a three-year period. This system is based upon the exclusion of children who are not appropriately labeled learning disabled from those who are eligible for remedial services. The flow chart shown in Figure 10 can be used as a graphic aid to understand this procedure.

Figure 10

Model of MLDS Screening System

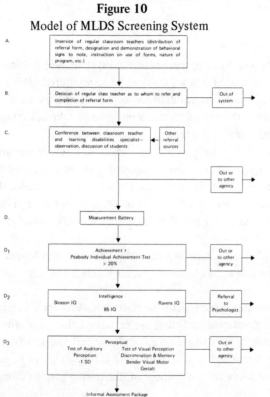

A. Inservice of regular classroom teachers (distribution of referral form, designation and demonstration of behavioral signs to note, instruction on use of forms, nature of program, etc.)

B. Decision of regular class teacher as to whom to refer and completion of referral form — Out of system

C. Conference between classroom teacher and learning disabilities specialist—observation, discussion of students — Other referral sources

Out or to other agency

D. Measurement Battery

D_1 Achievement + Peabody Individual Achievement Test > 20% — Out or to other agency

D_2 Intelligence — Slosson IQ — Ravens IQ — 85 IQ — Referral to Psychologist

D_3 Perceptual — Test of Auditory Perception -1 SD — Test of Visual Perception Discrimination & Memory Bender Visual Motor Gestalt — Out or to other agency

Informal Assessment Package

A.   Inservice of Classroom Teachers

Several pitfalls are inherent in any teacher referral system, and the screening system described has been refined to eliminate many of the difficulties that can be encountered. It is the contention of the MLDS staff that the screening of a large number of children can best be facilitated by a teacher referral system. Referrals and observations take place at the end of the academic year to take advantage of the classroom teacher's extensive experience with the referred children.

An inservice session is held during which the classroom teachers are familiarized with the nature of the learning disabilities program and become acquainted with the behaviors typical of a child who is learning disabled. Such training provides the classroom teacher with an overview of the program and provides a solid basis for referral decisions. To meet this end, a list of descriptors has been developed to identify areas of systematic focus to be assessed by the learning disabilities specialist. The complete list of these descriptors is presented in Chapter 5.

It is recognized that these areas are not mutually exclusive, but by encouraging the classroom teacher to think in terms of these possible areas of evaluation, his ability to observe objectively the behavior of the child will be enhanced.

To make these descriptors more realistic to classroom teachers, a corresponding list of definitions and sample behaviors has been developed, and these are presented along with the descriptor list. Sample behaviors are stated in a format similar to that found on an objective test and serve as a graphic representation of the actual behaviors in which we are interested. Some items were taken wholly or in part from standardized instruments, while others were designed solely for the purpose of illustrating specific behaviors. These definitions and sample behaviors are presented in Chapter 6.

The combination of descriptor list and sample behavior list provides an outline for the inservice session, familiarizes the classroom teachers with the parameters which should be observed during the referral process, and provides a commonality among referrals that makes the diagnostic process more meaningful by providing a common set of language terminologies.

During this inservice session, the classroom teachers are exposed to the referral form used by the MLDS (Appendix A). The items to be evaluated are discussed, and questions are answered concerning the completion of this form (see Inservice Chapter).

Inservice training of both learning disabilities and classroom teachers generally breaks down the state of isolation found in many classroom settings and helps the development of skills which can prove useful in many situations. Support team members such as psychologists are available in an inservice and consultant capacity.

It is apparent that the success of such a screening system depends largely upon the referral information provided by the regular classroom teachers. To facilitate the referral process, the staff of MLDS depends upon the inservice of the classroom teachers to provide them with sufficient information adequately to aid in the identification of learning-disabled children. It is often the case that one teacher readily refers a large portion of the class for evaluation, while another is reluctant to make any referrals. At this stage of the screening process, we are anxious to promote some over-referrals in an attempt to assure the inclusion of most learning-disabled children in the targeted population. Therefore, some false-positive referrals should occur in the process of encouraging teachers to refer when in doubt. Since over-referral may be objectionable on the basis of the criticisms leveled at the labeling process in general, the MLDS inservice sessions cover the dangers of the self-fulfilling prophecy (Palardy, 1969; Rosenthal and Jacobson, 1968) and the halo effect (Foster et al., 1974). It is further hoped that the label of learning disabled may be qualitatively different from that of other disability categories. The MLDS is conducting research in an attempt to investigate this contention.

It must be noted that the screening system does not limit its referral source to classroom teachers, although their suggestions furnish the bulk of referrals evaluated. Children can be referred for evaluation by administrators, guidance counselors, psychologists, nurses, and other support personnel. Referrals have also been accepted when made at the request of parents, although school personnel are always informed of such contacts.

B.   Completion of Referral Form

Following the inservice session on the use of the referral form, classroom teachers decide which children in their class they feel would be most appropriate for referral. The necessary form is completed for each of these children based on the teacher's knowledge of the child's abilities and behaviors. These forms are returned to the learning disabilities specialist and provide a basis for the conference between the specialist and the classroom teacher. Despite the large number of children typically referred, the screening system has now eliminated approximately 80 percent of the school population from consideration for learning disabilities services. During this process, the classroom teachers generally become familiar with the program offered and have developed some skills in the objective observation and evaluation of behavior.

C.   Conference Between Classroom Teacher and Learning Disabilities Specialist

After reviewing the completed referral forms, the learning disabilities specialist schedules an observation and conference session with each of the classroom teachers. Often it is necessary to schedule separate conference and observation periods, always at a time convenient for the classroom teacher. During this step, the referral forms are discussed and the referred children are observed in the classroom setting. The discussion which follows the observation is often sufficient to eliminate a portion of the referred children from consideration for the learning disabilities program. It must be kept in mind that over-referrals have been solicited and that this step allows for the deletion of many referrals which were inappropriate.

D.   Individualized Testing

Children not eliminated from the learning disabilities program on the basis of teacher referrals or the conference between the learning disabilities specialist and the classroom teacher are evaluated next with an individually administered test battery. This battery consists of six different measures which evaluate the broad areas of academic achievement, intelligence, and perceptual skills.

Academic Achievement

The MLDS has found the Peabody Individual Achievement Test (PIAT) to be an appropriate measurement device in the area of academic achievement. Subtests measure the skill areas of spelling, arithmetic, reading comprehension, word recognition, and general information. This instrument is administered by the learning disabilities specialist and constitutes the first stage of the screening battery. Scores are computed as percentiles for an age equivalent sample, and a child who scores below the 20th percentile on at least one subtest of this measure is considered to have displayed an academic problem. Children scoring above the cutoff point on all subtests have not demonstrated such a deficit and are not eligible for learning disabilities services. Such children are eliminated from further screening and may be referred to another service agency if such referral is warranted in the eyes of the learning disabilities specialist or the classroom teacher.

Intelligence Testing

This portion of the test battery consists of the Coloured Progressive Matrices Test (Raven's) and the Slosson Intelligence Test (SIT). The Raven's provides a measure of nonverbal intelligence, and the SIT, a measure of verbal intelligence. Both instruments are administered by the learning disabilities specialist, and an IQ of 85 or above on either measure is necessary for inclusion in the learning disabilities program. A comparison of these two scores provides the basis for a language assessment portion of the screening system. A discrepancy of 16 or more IQ points between the measures is a significant indication of a language disability, and such a pattern makes a child eligible for services despite the results of the perceptual battery. In such cases, the nonverbal IQ is usually inflated relative to the verbal IQ, but the opposite pattern of results is also accepted as indicative of a learning disability (Clements, 1962). Children who fail to earn an IQ of 85 on either of the intelligence instruments are eliminated from further testing.

It should be noted that our learning disabilities specialists are not formally trained psychologists and realize that they are not qualified to pass final judgment on a child's intellectual ability. The IQ scores are considered to be of little value to educational planning except for the range of verbal or nonverbal function which the child can demonstrate. Such information can be easily misunderstood, and confidentiality of these data is necessary.

In cases where IQ information eliminates a child from eligibility in the learning disabilities program, a certified psychologist assesses the child to determine if other services or programs might be beneficial. If, in the psychologist's opinion, the services offered by the learning disabilities program are appropriate for the type of disabilities demonstrated by the child, the child is recommended for admission to the program. Final placement decisions are left to the administrator responsible for the program. The psychologist should be available to help with placement decisions whenever difficult evaluation problems arise and to supervise the entire screening procedure.

Perceptual Testing

Three instruments are employed to measure behaviors associated with auditory, visual, and visual-motor perception. The Test of Auditory Perception (TAP), developed by Foster and Sabatino (1974), is employed to assess three areas of auditory perception: (1) phoneme discrimination, (2) memory for word units, and (3) sequencing. The Test of Visual Perceptual Discrimination and Memory (VPDM) assesses visual perception and visual memory skills, and the Bender Visual Motor Gestalt Test (BVMGT) serves as a measure of visual-motor development.

Data from the perceptual measures are converted to standard scores. A score of at least minus one standard deviation from the normative mean for the appropriate chronological age group is necessary for the demonstration of a perceptual problem. This variation would roughly correspond to the 16th percentile of a normal distribution. A child who scores below this cutoff point is now eligible for service. At the completion of the perceptual assessment, the screening process is complete. Children scoring above this point and not demonstrating a significant language handicap are not eligible for services and are referred to other agencies when appropriate.

Use of Learning Disabilities Teachers as Psycho-Diagnosticians

Even with a well-developed referral system, a great deal of individualized assessment is necessary. The lack of availability of psychologists and trained psychometricians in many states makes it difficult to complete this formal assessment. To circumvent the possible absence of trained psychometric personnel, the MLDS has developed an inservice system designed to train learning disabilities teachers in the fundamentals of testing procedures so that the staff can conduct its own formal testing. This practice allows for efficient use of learning disabilities personnel, who are generally in agreement that test data are more educationally meaningful when the teaching staff is integrally involved in its compilation.

Learning disabilities teachers are first introduced to the appropriate instruments as well as to basic psychometric considerations through a combination of lectures and demonstrations. Materials and instructions are provided so that teachers can become familiar with each test. After the clarification of questions which arise, the teachers administer the measures to each other and finally to volunteer children in the appropriate age range. Scoring and administration are carried out under a psychologist's supervision until these skills have been well developed. It is felt that this inservice training is a viable way to develop basic psychometric skills and that each teacher can learn to administer each instrument in a manner consistent with the degree of validity necessary in accordance with the uses to which the data are to be applied. This inservice extends over a one-week period before the school year begins and must be conducted by a trained psychologist. This resource person should be available for consultation during the screening period.

Limitations of the Screening System

Like any screening model designed to make decisions about a large number of children, the system developed by the MLDS has inherent strengths and weaknesses. The testing and referral process, although streamlined to the extent possible, is time-consuming and requires a good deal of conscientious effort on the part of all involved. It is felt that this method is, however, about as brief as possible without sacrificing the validity of the information. Further, the system proper is not specifically designed to identify the marginally underachieving, bright learning disabilities child. When referred, such children are screened for language/ perceptual handicaps and may be eligible for services on the recommendation of the staff psychologist. While any screening system needs operational criteria to be useful, our policy is not to generate cutoff points which are inflexible to the extent that services cannot be offered to marginally qualified children. The screening criteria are viewed as selection guidelines rather than as a replacement for professional decisions based on a broad spectrum covering many parameters.

A number of strengths are inherent in the system and have been noted throughout this chapter. These include the overall effectiveness and efficiency of the system and the use of extensive classroom teacher experience in making referrals. Communication between learning disabilities specialists and classroom teachers is facilitated, and each has an important role in the decision-making process. The use of learning disabilities specialists as diagnosticians gives them first-hand knowledge of the test-taking behaviors of each child and offers an opportunity for clinical observations and the opportunity to establish a relationship with the child.

Data from the screening battery serve a three-fold purpose. They identify a population appropriate for inclusion in the learning disabilities program. They are useful as the preliminary guidelines of a pre-post test evaluation of program effectiveness, and, in conjunction with other information on educational assessment, they may lead directly to the establishment of instructional goals and prescriptions (see Chapter 5).

Development of Screening System

This section deals with several methodological changes which have been implemented over a period of three years. It is hoped that others developing similar screening-diagnostic processes can profit from our past experiences.

The screening model used in the first year of operation attempted to steer away from teacher referrals as a basis of screening. Instead, all children in a given area were tested on academic achievement, and the lowest portion of these children were further evaluated on intelligence and perceptual skills. Testing took place at the beginning of the academic year and was conducted in the regular classroom. This methodology necessitated the use of group achievement tests, which proved to be totally inadequate with first- and second-grade populations. In an attempt to provide data which would be of further use to the local school district, tests were chosen to correspond with the measures typically used by the schools in that district. The group tests proved problematic due to test-taking difficulties, misinterpretations by classroom teachers, and poor overall reliability. Certain children were earning grade equivalent scores at a second-grade level by completing the IBM answer sheets without looking at the test questions. Such results forced us to avoid group academic achievement measures and to depend on our own resource teachers for test data. We have found that the choice of instruments must be made to fit program needs rather than existing evaluation programs.

The use of individually administered measures necessitated the development of a teacher referral basis for screening which, in turn, led to further difficulties. Early referral forms were designed to elicit a free response from the classroom teacher. This format yielded some very adequate referrals, but far too many classroom teachers responded with "needs testing" or a longer form of the same statement. The more specific referral form now in use has eliminated this difficulty and has proven to be a useful adjunct to the referral procedure, as it requires the teachers to make judgments based on actual observations.

The choice of instruments used in this screening model is based upon two years of experience with various devices. As mentioned earlier, group tests were abandoned in favor of more appropriate individually administered instruments. Individual assessment offers the advantage of affording the learning disabilities specialist an opportunity to interact with each referred child personally, adding clinical impressions to the supply of information about the child. Individual testing, properly handled, can be a positive experience for the child, and these testing sessions also afford the specialist the opportunity to establish rapport with the child who may be taught later.

The Peabody Individual Achievement Test (PIAT) was chosen as the instrument of preference for assessing academic achievement for several reasons. It is straightforward in its administration format, it covers a broad range of academic areas, reliability and validity data are adequate, and it is often intriguing to the child being tested.

The Slosson Intelligence Test (SIT) was chosen as the verbal intelligence measure and has proven adequate for this purpose. Scores correlate highly with the longer Stanford Binet Intelligence Scale and are highly reliable. The Coloured Progressive Matrices was incorporated as a supplement to this measure and as a means of assessing nonverbal language development difficulties. In many cases, the inclusion of this instrument made children who would otherwise have been eliminated eligible for services. One child earned a score of 72 on the Slosson Intelligence Test and an IQ of 132 on the Coloured Progressive Matrices. The child was definitely not retarded, although the Slosson Intelligence Test score alone would have made her intellectual ability seem suspect.

As mentioned earlier, the Test of Auditory Perception (TAP) and the Visual Perceptual Discrimination and Memory (VPDM) were used to supplement the measures available in these areas and have been useful both as screening devices and as aids in making instructional decisions. The BVMGT is a popular measure of visual-motor skills, although its poor overall reliability makes overdependence on this measure undesirable. It is included because of its brevity, the clinical impressions possible through its use, and the information that the pre- and posttest scores provide concerning program effectiveness.

A number of instruments were employed in earlier MLDS screening systems but were discarded because of poor reliability, validity, time, or administration or lack of useful information being provided to the specialists through their administration. These discarded measures include several group achievement tests, as well as various individually administered measures.

Screening Instruments Employed by the MLDS

The following is a brief description of each of the instruments used by the MLDS in its screening package.

Teacher Referral Form

This is a nonstandardized, informal assessment device which classroom teachers complete for each child referred as a prelude to the screening process. Items are completed, drawing from the teacher's experience with the child in an attempt to develop a picture of the child's academic skills, perceptual language function, and social-behavioral development in the school milieu.

The form is three pages long and includes space for (1) demographic information (name, age, etc.), (2) evaluation of academic skills in various areas, and (3) evaluation of other skills areas. Nonacademic items refer to the developmental areas of: (1) language, (2) visual perception, (3) auditory perception, (4) behavior, and (5) arousal-attention. Directions are clear, and completing the form presents little difficulty to a teacher familiar with the concepts being evaluated and the child referred. This form is presented in the Appendix.

Peabody Individual Achievement Test (PIAT)

The PIAT (1970) was developed by Dunn and Markwardt and is published by the American Guidance

Service. It is an individually administered measure of academic achievement and taps the areas of mathematics, reading recognition, spelling, and general information. A basal and ceiling system shortens administration time of this measure.

The instrument is enclosed in two hardbound books which can be set at a 45^0 angle to the perpendicular
for test administration. This permits, for some subtests, the presentation of stimulus items to the examinee,
while cues are available on the hidden page which aid the examiner in administration. The format is well
planned and facilitates administration. In addition, the unique format and nature of test items makes the
PIAT interesting to the children being evaluated, facilitating the screening process.

The measure provides normative data extending from kindergarten through the twelfth-grade level.
Scores can be expressed as grade equivalents, percentiles, or standard scores with a mean of 100 and a
standard deviation of 15. Test-retest reliabilities are available for each subtest at each of six representative
grade levels. Total test reliabilities range from $r = .82$ at the kindergarten level to $r = .92$ at the eighth grade
level, with test-retest reliabilities for individual subtests ranging from $r = .42$ to $r = .89$.

Slosson Intelligence Test (SIT)

The Slosson Intelligence Test (Slosson, 1974) relies largely on verbally loaded items and is useful for
children below the age of four through adult populations (items are presented as low as the 2.0-year level).
The measure employs a basal and ceiling format which greatly shortens administration time. Scores are
expressed in terms of mental ages, which are used to compute intelligence quotients.

The test instructions are concise, and items are not difficult to administer. The measure was designed for use by a large number of professionals including teachers, social workers, etc. The measure shows a very high relationship with the Stanford Binet Intelligence Scale. A test-retest (two-month interval) reliability coefficient of $r = .97$ is reported by the authors, but this figure is probably inflated by the extended age range involved in the study.

Coloured Progressive Matrices (Raven's)

A measure developed in England by J. C. Raven (1965), the Coloured Progressive Matrices is a non-verbal test of reasoning ability and is distributed in this country by Western Psychological Services. Different forms are available which make the test appropriate for use with young children through adult levels.

The test format consists of three sets (A_1, A_B, & B) of twelve items each. Items present a partially incomplete matrix to the examinee whose task is to complete the design by choosing one of six possible response choices. The measure is highly nonverbal in nature and serves as a useful adjunct to the Slosson Intelligence Test.

Normative data in the age range of five to eleven and one-half years are somewhat inadequate, having been compiled on 608 English school children. Scores can be reported which can be used in the computation of intelligence quotients. Test-retest coefficients are adequate and range from $r = .86$ to $r = .99$. Due to the normative sample, this measure is inadequate as a singular measure of intelligence. Its format and nonverbal character, however, make it a useful adjunct to a verbally loaded measure as part of a screening system.

Bender Visual Motor Gestalt (BVMGT)

The BVMGT (1938) is a test of visual motor development and consists of nine geometric designs which the subject is to copy onto unlined paper. The model is constantly in view during this process. The original designs were constructed by Wertheimer (1923). Various scoring systems have been developed for use with the BVMGT, and perhaps the most commonly used is that developed by Koppitz (1971). Using this system, the examiner scores certain key errors which were found to differentiate between normal and abnormal groups. The instrument receives wide usage and is at various times construed to be an indicator of brain damage, perceptual functioning, perceptual-motor functioning, intelligence, and emotional stability. Test-retest reliability coefficients using the Koppitz scoring system range from r = .60 to r = .67 (Koppitz, 1971).

Test of Visual Perceptual Discrimination and Memory (VPDM)

The VPDM (Foster and Sabatino, 1974) was designed as a nonmotoric measure of visual perception and memory based on Wertheimer's (1929) designs. The measure consists of 18 items, each in a multiple-choice format. The examinee is presented with a stimulus design and must choose which of six possible response choices is identical to that design. Scores are reported as age equivalents, and normative data are available on 450 elementary-age children in the mid-Pennsylvania area. Test-retest reliabilities (four-month interval) range from r = .60 to r = .76.

Test of Auditory Perception (TAP)

The TAP was designed as a measure of auditory perceptual development. The measure consists of three subtests and is presented with the aid of prerecorded test items. The subtests measure the areas of auditory discrimination, word recognition, and auditory sequencing. Scores are expressed as age equivalents. Normative data are available from 450 mid-Pennsylvania elementary-age school children, and KR-20 reliabilities range from $r = .75$ to $r = .89$ for the three subtests.

Beyond Screening

This chapter was designed to examine a particular screening system used to identify, not classify, learning-disabled children. It was not designed to replace any professional now employed in the school systems. It was designed to promote better utilization of their time and talents. Nor does the screening system discussed attempt to replace any diagnostic assessment felt necessary. In fact, it is designed to facilitate such systems. The brief review of formal and informal assessment practices was not designed to be exhaustive or definitive in nature. Rather, it should be read as a set of observations and perceptions on these topics, replacing a summary by surfacing critical questions.

Formal Assessment

Most formal assessment instruments have been constructed to measure or describe specific or global behaviors, by reinforcing the performance of one person against the normative function of others of his age, grade, or sex, etc. Most of the personality, perceptual, language, or academic achievement skills measured are school-related behaviors on school-related tasks. But, since we fail to define learning except in operational terms, we seem to be assessing the top of the iceberg. The variance accounted for when we administer test batteries of perceptual, language, and academic tests is always shockingly low. The problem is that our tests are designed to get a piece of the whole in a concurrent and predictive fashion. That is, they are designed to tell what is or what will happen with a behavior or an academic task in relationship to that test score. They are not designed to say that if this or that intervention is employed or if no intervention is employed, thus or so will happen.

Standardized tests permit a comparative statement of how one person does, based on his performance, in reference to the group. In preparing an instructional objective that information is meaningful because it says something of the interest, reading, language, and perceptual complexity that a teaching material may possess. It does not say, nor was it designed to say, which teaching material to use.

A few tests do not fit the last criterion because they are designed to be used to initiate a level of activity as well as to state which specific activity to use. The problem is that most of these tests are to be used with a specific set of teaching materials, which are based on the construct that such a trait exists in nature. We are all familiar with Cohen's (1969) and Mann's (1971) feeling toward nonacademic (perceptual motor aptitude) training.

Finally, and most importantly, is the question of test reliability. Nunnally (1967) stated that:

In those applied settings where important decisions are made with respect to test scores,

a reliability of .90 is the minimum that should be tolerated and a reliability of .95
should be considered the desirable standard (p. 226).

Few of the popular tests can claim test-retest reliability in the .90s. The nine-item Bender Visual Motor Gestalt Test, the most commonly administered test, especially by school psychologists, has reliability of .39 to .66. It is therefore hardly suitable for preparing an educational prescription. But there is no need to criticize the Bender, because few claims were ever made for it by its test authors. The stability of the Frostig Developmental Test of Visual Perception is .69, the subtest ranging from .29 to .74. And the Illinois Test of Psycholinguistic Abilities has a reliability of .66 to .91 for the total test, .21 to .90 for individual subtest.

But what is more important is the difficulty in attempting to specify basic skills which may relate to, underlie, or be germane to academic learning. Again, it is difficult to say what human traits or aptitudes comprise a human information processing system capable of learning academic subject matter. And we really do not know which aptitudes are compensatory one for another, in support of or when it becomes impossible to learn because one or more are inoperative. In essence, we do not have definitive data to support a specific aptitudinal breakdown of the human traits that presumably underpin learning. To maintain test stability, it is necessary to keep the number of items at a reasonable length and to ascertain a given aptitude reliably. Thus, the practical test design problems associated with measuring aptitudinal breakdown are generally reflected in the amount of test time and the range or number of specific aptitudes that can be identified in nature as real traits relating to academic learning. Then the question becomes how specific is specific. Let us use the Bender Visual Motor Gestalt Test as an example. It is a short test that is designed to measure visual perceptual discrimination. Although it is used as a projective, indicative of brain damage, etc., it is at its best when scored with a Koppitz scoring system—a measure of the development of visual-motor development. But that seems to be the problem. Given the opportunity in factorial studies, such as the ones reported by Banantyne (1969), the Bender (or BVMGT) loads factorially with motor tests when it is administered to children that could have motoric types of impairments. That suggests that when a test such as the Bender Visual-Motor Gestalt Test is administered, it could assess visual perceptual discrimination, manual motor performance, and possibly visual perceptual memory component. All of these assumptions are, of course, based on the examinee having normal visual sensory function.

In short, most formal assessment instruments lack reliability, and even if they were reliable, we are not always sure what they ascertain. Therefore, the question of the human traits being measured as component aptitudes of some behavioral complex becomes more difficult to understand, especially when each component is to be viewed as a strength or weakness in relationship to every other component in deciding the instructional objective to be prepared.

The critics of the information-processing theorists have generally contested that such theory is decidedly shallow in accounting for what really happens with the learner. It is the feeling that most assessment systems of so-called information-processing behaviors fail to consider reward preference, achievement motivation, self-concept, self-expectancies and expectancies of meaningful others, values, particularly those of the family, and the learning style of the individual.

Hickey and Hoffman (1973) contend that most educational diagnosis assesses achievement levels. It is their belief that other aspects should also be assessed. They recommend that the following also be assessed:

Cognitive style (concrete/abstract)

Learning style (visual/auditory/kinesthetic)

Need for teaching structure (remedial, speech class)

Preferred mode of instruction (independent study, one-to-one, small and large group).

Once this data is obtained, then prescriptive learning packages or activities must be developed which take into consideration the various combinations of these components in treating the concept around which the generalized learning package is based (p. 37).

Informal Assessment

It should be obvious to the reader that among the other more common failings of a formal assessment procedure is the "one-shot approach." I have known instances when school psychologists have literally lined students up in the hallways for 20-minute assessments using the same (and only one) standardized test on each child.

To reiterate, to know how a child compares to others is to know what he has learned. In preparing educational prescriptions that may be of limited value, it is not nearly as important as knowing what he can learn, and even more importantly *how* that information is best received. It is imperative that so-called diagnosis be looked upon as one segment of a continuous process leading toward effective instructional programming. It is my observation that diagnosticians are not shy of information once they have administered several tests or a formal test battery. In fact, their problem becomes one of organizing and interpreting the data—hopefully in instructionally meaningful terms. Either the lack of that skill or the impossibility of getting instructionally relevant data from most formal tests has resulted in many special educators and school psychologists becoming dependent on teacher-made informal devices, since the basic response in the construction of an informal test is "what should I teach the child." That question automatically breaks down into a reading and mathematics component. Informal tests may well be used to ascertain other academic skill areas, but practically always reading and mathematics. Merely to state a child's grade score, age equivalent score, or scaled score does not permit the programming of actual teaching material.

It is not good enough to know that he has reading vs. math strengths or weaknesses. It is not even good enough to describe strengths and weaknesses within an area such as mathematics. Sternberg writes, "It seemed all that was necessary to measure a student's achievement level in mathematics and to diagnose his strengths and weaknesses within this area was to measure how well he could compute with whole numbers and fractions, and how well he could use computation to solve basic verbal problems" (Sternberg and Sedlak, 1974, p. 12).

What Sternberg is saying is that measurement of a child's operational performance on addition, subtraction, multiplication, and division cannot provide the assumption that the child really understands these operations. The examiner must have a feel for the rules that the learner is applying to the learning process.

What is being recommended then is the use of diagnostic instruments; these instruments must: (1) provide a depiction and delineation of specific mathematical behaviors through behavioral or performance objectives; and (2) indicate or prescribe instruction based upon a student's performance on a given formal or informal instrument or behavior observation device. Norm-referenced diagnostic tests or achievement tests do not meet these two requirements. The only appropriate path to follow seems to be in the use of criterion-referenced tests or inventories.

Glaser and Nitko (1971) defined a criterion-referenced test as a measure ". . . that is deliberately constructed so as to yield measurements that are directly interpretable in terms of specified performance standards" (p. 653). Criterion-referenced tests are usually representative samples of tasks that are to be learned. The assumption being that the level at which the material is successfully passed is identified, the teacher will know the student's level of mastery on that given material and be in a position to determine the next instructional objective.

The primary problem with criterion-referenced measurement is that students may be assigned to mutually exclusive instructional mastery states, depending upon the flow or sequential order of the material being taught and the particular subject areas of subsets covered in a given criterion-referenced test (Hambleton and Novick, 1973). The mutually exclusive categories are typically mastery and nonmastery (Millman, 1973). Criterion-referenced tests have the same difficulties with reliability and validity that formal assessment procedures may have. The means for arriving at instructional decisions are never easy or magical, and the use of outside reference measures, in particular standardized tests, will always be a necessity.

Criterion-referenced measurement can probably be classified as an informal testing procedure. It is generally considered to be an extension of an individualized instructional program. It attempts to answer the question as to the learner's current degree of attainment on some prescribed piece of instructional material. A criterion test may be used to evaluate the student's mastery of instructional objectives taught. It may serve to denote that point at which the next lesson should be initiated or when teaching methods and/or materials are to be altered.

Millman (1973) has described a derivative of a criterion-referenced measure. It is a domain-referenced measure, and it ascertains a unit of information from a limited number of skills and knowledges so that it makes sense to establish a single proficiency standard.

Cox (1975) reflects on the fact that research on what teaching methods are appropriate for remediating diagnostically specified problem is "nonexistent." He notes that research findings (Risdon, 1956; Smith and Lovith, 1973) tend to support the supposition that: (1) systematic errors are remediable; and (2) without proper instructional intervention a significant number of children continue to make the same errors years later.

Cox offers no simple remediation technique but wisely suggests that teachers use their professional judgment to select appropriate manipulative and instructional stretegies. Potentially fruitful research regarding the development of specific teaching techniques designed to remediate specific errors is underway. Thus far the solutions are tentative at best. Until a verdict is rendered, if indeed one is offered, teachers must continue searching for instructional alternatives that work with students who make systematic errors.

The Appropriate Assessment Arena

The changing emphasis from formal to informal tests, including criterion-referenced measures, has an additionally important connotation. One problem that was articulated is the present inability to transform test results into meaningful educational prescriptions. One of the reasons that formal tests have failed so miserably is they are frequently administered in an inappropriate examining setting. They are frequently administered behind closed doors in a small room, with a "Do Not Disturb" sign on the door. That, in my opinion, is an inappropriate assessment arena because it fails to answer three questions that must be answered in preparing an instructional prescription. These questions are: 1) *What* has been used to teach the child to date? 2) *How* has it worked? 3) *Why* was that material or technique used?

These questions cannot be answered short of eliciting observations in the teaching arena. It is my opinion that the best developmental history, behavioral observations, and psychometric profile are not enough. These three things, found in most school psychological reports, will possibly answer the issue of the least restrictive placement alternatives, but they will not assault the issue of the most relevant instructional strategy. The data necessary are an educational history and a direct set of observations through time, made by the teachers in the instructional arena in which the child is functioning.

There have, of course, been some attempts to formalize and structure classroom observation until they yield more precise data. But most of the formal observation systems to date have not addressed the issue of what and how something is being taught, and the importance of this issue looms as an unfulfilled promise at this time. Fink (1970) called for systematic and precise analyses of special class environments, providing a procedural format for such efforts. Craig and Collins (1970) have adopted Flander's (1965) observational scheme for specific application in classrooms for deaf children. Hammill (1971) adds that the goal of observation should be ". . . to expand, probe, verify, and, if need be, discard the conclusions and recommendations of formal assessment" (p. 348). Lovitt (1967) noted that:

The diagnostician is concerned not only with the reliability of baseline performance, but also with the validity of his evaluation. In behavioral diagnoses, a valid measure of performance is provided through objective observations of behavior, for example, direct analysis of reading or attention span, rather than subjective inferences of behavior (indirect assessment through the use of standardized tests) (p. 234).

Reporting Results

This is another area in which the teacher-school psychologist relationship could profit from new approaches. Psychological reports have been at best a feeble form of communication between psychologist and teacher. It is my current belief that a moratorium should be declared on psychology reports. The diagnostic summary and recommendations are the important parts of the psychological report. School psychologists should work to reduce verbiage in reports to a more clearly readable learning profile. With appropriate preparation in staff meetings, such a profile would offer specific educators a diagnostic summary and a graphic picture of academic achievement. In the hands of a psychologist-educator team, this information could contribute to the establishment of viable instructional objectives and to more exact learning and behavioral management techniques in the form of teaching prescriptions. An example of a learning profile is shown in Figure 11. The essence of this figure is an ability-achievement profile established on the basis of an ideographic assessment of those (perceptual and language) behaviors which seem to relate to academic achievement. Academic skills are also reported here. Once a chronological age line is drawn across the face of the profile, a predicted achievement level (PAL) can also be plotted based upon the verbal function (the WISC subtests of vocabulary, information, and comprehension).

Figure 11

Psycho-Educational Diagnostic Profile

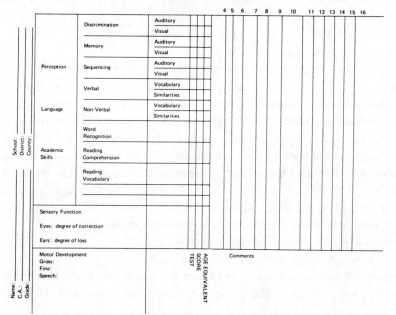

The remaining test information is obtained from commonly used clinical tests, and these, as well as the academic achievement tests, are converted to developmental age equivalents. (For suggestions on appropriate tests, see Sabatino, 1968; Sabatinc and Hayden, 1970c). The profile is an easily read diagnostic indicator of behaviors postulated to underlie academic achievement, and it serves as a baseline against which further diagnostic and academic or behavior training can be evaluated. Moreover, teachers can be instructed through inservice sessions to use it meaningfully.

The question then becomes one of what to assess and how. Should school examiners administer test batteries by consistently utilizing the same tests in order to prepare a learner characteristic profile? Or should particularly selected tests be used depending upon the type and amount of handicap? It is my belief that tests of choice can be identified, based upon reliability and validity, providing an examiner a choice as to which test to use. Examiners desiring to describe a consistent set of behaviors will substitute one test for another when handicapping condition(s) make it impossible to administer a given instrument. It is my opinion that tests are better reported on graphic profiles than described in essay form. The reasons are:

1) The test gibberish used by most examiners can be eliminated in using a profile.

2) Inservice training can be developed to promote consistent communication skills associated with the meaning of the terms used in a profile.

3) Consistent use of terminology should enhance the utilitarian nature of behavioral description, providing explicit instructional meaning.

4) The cost effectiveness of using a behavioral descriptive profiling system is an important consideration. It is true that paraprofessionals can administer many of

the instruments with good reliability, resulting in a freeing of the professional school psychologist from the enslavement of the dreaded testing role.

5)   Important, however, are the implications for learning the rules bridging formal assessment results into instructional prescriptions. It is probably safe to say that currently there are no valid means of going directly from formal test results to educational prescriptions. The sad aspect of that statement is the hundreds of thousands of man hours that are spent each year across the United States in formal psychological and educational assessment to do just that.

What should constitute a responsible formal assessment battery? It would appear that the two perceptual channels should be measured. Within each perceptual channel, both immediate discrimination skills and short-term perceptual memory should be measured. Perceptual integration, or the cross-modal utilization of perceptual information, appears to be a most sensitive measure of a child's prognostic ability to profit from remediation (Birch & Belmont, 1964). The receptive, expressive, and central language skills are important to ascertain. These learner characteristics and the skills associated with academic achievement comprise most of the components that might be considered in a profile. But to speculate on the learner characteristics that really underlie academic learning, and their relationship to one another, or their compensatory value is difficult. Educators have just not constructed and tested enough models related to the information processing abilities of man to state, with any degree of certainty, what is and is not applicable.

Appendix

ID NUMBER _____

MODEL LEARNING DISABILITIES SYSTEMS
TEACHER REPORT OF PUPIL TRAITS

PUPIL NAME _____ AGE _____ GRADE _____

TEACHER _____ SCHOOL _____ DATE _____

Please evaluate the child on each item in comparison to other children in the same grade by circling the appropriate grade level at which the child is functioning.

1. Word Recognition
    Pre-K   K   1.0   1.5   2.0   2.5   3.0   3.5   4.0   4.5   5.0   5.5   6.0   6.5
2. Word Analysis Skills
    Pre-K   K   1.0   1.5   2.0   2.5   3.0   3.5   4.0   4.5   5.0   5.5   6.0   6.5
3. Reading Vocabulary
    Pre-K   K   1.0   1.5   2.0   2.5   3.0   3.5   4.0   4.5   5.0   5.5   6.0   6.5
4. Reading Comprehension
    Pre-K   K   1.0   1.5   2.0   2.5   3.0   3.5   4.0   4.5   5.0   5.5   6.0   6.5
5. Arithmetic Computation
    Pre-K   K   1.0   1.5   2.0   2.5   3.0   3.5   4.0   4.5   5.0   5.5   6.0   6.5

6.   Arithmetic Reasoning
      Pre-K   K   1.0   1.5   2.0   2.5   3.0   3.5   4.0   4.5   5.0   5.5   6.0   6.5
7.   Spelling
      Pre-K   K   1.0   1.5   2.0   2.5   3.0   3.5   4.0   4.5   5.0   5.5   6.0   6.5
8.   Handwriting
      Pre-K   K   1.0   1.5   2.0   2.5   3.0   3.5   4.0   4.5   5.0   5.5   6.0   6.5
* *

Please evaluate the child in comparison to other children in the same grade on each of the following items, using this key:

0 = behavior is not displayed
1 = behavior is infrequently displayed
2 = behavior is frequently displayed

LANGUAGE
  9.   _____   Has difficulty in using oral language to express thought and ideas.
 10.   _____   Has not developed speaking vocabulary common to others his grade.
 11.   _____   Has difficulty understanding verbal directions.
 12.   _____   Has difficulty following conversation.

VISUAL PERCEPTION
 13.   _____   Has difficulty discriminating letter symbols.
 14.   _____   Can't remember written sequences of letters; e.g., has difficulty with immediate recall of what was seen.

15. _____ Has difficulty reproducing simple visual patterns or designs.
16. _____ Has difficulty copying from chalkboard.

AUDITORY PERCEPTION
17. _____ Has difficulty discriminating letter sounds.
18. _____ Has difficulty discriminating between similar sounding words.
19. _____ Can't remember isolated sounds; e.g., has difficulty with immediate recall of letter sounds.
20. _____ Has difficulty remembering verbal directions.
21. _____ Can't remember a series of isolated sounds.

BEHAVIORAL
22. _____ Is underactive; e.g., is lethargic, appears lazy, is inactive in classroom or on playground.
23. _____ Is overactive; e.g., is restless, fidgety, always "on the go."
24. _____ Lacks self-control; cannot apply classroom or school regulations to own behavior.
25. _____ Mood is unpredictable; frequent sudden changes in mood throughout school day.
26. _____ Excessive inconsistency in performance from day-to-day or even hour-to-hour.
27. _____ Is insecure; e.g., needs constant approval or reassurance.
28. _____ Is unusually aggressive toward peers.
29. _____ Is unusually shy or withdrawn.

AROUSAL - ATTENTION
30. _____ Is difficult to obtain attention.
31. _____ Is difficult to maintain attention; e.g., short attention span.

32. _____ Is easily distracted.

Has the child ever been retained? _____

    If so, in what grade? _____

Do you anticipate retaining the child in the child's present grade? _____

Are you going to promote the child to keep the child with peers, even though you feel the child may have academic difficulties in the next grade? _____

L E A R N I N G   O B J E C T I V E S
Chapter 3

Cognitive Objectives

At the completion of this chapter you will be able to:

1) State the definition of learning disabilities.

2) Identify the three measurable components found in the definition of learning disabilities.

3) Construct the screening process by which eligible candidates for learning disabilities services are identified under the Model Learning Disabilities Systems.

4) Differentiate specific learner behavior under the categories of language, visual perception, auditory perception, and behavioral traits.

5) Summarize the primary functions of formal and informal assessment.

L E A R N I N G   O B J E C T I V E S
Chapter 3

Affective Objectives

After reading the chapter, the author intends that you will:

1)   Be aware of an operational definition of "learning disabilities."

2)   Recognize the vital importance of inservice training in order to utilize the teaching staff as an integral part of screening learning-disabled candidates.

3)   Value the principle of screening candidates through the **MLDS** methodology.

4)   Understand that the most critical instructional diagnostic decision relates to the interaction between learner and curriculum.

READER'S NOTES

I. LEARNING DISABILITIES PRIMER

Although there is considerable difference concerning the meaning of the term *learning disabilities,* many authorities agree that the inclusion of three major components is essential:

1. _____

2. _____

3. _____

[Refer to p. _____ in manual.]

II. MLDS SCREENING MODEL

The purpose of the screening model is to operationalize the definition of *learning disabilities* and to provide an effective means of screening a large number of potential candidates for learning disabilities services. The process incorporates a combination of strategies, including:

1. _____

[Refer to p. _____ .]

READER'S   NOTES

SCREENING   PRIMER

2. _____

3. _____

Children are eliminated from eligibility at various referral stages, the target population being those who meet the criteria necessary for inclusion in the learning disabilities program.

Figure 1 is presented to summarize the basic steps in the screening process.

MLDS Inservice Training

Classroom Teacher Observations

Classroom Teacher Referral

LD Specialist/Classroom Teacher Conference

Individualized Testing (6 measures)

Figure 1.   Screening Model

[Refer to p. _____ .]

READER'S NOTES

SCREENING PRIMER

It is apparent that successful screening of learning-disabled children depends a great deal on the referral information provided by the classroom teacher. Consequently, the classroom teacher must be aware of the importance of inservice training and proficiency in utilizing observation skills with the aid of the MLDS descriptors.

The basic rule in making referrals to LD Specialists is not

[Refer to p. _____ .]

to under-   (CIRCLE ONE)
to over-

refer candidates. Referrals are also accepted by other school personnel as well as parents, though school officials are notified of such requests. The MLDS inservice training provides classroom teachers with several beneficial learning experiences, such as:

[Refer to p. _____ .]
1. _____

READER'S NOTES

SCREENING PRIMER

2. _____
3. _____
4. _____
5. _____

To aid the reader in further clarification of descriptor usage, which plays a vital role in the referral process, the following activity is presented.

In this activity, please read the statements and place the letter under the category in which it belongs. For aid refer to the supervisor or Appendix _____ in the Manual.

DESCRIPTOR CATEGORIES

  I. LANGUAGE

[Refer to p. _____ .]

READER'S NOTES	SCREENING PRIMER

SCREENING PRIMER

II. VISUAL PERCEPTION

III. AUDITORY PERCEPTION

IV. BEHAVIORAL

V. AROUSAL-ATTENTION

EXCERPTS

A. "I can never understand what John is trying to tell me."
B. "Susan's vocabulary is much lower than that of her classmates."
C. "Glenn, would you please do as I tell you. Just once!"
D. "For some reason, Jonathan does not distinguish M from N or S from Z."
E. "No, Jane, that was an apple I just showed you, not an orange."

READER'S NOTES

SCREENING PRIMER

F. "Amy, are you still having difficulty drawing those circles?"

G. "Jeff, the door is what you open to come in and the floor is what you step on—not the other way around."

H. "Glenn, I told you five minutes ago to close that book— it's hard to believe you can't remember these things all the time."

I. "Todd seems so lazy; he's never very active on the playground."

J. "I can't seem to stop Glenn from fighting with his classmates."

K. "I can't keep Shirley interested in something for five minutes."

L. "Albert seems to be distracted from his endeavors at the slightest provocation."

Learners who are *not* excluded from the learning disabilities program on the basis of teacher referrals or the conference

READER'S NOTES

[Refer to p. _____ .]

SCREENING   PRIMER

held between LD Specialists and the classroom teacher are
evaluated next with an individually administered testing
battery. This battery consists of 6 different measures covering
the broad areas of:

1. _____
2. _____
3. _____

For further clarification of instruments utilized under each of
the above areas, the following activity is presented. (For aid
in understanding the administration, purpose, and content of
each instrument, refer to Pages _____ in your Manual or your
inservice LD specialist.)

Please place the letter symbol representing a particular Test
in the block correlating the area such test is used in with the
area in which it functions:

READER'S   NOTES

SCREENING   PRIMER

1.   ACADEMIC ACHIEVEMENT

2.   INTELLIGENCE TESTING

3.   PERCEPTUAL TESTING

A.   Peabody Individual Achievement Test (PIAT)
B.   Ravens Progressive Matrices Test (RAVENS)
C.   Slosson Intelligence Test (SIT)
D.   Test of Auditory Perception (TAP)
E.   Multiple Choice Bender (MCB)
F.   Bender Visual Motor Gestalt (BVMGT)

The above battery serves a threefold purpose, which includes

[Refer to p. _____ .]

_____ ,

_____ ,

_____ .

READER'S NOTES	SCREENING PRIMER
	OVERVIEW REVIEW

READER'S NOTES

[Refer to p. _____ .]

[Refer to p. _____ .]

[Refer to p. _____ .]

[Refer to p. _____ .]

[Refer to p. _____ .]

SCREENING PRIMER

OVERVIEW REVIEW

The definition of learning disabilities is _____
_____
_____
_____ .

The three components of the above deinition that can be operationally measured are _____
_____ , _____
_____ . Academic achievement deficits may be found in any of the skill areas of _____ ,
_____ , _____
and _____ .
The MLDS makes use of a _____
(type) score for deciding academic difficulties and generally operates on the assumption that a score below _____ (%) on any achievement subtest, in the presence of normal

SCREENING   PRIMER

[Refer to p. _____ .]

intelligence, is indicative of academic dysfunction. Intelligence
is defined as _____

_____

_____ .

[Refer to p. _____ .]

Effective measurement of this basic psychological process requires the administration of nonverbal and verbal tests. The
MLDS suggests a verbal and nonverbal I.Q. of _____
as the lower limit for accepting a child having demonstrated
the ability to develop language concepts at a rate comparable
to that of normally developing children of his age. A difference

[Refer to p. _____ .]

of _____ or more between verbal and nonverbal
measured intelligence is considered sufficient difference to
make the candidate eligible for services whether or not a perceptual handicap is present. The definition of perception is

[Refer to p. _____ .]

_____

_____

_____ .

In determining perceptual development it is vital that both

READER'S NOTES

SCREENING PRIMER

auditory and visual components of the perceptual process be measured.

The MLDS screening model is an attempt to operationalize the _____ definition of learning disabilities and provides an effective means of screening

_____   _____

of potential candidates. To meet this end, the process incorporates a combination of strategies, including _____

_____ , _____

_____ , _____ .

The classroom teacher plays a very _____ role in the screening of potential learning-disabled children.

[Refer to p. _____ .]

[Refer to p. _____ .]

[Refer to p. _____ .]

[Refer to p. _____ .]

READER'S   NOTES

SCREENING   PRIMER

DEFINITIONS

[Refer to p. _____ .]

MLDS: _____
_____
_____

[Refer to p. _____ .]

Learning-Disabled Children: _____
_____
_____

[Refer to p. _____ .]

Intelligence: _____
_____
_____

[Refer to p. _____ .]

Perception: _____
_____
_____

READER'S NOTES	SCREENING PRIMER
[Refer to p. _____ .]	Screening Model: _____ _____ _____
[Refer to p. _____ .]	Descriptor: _____ _____ _____
[Refer to p. _____ .]	LD Specialist/Classroom Teacher Conference: _____ _____ _____
[Refer to p. _____ .]	Individualized Testing: _____ _____ _____
[Refer to p. _____ .]	Psychometric Skills: _____ _____ _____

4   A Review of Instructional Development with Learning-Disabled Children

David A. Sabatino

Let us suppose, in order to present the difficulty in its entirety, that we have discovered with certainty that one of our pupils suffers from a distressing inability to understand what is said in class; the child can neither understand well, nor can he judge well, nor can he use his imagination; even if he is not abnormal, he is still remarkably retarded academically. What are we to do with him? What are we to do for him?

If one does nothing, if one does not intervene actively and usefully, the child is going to continue to lose time, and the ineffectiveness of his efforts would lead us to believe that he will end up completely discouraged. The situation is a very serious one for him, and since this is not a matter of an exceptional case, because children who have difficulty understanding are legion, one may well say that the matter is a very serious one for all of us, for society; the child who loses in class the taste for learning is not likely to acquire it when he leaves school (Binet and Simon, 1911, p. 140).

Types of Remediation

I T is difficult to organize the types of instruction utilized with learning-disabled children. At least four major classification types can be identified, around which a review of the literature can be structured. These are: (1) academic remediation; (2) perceptual-motor; (3) language training; and (4) psychotherapy and behavior modification. Academic remediation involves direct work using academic types of teaching material, e.g., direct work on word recognition, phonic skills, sight vocabulary, reading comprehension, math remediation, etc. The ability or aptitudinal training areas of perception and language are included because of their continued use in educational programs for learning-disabled children. Psychotherapy and behavioral modification are used to ameliorate the adjustment and behavioral problems of learning-disabled children. And finally, a brief discussion is provided of the diagnostic-prescriptive process, which draws on all four of the major treatment typologies as specific intervention techniques with learning-disabled children.

The intial effort was to review these four major educational management procedures and then review any research conducted to evaluate the effectiveness of a given teaching technique. It would appear that research information on what works, with whom, and under what circumstances is shockingly absent. The reason seems to be a prevailing attitude that research is important but that what works with a child is more important. Orlando captures these sentiments in his review of research on exceptional children:

> The success achieved in some of the current research in reading and the learning-disabled
> child is important; however, at present it seems more logical to concentrate on the pre-
> vention of failure from the very beginning (Orlando, 1973, p. 261).

A controversy that has recently been given a great deal of attention is the effectiveness of ability training (perceptual and language training). Mann (1970) and Cohen (1969) have repeatedly emphasized that if the end goal of remediation is to obtain changes in a positive direction in reading, writing, spelling, or math skills, then academic achievement, not crawling or copying or listening to noises, should be taught. One argument (Balow, 1965) is that academic remediative skills, built on poorly developed perceptual or language skills, deteriorate rapidly. That is, children taught academic remedial approaches without ability training learn to achieve in reading (or whatever is being taught) faster but forget what is taught sooner and fail to display long-term skill development. In the absence of definitive, substantial research, an era of subjective controversy still exists on the form of remediation producing the greatest results with a definitive population, sample, or subsample of learning-disabled children or youths.

Academic Remediation—The Need for Radical Departures

Frequently, remediation is regarded as a concentrated effort using standard developmental teaching methodology, in most cases provided through individualized instruction. Gillingham and Stillman describe a program utilizing the visual-auditory kinesthetic approach in their *Remedial Training for Children with Specific Disability in Reading, Spelling, and Penmanship* (1960). Their technique is based upon teaching letters and sounds which are later blended into words for reading. The procedure employs three "associations" based on the visual, auditory, and kinesthetic elements of the "language triangle." The first association deals with matching the visual symbol with the name and sound of the letters. The second involves matching the sound of the letters with the name of the letters, while in the third association, the child traces, copies, and then writes the letter from memory. Then the letter sound is made and the child writes the letter symbol.

Other important factors in the remediation of reading disabilities are reviewed in a study by Bluestein (1967). It was found that girls progressed less well than their male peers during remediation. Bluestein hypothesized that, while a significant percentage of disabled readers are males, disabled female readers "are, in a sense, even more 'atypical' and present special problems that require a different remedial approach." Initial achievement in preremedial reading and arithmetic was found to relate to remedial reading improvement. Bluestein also hypothesized that failure among both male and female learning-disabled pupils in the program increased their frustration and lowered potential for future achievement. She suggested an optimum age level as well as an optimum length of remediation, beyond which results are unlikely to occur.

To remediate "deficiencies" in the child's learning skills, Shelquist, Breeze, and Jacquot (1970) provide a Resource Handbook of concrete activities, exercises, and training techniques. Word discrimination, perception of letters, and learning of letter names are dealt with, and the development of visual and motor skills is stressed.

Ferinden, Van Handel, and Kovalinsky (1971) recommend teaching learning-disabled children without segregating them from the regular classroom. They initiated a Learning Disabilities Program which undertook the remediation of academic skills as well as other abilities. Reading skills were developed using highly motivational techniques such as dramatization of stories and discussion of real-life problems. Before a vocabulary list was compiled, letter formations, graphic representations of letters associated with letter names, were traced and said, copied directly from print, and then written from memory. The final activity required the child to write the letter symbol in response to the letter sound. Also used was a language-experience-type approach which required the child to dictate a story that was later reread, mimeographed, and given to him for his "personal reading booklet." Vocabulary for later word analysis work was drawn from the child's own experiences. Later vocabulary work was expanded to include work with synonyms, antonyms, word families, rhyming, and finding smaller words in larger ones.

Gold (1968) describes a remedial program implemented at the Learning Disabilities Center in Binghamton, New York. Reading and social studies were the areas in which pupils had the most difficulties. A typical work session included reading in a basal reader, reinforcement activity for development of word analysis and recognition skills, reading from supplementary books, and some use of workbooks. To teach word attack skills, a linguistic approach was employed which called for a balance between phonetically regular words and high utility words. Materials used included word games, audiovisual media, and typewriters for use with students who lacked alphabet identification skills. The language-experience approach and the phonovisual method were also used as supplementary activities.

The program described by Johnson (1957) emphasized training auditory or visual strengths and weaknesses. Materials and methods were chosen, for the most part, on the basis of these factors. For "visual dyslexics," an elemental or phonic approach was used in order to help the child unlock the code by converting the auditory to the visual as simply as possible. To help the child perceive letter and word differences, methods such as color cues, increased letter size, kinesthesis, or extensive verbalization were used. For "auditory dyslexics" the whole-word approach was employed initially. The child was taught a sight vocabulary of mostly nouns and verbs which could be associated with an object, picture, or experience. Words were introduced in units or families. Later, decoding skills, rhyming, discrimination, blending, and other auditory tasks were presented to the child. Often the child was asked to close his eyes; this modification enables many children to hear similarities and differences in words. Other procedures included intensifying the auditory stimulation by talking very loudly, matching pictures with words and grouping them, having children watch the mouth as words were said, and employing actions of kinesthesis while working on auditory perception.

In another study concerned with reading disability and learning-disabled children, programmed reading was presented and reinforced to a group of children with reading disabilities (Haring and Hauck, 1969). As a result of the programmed presentations, the children in the study averaged approximately one to two hundred correct responses per session. The children worked in increasingly longer sessions and increased their reading level scores from one and one-half to four grade levels in five months of instruction.

Heckerl and Webb (1969) studied the effects of remedial reading programs for 240 children from kindergarten through third grade. These programs were based on clinical impressions during diagnosis and teaching. Remedial sessions of forty-five minutes were provided for each student, and in addition, consultation and special materials were provided for the classroom teachers. At the end of the one-year program, pretest and posttest comparisons were statistically significant in oral reading, word pronunciation, and spelling tests. The results indicated that diagnostic impressions can lead to accurate and effective programming for the learning-disabled child.

Sabatino and Hayden (1970) reported that when chronic, ten-year-old male nonachievers were randomly assigned to an experimental and control group, the experimental group (fourth-grade boys) made statistically significant progress in word-recognition (sight vocabulary) training by the fourth week of the program. By the tenth week of the program the experimental group had gained nearly a full year of academic achievement results over the control subjects. The experimental subjects received a set of training activities that did not require language. These materials were visual-perceptual discrimination forms, fine-form discrimination, letter shapes, and finally letters in isolation and in words, and word shapes. The control group received the same activity with traditional letter-naming exercises.

Sabatino and Streissguth (1972) also found that a letter-and word-discrimination training program improved reading significantly when letter names were not used with second-grade males who had failed the academic year before and were still reading at less than 1.5 grade level (statistically significant at the .05 level).

Sabatino and Hayden (1970) have hypothesized that children with severe visual perceptual difficulties must not be taught to compensate using language, except for language cueing and cluing of the perceptual material, when they are under ten chronological years. After age ten, perceptual training seems to accomplish very little and must be used only when it can be justified. Language training and direct remediation appear to provide greater effectiveness.

In the absence of definitive research that provides concise guidelines for when to use what type of instructional material, we must select a curriculum or teaching strategy on the basis of justifiable professional judgment. Certainly, the professional judgment, operating in the absence of rules for stating what instructional objective is best and what material most effectively satisfies a given instructional objective, will depend on the preparation, experience, and material available to a given learning disabilities teacher. This chapter is designed to review what is known and to prepare the reader for chapters 5 and 6, which specify the MLDS diagnostic-prescriptive system and acquaint the reader with the voluminous lists of commercially available material.

Perceptual Training

Perceptual training techniques directed at the modification of abilities continue to separate educators into two camps: believers and nonbelievers. Mann (1970) states that it is futile to fractionate specific abilities into their components because of their dependence upon one another. The problem seems to be the relationship between the training of perceptual behaviors and the gains in academic achievement. A case in point is the way children perceive letters and words. Vernon (1959) writes ". . . we must conclude that the acquisition of facility in well-integrated perceptual processes requires prolonged practice." Gorelick (1965) found that visual-form training during a prereading training period had little effect on later reading. Taylor (1963) concluded that children learn to read by reacting totally to a word pattern. Wheelock and Silvaroli (1967) found that discrimination of word-form training improved reading. Pick's (1965) work parallelled the findings that discrimination training is good if a tactual dimension is added to the visual. Goins (1959) and Muehl (1961) proposed that preschool children who learned to discriminate form read more proficiently by school entrance age.

There seems to be little evidence to support the suggestion that a transfer exists between perceptual training and remediation. But it is our view that there must be connecting links or "bridges" between perceptual training and remediation. The principle feature of perceptual training is the learning of rules of distinctive-feature analysis and their consistent application to letter recognition and phonetic sound discrimination. Most perceptual training programs, however, stop short of any sequentially connected remedial program. Therefore, perceptual training cannot be expected to generate transfer to academic remediation. One of

Frostig's examples is developmental and remedial visual-perceptual training programs (1964) which center on the development of visual- and motor-perceptual skills rather than on providing instruction specifically in reading, spelling, writing, and other subject areas. Although knowledge of subjects is important, it is not enough to establish an optimal program for learning-disabled children. It is necessary to analyze each child's style of learning, preferred sensory channels, and areas of perceptual and cognitive deficits or strengths in order to determine the most effective teaching method. Frostig's Developmental Test of Visual Perception provides an analysis of individual strengths and weaknesses in the areas of eye-motor coordination, figure ground, constancy of shape, position in space, and spatial relations. The commercially prepared developmental and remedial visual perceptual training program devised by Frostig is then used to ameliorate specific disabilities assessed by the test and to focus on readiness training involving all abilities normally developed by the age of first grade. Exercises that develop fine and gross motor coordination and eye movements and enhance body image and self-concept are provided as a basis to adequate perceptual functioning, as well as individual perceptual training, in each of the five areas of measured visual perception.

Other contributors to the field of visual perception have been Fitzhugh and Fitzhugh (1966). Through their clinical experience, they have produced a series of eight workbooks, dissimilar in format but similar in intent to the visual perceptual training of Frostig. The Fitzhugh Plus Program centers on two specific areas of learning, including spatial organization and language and numbers. Through exercises in spatial organization, the child is trained to improve his perception and to comprehend and manipulate objects in space and time. Through language and number exercises, the child is helped to improve his ability to identify letters, numbers, words, and pictures and to increase his understanding of linguistic symbols and arithmetic operations. The program is based on a matching design, with correct answers indicated when the child's response turns green after being filled in with a special pencil. The authors of the program recommend use of the workbooks for one hour per day over a six-month period, using a pretest and posttest model to evaluate educational growth. The program, although not a complete educational scheme, is a comprehensive supplementary, remedial, or preparatory self-instructional approach to remediating learning disabilities.

Getman (1965) also emphasizes a developmental approach to visual perception. His remedial program is based upon four concepts which are repeatedly emphasized throughout his work:

1. educational success depends heavily upon visual perceptual adequacy;
2. direct experience enhances perceptual development;
3. as the child learns to perceive he learns to learn as well;
4. perceptual success follows a logical, systematic sequence of development (Myers and Hammill, 1969).

The training of visual perception is founded upon the basic sequence of growth and development associated with the first five years of life. Getman's sequential development is organized into interrelated developmental stages—general movement patterns, special movement patterns, eye movement patterns, and visual perceptual organizations. The training procedures used correspond to these developmental stages and include activities to facilitate complete development within each category. The training program concentrates on practice in general coordination (Angels-in-the-Snow), balance (walking board), eye-hand coordination (chalkboard activities), eye movements (ocular fixation and pursuit), form perception (tracing shape templates), and visual memory (tachistoscope exercises). Although Getman's model provides comprehensive coverage of the visual-perceptual deficits in learning-disabled children, it is often criticized for its lack of attention to other deficiencies that may require remediation.

Visual-perceptual theories relating diagnosis to remediation have dominated the study of learning disabilities. However, other theories have had significant effects upon the field. The multisensory approach to learning disabilities has been advocated by both Fernald (1943) and Cruickshank (1961). Fernald had been treating the learning-disabled child in the Clinic School at the University of California since 1921. Her early work dealt mainly with children with adequate intelligence who had difficulties in reading, spelling, or language. Her remedial approach, therefore, was geared to developing reading, writing, and spelling in learning-disabled children. Making use of all sensory avenues, the child chooses words, composes sentences and paragraphs that suit him, and then learns to read what he has written by reading it back to the teachers. In the first stage, a word chosen by the child is printed in large letters on a card. The child then traces the word with his finger, saying the word aloud as he does. This process is repeated using the visual, auditory, haptic, and kinesthetic modalities until the word can be reproduced from memory. The next step is the same as the first, except that the tracing is dropped. In the third stage, word cards are not used, and the child looks at the printed word, says it, and writes it while he is saying it. The final stage teaches the child to recognize new words from their similarity to words or parts of words he has already learned. Work at this level can be continued until the student is ready to be placed in his appropriate grade.

Cruickshank (1961), another advocate of the multisensory approach to learning disabilities, believes that educational programs for normal children are completely unsatisfactory for learning-disabled children. He suggests an educational environment designed to meet the needs of each child and teach directly to each disability. His remedial program is based on four essential principles comprising a good teaching environment:

1.   the reduction of unessential visual and auditory environmental stimuli;
2.   the reduction of environmental space;
3.   the establishment of a highly structured daily program;
4.   the increase of the stimulus value of the instructional materials themselves (Myers and Hammill, 1969).

The program also includes the use of color in the teaching techniques and materials. Through individualization with each child and his unique disability, a multisensory classroom is established. Remediation in visual discrimination and other visual tasks is enhanced through the use of color coding; auditory training is provided for children with the inability to distinguish sounds; tactual and kinesthetic perception is enhanced through manipulation of materials, including sandpaper numbers and letters; motor development is enhanced through classroom activities and materials such as the balance beam, jump rope, and jumping board. In teaching academic subjects, Cruickshank recommends the use of a developmental kinesthetic approach to writing and concrete and practical arithmetic, with the teaching of reading as the last task.

Strauss and Kephart (1967) further extended the remediation of learning-disabled children through a perceptual motor theory. Although their theory of perceptual motor learning development is more systematic than their remedial method, the sensorimotor program has become a milestone in the education of learning-disabled children. Kephart's program for sensorimotor training is sequenced from gross motor development to specific perceptual training activities. The areas emphasized for development include gross-motor abilities, eye-hand coordination, laterality, directionality, ocular control, dexterity, form perception, and space discrimination. Remedial activities begin with sensorimotor activities and then advance to academic tasks. Kephart incorporates chalkboard training, rail-walking, balancing, ball play, template tracing, and many other activities into his remedial curriculum. As motor ability improves through this training program, so should the child's perceptual ability be improved. It is theorized that the child's cognitive abilities will finally be favorably affected.

A theory similar to that of Strauss and Kephart is postulated by Barsch (1965). He believes that a curriculum for learning-disabled children should have as the primary objective the correcting of whatever impediments stand in the way of the child's taking full advantage of the offerings of the regular curriculum. To accomplish this objective, Barsch developed his theory of movigenics. Movigenics is the study of the origin and development of movement patterns leading to learning efficiency. The movigenic curriculum is a planned program of activity through which a child with a learning problem receives an opportunity to explore and experience himself in space and to integrate these experiences into progressively more complex relationships.

Barsch's classroom design enables the movigenic curriculum to be put into practice through the manipulation of space and objects. Desks, books, and workbooks are removed to provide open space, and window panes are covered with black plastic sheeting to allow complete control of lighting. Lines are marked on the floor to provide guides for chalkboard writing, walking routes, and other activities. Barsch advocates a space for crawling and rolling, preferably covered with carpet, and requires that the children participate in all class sessions barefooted or in stocking feet. Initially, Barsch's teachers wore white blouses and black slacks to minimize distraction, but later switched to more colorful clothing.

Effectiveness of Perceptual Training

Research on the effectiveness of perceptual-motor curricula is anything but definitive. O'Donnell and Eisenson (1969) and Robbins (1966) found that Delacoto's motor training and patterning did not improve reading. Fahlik (1969), using Kephart's Purdue Motor Survey, did not find increases in reading at the kindergarten or second-grade level. Painter (1966) reported on a rhythmic and sensory motor training program comprised of thirty-eight activities related to curriculum; the remaining were from Kephart's (1960) perceptual-motor activities and specific rhythmic patterns including sequencing on unilateral, bilateral, and cross-lateral movement. Generally, the findings support the supposition that motor and perceptual behaviors are different and require different sets of training activities. Bates (1969) investigated the effect of perceptual-motor training on both learning aptitude (basic behavior) and academic achievement. She failed to establish any conclusive or consistent relationships between these training procedures and increased academic achievement.

Beck et al. (1965), however, did report positive results in their rehabilitative program for emotionally disturbed children based on perceptual motor deficits. A comprehension evaluation battery was also provided for assessing primary adaptive functions.

The need for teacher awareness of perceptual problems as well as the need for training techniques was emphasized in the Child Development Program as described by Roth (1970). It was felt that personality variables of the teachers were more important than skill and training in dealing with perceptually handicapped children. Aside from adequate selection and training of teachers, the program aims were centered on developing and integrating sensory motor areas, developing social skills needed in problem solving, and developing an individualized curriculum. A secondary aim was to acquaint parents and teachers with the nature of perceptual difficulties.

Jacobs (1968) administered the Frostig Visual Perception Training Program to groups of prekindergarteners, kindergarteners, and first graders. He also tested for transfer effects with the Metropolitan Readiness Test at the kindergarten level. The results were positive but not statistically significant. Beck and Talkington (1970) found that after training on the Frostig program, the only significant posttest increases were in Frostig subtests and not in academic achievement measures.

Keim (1970) contributes further study of the merits of visual-motor training procedures at the kindergarten level. There are several such training programs available, all of which apparently require more investigation before assessing their relative worth. This fact, however, does not seem to prohibit their wide-scale use and acceptance by school personnel. Generally, studies report on visual perceptual training of gross and fine form discrimination skills, but not reading ability (Gibson and Gibson, 1955). A substantial body of literature suggests that good readers do respond to total word patterns (Wheelock and Silvaroli, 1967) and not to specific letter shapes. The literature does tend to support the supposition that if the distinctive features of letters and the forms of words are added to visual perceptual training in form discrimination, children with reading difficulties and fairly adequate visual perceptual function should show improvement in reading skills.

Falik (1969) used as the rationale the developmental sensory, sensory-motor perceptual process based on body awareness for a study with kindergarten to second graders. In short, he studied the way in which visual perception is integrated with and/or developed out of total body perception (Kephart, 1960). He further extended this study to include the "perceptual learning" process of gradual differentiation of elements, dimensions, or qualities of the perceptual world (Gibson and Gibson, 1955). The purpose was to determine whether a curriculum based on principles of perceptual-motor development would effect readiness and show other signs of maturity. He found no beneficial effect of a perceptual-motor curriculum with an emphasis placed on the motor aspect.

Miller (1974) compared four curricula—a visual-motor curriculum (the Frostig Program), a visual discrimination Word Form Constancy Program (Sabatino, Miller, and Sabatino, 1973), and the linguistic based Merrill Readers, with a diagnostic-prescriptive approach, using material from the other three curricula. Listed in order of greatest achievement gain in the first to third graders was the diagnostic-prescriptive approach, the Word Form, the Merrill, and the Frostig. There were no statistically significant differences, however, between the diagnostic-prescriptive and the other three approaches.

Klein and Marsh (1969) investigated the effects of perceptual training upon selected measures of reading achievement. Eighty-seven second graders with average intelligence and either reading or perceptual deficits were assigned to one of three matched groups. One group received a twenty-five-minute perceptual training period per week, one received a traditional remedial approach, and one served as the control, with regular classroom instruction. Pretest and posttest scores on measures of intelligence, perception, and word recognition were evaluated. Unlike Sabatino (1971), they reported that the traditional remedial group showed significantly higher posttest scores than the perceptual training or control group.

Interesting results were reported in two studies dealing with deficit-centered training programs for learning-disabled children (Sapir, 1967; Sapir, 1969). In 1967, Sapir conducted a study of 54 children with deficiencies in body schema, perceptual motor skills, and language development, who were randomly placed in one of two remedial groups. Children in the experimental group were taught via deficit-centered classroom instruction (a program concentrating on weaknesses and their remediation). The control group was taught using the traditional remedial approach. Results showed significant differences for the experimental group in mean change in WISC scores, visual perception and language functioning, and perceptual motor skills. Other positive changes noted were in auditory visual integration and language development; however, little difference was measured in academic achievement. In a follow-up study in 1969, Sapir placed 18 first graders (with learning deficits) in one of two groups. The experimental group contained 12 children and was organized as a self-contained class with deficit-centered training. The control group had 6 deficit children mixed in with 12 normal children in a class using a traditional curriculum. Once again, the experimental group did significantly better on many (not all) perceptual, intellectual, and language tests, but the data on academic achievement failed to show significant differences.

Another attempt to show a correlation between ability training and academic achievement is found in a study by Litchfield (1970). Eighty first, second, and third graders, identified as having visual, motor, and perceptual deficiencies, were randomly divided into experimental and control groups (assessment measures served as pretest information). The experimental subjects received one-half hour of visual motor training per day for six months, while the control group received no specialized training. Pre- and posttest comparisons showed no improvement of the experimental group over the control group in academic achievement. Fine screening results showed more improvement in visual motor perceptual functioning by the experimental group.

Sensory motor training and motor training have also been studied in relation to the learning-disabled child. Maloney (1967) investigated the "generalizability" of Kephart's sensory motor training system and found that sensory motor training generalized to body image development but not to finger localization. Ayres (1968) studied the effects of sensory motor activity on perception and learning and has hypothesized that educationally handicapped children in special classes receiving sensory motor training show a greater change in perceptual motor, language, and academic achievement scores than children receiving an equivalent amount of classroom instruction. Unfortunately, posttest scores failed to support this hypothesis. Best (1967) linked structured physical activity with motor skill development in learning-disabled children. In a study comprised of 24 students in a perceptual development class, an eight-week training program of structured activities was used with subjects in the experimental group. The control group received no special training, only regular play. The Johnson Test of Motor Skill Development was used as a pre- and posttest measure. The results indicated a statistically significant difference between experimental and control groups, with increased motor skill development in the experimental group.

The use of a multisensory approach to remediate learning disabilities was investigated by Patterson (1968). In a study of 750 children, 15 percent were found to have evidence of minimal brain damage or dyslexia when screened through psychoeducational devices. This population received a highly structured language arts program in homogeneous transition groups while remaining in regular homerooms. In addition, they participated in motor training, rhythm, and patterning programs. As a result of the multisensory stimulation and training, the subjects increased an average of 1.7 years in reading ability.

A study by Stark (1967) explored three separate projects designed to develop and evaluate materials and procedures for the perceptually handicapped child with learning difficulties. The first project presented stimulus pairs (language pairs) to children in varying modality conditions, the result being an improvement in the visual modality and in some combined (integrated) modalities. There was no improvement, however, in the overall auditory discrimination performance of the child. Stark's interest in the language-disordered child continued to provide insights into remedial approaches and materials for his use. Project two of this research studied the nature of auditory sequencing abilities in an optimally controlled environment and explored means of improving those abilities. The third project developed instructional materials for the language-disordered child, making use of visual stimulation along with an auditory program designed to provide phrase structure in regulated units. Although Stark's study provided no clear-cut research information, his investigations into the process of language remediation of learning-disabled children have been important and significant to the development of new programs for these deficiencies.

The conclusion may be that most widely used perceptual-motor training programs have been developed without a body of empirical evidence to substantiate their validity. The question of validation, however, may reside in Gibson and Gibson's (1955) review of the research pointing out that perceptual training seemingly improves only the perceptual function it was designed to train. To illustrate the point, King (1964) has shown that visual discrimination and training of letters improve letter recognition skills but not word recognition skills.

Muehl (1961) found that the most appropriate method for teaching sight words varied with the similarity of the group of words introduced. That is, when gross-form and letter pretraining are provided to kindergarten children, a transfer of training will occur if there is a similarity between the pretraining experience and the reading-readiness task to be accomplished. Other investigators (Taylor, 1963) have felt that letter discrimination within word units provided a most effective means of perceptual training. Elkind and Deblinger (1969) reported that work with serially ordered letters, anagrams, scrambled words, symbolic transformations, tenses, and coding improved word-recognition skills. Gorelick (1965), using a training program of word-form configurations and word pictures, found no significant gains in word-discrimination abilities. Pick's (1965) work in perceptual discrimination indicates that the "detection of distinctive features (of words) may be the necessary and sufficient condition for improvement in (perceptual) discrimination" (p. 332). It was postulated by Vernon (1959) that perceptual training, independent of direct training in letter and word recognition, would not result in word recognition or reading comprehension improvement.

Hammill and Wiederholt (1973), in a review of visual perceptual training, still contend that there is no merit to what they term "nonsense." Sabatino (1973), in a comprehensive review of auditory perceptual remediation research literature, concluded that greater and more efficient gains were made in academic remediation when underlying work had taken place to train auditory perceptual abilities before beginning academic remediation. The controversy over what to teach a learning-disabled child continues, primarily because we have little research—most of it poorly designed—and consequently we are without conclusive data.

Motor, Tactual, and Kinesthetic Training

Auditory and visual sensory modalities have been described as providing about 80 to 90 percent of all information received. The blind child has been taught to develop the haptic and tactual senses in order to learn Braille symbols. Whether severe visual perceptual deficits could be trained directly or by tactual or haptic procedures is not well established. Gibson (1962) concludes that there is no sensory receiving system as efficient and effortless as the ear or eye. Lobb (1965), in an effort to determine the effectiveness of transfer between vision and touch, confirmed that visual learning has superior transfer over tactual. All the attempts to create an experimental conflict between sight and touch showed that vision was completely dominant under all experimental conditions.

A review of motor training programs (Barsch, 1967; O'Donnell and Eisenson, 1969) seems to suggest that tactual and kinesthetic learning is effective when combined with either visual- or auditory-perceptual functions, when it is used specifically to increase memory function. In essence, it would seem that information is more difficult to grasp through gross motor or tactual presentation, but once learned, the result is prolonged retention. One speculative conclusion is that motor, tactile, haptic and/or kinesthetic training is not efficient and is therefore effective only with children who do not learn through more direct teaching approaches utilizing the two primary sensory modes, the eyes and the ears.

Language Training

Verbal language is composed of spoken words, conceptual units which are manipulated and constructed into meaningful wholes. The sum of these compositions and meanings (verbal language) provides more meaning than the sum of the individual words (Morley, 1956; Bloomer, 1959). In his writing, Myklebust (1967) states that the language impairment of aphasic children may result from disturbances of one or a combination of three main types of language functions: inner, receptive, and expressive.

Inner language, which is the first function to develop, refers to the ability to organize, understand, and interpret perceptual symbolic information and store it for future use. Without the development of inner language, no other kind of symbolic processes can develop (Myklebust, 1956). Global or central aphasia results from a dysfunction at this level and is characterized by infrequency or absence of vocalization, extreme dysfunction of auditory perceptual skills, withdrawal due to frustration, confusion in verbal communication, and the least promising prognosis.

Receptive or sensory aphasia is the result of a dysfunction of the aural interpretation and understanding of the verbal speech of others. The language facility of children with receptive aphasia can vary widely. Children who use scribble speech or jargon have both proper intonation and gesture, but their vocalizations are rapid and without meaning. Children with receptive language difficulties cannot understand, imitate, or use real language but have a good prognosis (McGinnis, 1963). Eisenson (1966) says that these children may actually hear jargon because they cannot remember the sequence of sounds.

Expressive language refers to the verbal expression of thoughts and requires both central and receptive language for adequate functioning. Developmentally, it is the last function to become operational and has a tendency to lag behind receptive language in performance level. A language dysfunction at this level is referred to as expressive or motor aphasia. Receptive language abilities are intact, and although such children can respond nonverbally to spoken language, they cannot respond verbally. Expressive aphasia is characterized by a partial or complete inability to imitate movements governed by articulation. The major language-training programs are those developed by Bangs (1957), Barry (1961), McGinnis (1963), Agranowitz and McKeown (1964), Lea (1965), Scagliotta (1966), Myklebust and Johnson (1967), Eisenson (1972), and Fygetakis and Ingram (1973).

Bangs (1957). The philosophy of this program is that socialization and an awareness of the need to communicate are prerequisite to language learning. Formal or direct language training is not attempted. Rather, a natural, informal atmosphere is provided where speech can be expressed spontaneously. The goal of language exposure is to make the child aware of the need to communicate.

Barry (1961). Her first objective is to remediate behavior rather than language. She outlines specific techniques for remediating this difficulty as well as problems in body image and perception—which are also preliminary to language remediation. Like Myklebust, she believes that only deficient areas should be remediated, rather than all areas equally.

McGinnis (1963). The program consists of three main steps. The first develops attention and sequential memory, introduces the phonemes for vowels and consonants, and teaches fifty nouns. The second level increases memory span and comprehension. The third level improves all language areas and exposes the child to more creative and abstract language usage.

Agranowitz and McKeown (1964). The Agranowitz and McKeown handbook provides numerous concrete suggestions for therapy in each of the areas they discuss. They do not provide specific behavioral objectives or a complete curriculum, but rather a hierarchical checklist to be used in assessing and working with the child. They feel that perceptual deficits cause the child's language impairment and begin language remediation at the nonverbal level, using a multimodality approach.

Lea (1965). Lea has developed a program called the Color Pattern Scheme. In it, words are color-coded according to the function they serve in a sentence. Different sentence patterns are also color-coded to illustrate syntactic patterns. In stage one of Lea's program, a two-hundred word vocabulary is taught. The words are also constructed into sentences emphasizing phrase and sentence patterns. Stage two builds more vocabulary and increases the complexity of sentence construction and of verb tense usage. Unlike programs which teach phonemes or syllabic production first, Lea maintains that it is more practical and effective to introduce whole words—nouns, then verbs, prepositions, adjectives, pronouns, etc. As in McGinnis's program, the written and oral forms of a word are taught simultaneously, and a format is used similar to McGinnis's for introducing questions and teaching appropriate responses.

Scagliotta (1966). This program is intended for use in the home with preschool children. Parents are responsible for all of the training, which includes work in auditory discrimination for inanimate and animate nonlanguage sounds, speech motor skills, and formal language development—categorizing and comparing objects, responding to questions, expanding the child's experiences through trips, etc.

Eisenson (1972). Eisenson presents a complete remedial program, including methods for diagnosis. He specifies that his program is a guide rather than a specific curriculum or prescription, although it is a rather precise guide giving specific hierarchies for moving a child from one level of competency to the next. The program consists of five levels, and placement within this system is determined by the length of the utterances the children produce. Like Myklebust, he feels that a unimodality approach is best in the beginning of therapy, claiming that aphasic children have difficulty in coping with multisensory information.

Fygetakis and Ingram (1973). Fygetakis and Ingram believe that language learning is a rule system rather than simply a collection of stimuli and responses. Their study is an application of operant techniques to recent linguistic findings. This is accomplished by systematically introducing a sentence construction one level above the child's present level of language functioning. The authors describe their method as follows:

In the programmed conditioning procedures, the child makes progressively closer approximations to the target construction by imitating increasingly longer units of the model sentence. When the child has reached the level of imitating the entire construction, the model sentences are systematically faded out as the program progresses. By the end of the program, the child is formulating his own sentences which exemplify the underlying grammatical relationship (p. 7).

Myklebust and Johnson (1967) established the following as important educational procedures to be incorporated in language training:

1. Communication input is more important initially than a child's expression.

2. Provision for amplified meaning should be made for auditory units by structuring, isolating, and timing the presentation of any message until it is comprehended.

3. Simultaneous and repetitious use should be made of selected vocabulary, emphasizing the meaningful words that reflect experiences, teaching the concept, emphasizing the auditory configuration, or distinguishing characteristics of the word.

One of the more prominent structured language training programs was developed by Bereiter and Engelman (1966). The objectives are to have children acquire the ability to refer to familiar objects in simple, complete sentences, to use these sentences in both the affirmative and negative forms, and to ask relevant questions in a learning situation. The program begins by employing words and sentences to make simple language deductions, which are followed by a deliberate and painstaking drill on language analogies and generalizations.

Orton (1937) described a relationship between strephysymbolism (word blindness) and disabilities in writing, reading, and speech. The cause, he theorized, was ambivalence of the cerebral hemisphere, which resulted in a delay of normal cerebral dominance. This study prompted Gillingham and Stillman (1936) to reflect upon the use of language training devices to influence children who have reading difficulty. Later, Cole and Walker (1964) published a monograph on reading and speech problems as expressions of specific language disability. Many speech therapists and language clinicians have developed useful training procedures that are valuable when children exhibit aphasoid language difficulties (Agranowitz and McKeown, 1964).

The Gillingham and Stillman (1936) program is geared to children from third to sixth grade who are of normal or superior intelligence and have normal sensory acuity (visual and auditory) but have the tendency to reverse letters or words or to mirror-write, have difficulty in pronunciation, and have been unable to acquire reading and spelling skills by usual school methods. In contrast to functional sight word procedures, in which words are initially recognized by children as ideograms and then dissected by the teacher into letter sounds through phonetic analysis, Gillingham's Alphabetic Approach teaches the sounds of the letters first, then builds those letter sounds into words. Their remedial technique is aimed at establishing close association between the visual, auditory, and kinesthetic modalities in the brain.

Myklebust (1968), originally known for his work in the diagnosis and remediation of communication disorders in children, developed a remedial approach to psychoneurological learning disabilities. His aim is to acquire an accurate, differential diagnosis for children with learning disorders and to plan an educational program based on the information gleaned from the diagnostic investigation. Therefore, an accurate appraisal of the brain's capacity to receive, categorize, and integrate information, as well as of the intactness of the individual modality systems, is important. Myklebust and Johnson (1967) have outlined the fundamental principles that guide the remediation of learning disorders. Some important aspects of the program are individual teaching, teaching according to readiness and involvement, teaching to the tolerance level without overloading the sensory systems, using multisensory stimulation, providing training in perception when needed, controlling variables such as attention, rate, proximity, and size as needed, and developing both verbal and nonverbal areas of experience. The total remedial program is designed to facilitate development of psychoneural disabilities through structured clinical teaching to deficits in language, reading, arithmetic, and nonverbal learning.

Wiseman (1965) utilizes language for both diagnosis and remediation of children with certain types of learning disabilities. His remedial approach is based on the assumption that direct treatment of linguistic deficits can bring about the reduction of certain forms of learning disabilities. He identifies auditory and visual decoding, association, memory, automatic auditory or visual closure, and vocal and motor encoding as key language abilities in children. Using the Illinois Test of Psycholinguistic Abilities (ITPA) as a basis for diagnosis, Wiseman assigned remedial exercises to correct those deficits profiled. The remedial approach is relatively simple, generating remedial exercises to fit each child's individual needs.

Revelle (1971) recommends several guidelines and procedures for work in written communication with learning-disabled children. Many of the suggestions given are based on the work of Orton (1937) and Gillingham and Stillman (1960). The basis of the technique is to keep a highly structured sequence of events, beginning with very simple concepts and working to more complex areas. Constant review and opportunities for daily success are essential parts of the program. Beginning with work in sequencing, the child is led by gradual steps to writing concise expressions of his thoughts and experiences.

Recent work in this field employs many commercial programs and materials. Reger, Schroeder, and Uschold (1968) make some recommendations. The Language Master by Bell and Howell may be used to program lessons in symbols, letters, words, and sentences. Houghton-Mifflin has published the *Listen and Do Program,* which establishes auditory-visual association patterns for prereading experiences. *Listen and Think,* by Educational Development Laboratories, is a "developmental program designed to develop the specific thinking skills necessary for good listening . . . and for good reading, too." *The Language Development Experience for Young Children* program by Engel, Reid, and Rucher and the *Listening Aids Through the Grades* program are similar listening programs. The *Echorder,* by RIL Electronics, is a machine which may be used for auditory training and language experiences. Other book series and filmstrips are also suggested.

Psychotherapy and Behavioral Modification

Psychotherapy and various forms of behavioral modification have been thought to alter those personality factors or overt behavioral symptoms that inhibit academic achievement. Abrams and Belmont (1969), however, discovered observable differences in benefit from two different types of psychotherapy in their attempt to determine whether any significant improvement occurred with the reading ability, intelligence, and behavior characteristics of severely retarded readers when various forms of individual psychotherapy were offered. The groups receiving specialized reading instruction made substantial gains in academic growth. Thus psychotherapy may improve personality, but its effect upon academic achievement is questionable.

The role of reinforcement played an important part in a study done by Wadsworth (1971). The effects of clinic tutoring, reinforcement, and intermittent reinforcement on the reading achievement of ten learning-disabled boys were studied. After receiving the three programs, in the same sequence, the results for each child were analyzed. Wadsworth found that clinic tutoring produced no significant gains in reading achievement but that reinforcement treatments produced significant gains. Valett (1966) proposes that the following guidelines are useful in constructing a behavioral modification system with learning disabled children:

1. Pupils must be educationally programmed according to their level of development and achievement.

2. Material to be learned must be systematically organized and able to elicit response and success from the pupil.

3. Success in learning (e.g., desirable behavior) should be immediately rewarded. If necessary, primary reinforcement (food, praise, etc.) should be used.

4. Immediate primary reinforcements should be part of a broader system involving varying rewards and social reinforcement.

5. Rewards should be obtainable after a reasonable period of effort. (Lessons should not be too long and may have to be broken down into smaller units with subsequent reinforcement as necessary.)

6.   The pupil must be able to understand the desired behavior change, the
rewards involved, and the operation of the total system. The system should
be available (e.g., written out) and as concrete as possible.

Operant approaches to behavior change have become increasingly popular (Bandura, 1969; Sherman and Baer, 1969; Ullman and Krasner, 1965). An extraordinarily wide range of deviant and maladaptive behavior has been treated, ranging from decreasing the frequency of thumbsucking (Baer, 1962) to increasing academic achievement.

Patterson, Shaw, and Ebner (1969) explored the efficiency and practicality of operant conditioning procedures in modifying the behavior of children typically labeled as "hyperactive" or "conduct disordered" in a classroom setting. It was hypothesized that: (1) one could, with the application of operant techniques, weaken or decelerate objectional classroom behaviors; (2) further weakening of the behavior is better accomplished through simultaneously strengthening a set of behavior that will interfere with the objectionable behaviors. The teacher was involved as a behavior modifier using a token system to maintain gains until the behaviors are under the natural conditions found in the classroom. Both the first and the second hypotheses were supported. The study showed that the application of operant techniques resulted in significant reduction of specific objectionable behavior in the classroom.

Considerable attention has also been given to the use of arbitrary reinforcers such as candy, points, and stars, as opposed to natural reinforcers that are indigenous to the situation, such as privileges, approval, and feedback (Ferster and DeMyer, 1967). However, there is a predominant reliance on primary reinforcement such as food or avoidance of pain.

Reinforcement practices in the classroom have proliferated in recent years (O'Leary and Drabman, 1971). Whether token reinforcement (O'Leary and Becker, 1967) or social reinforcement (Ward and Baker, 1968) were introduced to modify academic (Hewett, Taylor, and Artuso, 1969) and disruptive behaviors (Meichenbaum, Bowers, and Ross, 1968), both have met with rather consistent success. Scott and Pahre (1968) report the results of reinforcement used with audio-tutorial techniques in the remediation of a student who was unusually reticent in oral language expression and easily frustrated on test items. The technique used with him consisted of reading a story from the Readers' Digest *Skill Builders* and then having him relate the story in his own words. If the version was satisfactory, he was given free time for the rest of the period in which to do whatever he wished. If unsatisfactory, the student was given the option of retelling the story immediately or listening to the story again before retelling it. The study reports successful results, although the authors admit the need for research using more controls and a larger population.

Coyle (1968) found positive results in his study of counterconditioning, or desensitization, for use with readers disabled by extreme anxiety. Procedures consisted of teaching relaxation responses to the anxiety-causing situations through the process of gradual desensitization of the students to more active, progressive roles in the oral reading situation.

Other operant conditioning procedures with learning-disabled and handicapped children have produced some dramatic results. Self-destructive behaviors were extinguished (Lovaas, Frietag, Gold, and Kassovia, 1965; Wolf, Risley, and Mees, 1964), speech was developed (Lovaas, Berberich, Perloff, and Schaffer, 1966), and stuttering was decreased (Browning, 1967). The efficacy of positive and negative reinforcement, as well as punishment, has been demonstrated for a number of behavioral problems (Lovaas, 1968).

In general, the reinforcement technique is a powerful tool, and everyday classroom problems may be alleviated by instructing teachers to use attention, praise, and approval as social reinforcers (Becker, 1971; Madsen, Becker, and Thomas, 1968; Thomas, Becker, and Armstrong, 1968; and Ward and Baker, 1968). However, in some settings and for some children praise may not be sufficiently reinforcing; a token system may be more effective.

Whatever reinforcement is employed in the classroom, arbitrary or natural, it is usually the teacher who administers the contingencies for reinforcement. The importance of the teacher in modifying behavior has recently begun to receive particular emphasis (Becker, Englemann, and Thomas, 1971; Skinner, 1968). In the classroom the teacher alone is the arranger of the contingencies because she generally works by herself. This has led Bijou (1970) to refer to the teacher as the "Lone Arranger."

Kingsley and Spies (1969) explored the efficacy and practicality of operant conditioning procedures in modifying selected behaviors of neurologically handicapped children placed in special classes. It was hypothesized that: (1) the application of operant techniques would result in significant reduction of specific objectionable behaviors; (2) significantly greater reduction of objectionable behaviors would be found among children with higher initial rates of target behavior; and (3) nonmedicated students would experience significantly greater reduction of the objectionable behaviors. A behavior-counting technique was employed to measure baseline (initial) and terminal rates of emission of the target behaviors. The findings provided qualitative support of the first hypothesis. Insignificant changes were found among measures of impulsiveness. No support was found for the third hypothesis.

Operant techniques were found to be effective in reducing hyperactivity and distractibility behaviors of children who did not display exaggerated forms of the objectionable reactions during incipient stages of the intervention. The techniques were not effective with impulsive behaviors at any initial rate of emission, nor with hyperactivity and distractibility responses at high initial rates of emission. Medicated-nonmedicated status was not found to be effective with any of the target behaviors. Teachers employing this kind of intervention found the technique "somewhat time-consuming" but "generally effective in modifying behavior."

Diagnostic-Prescriptive Process

A simple but accurate description of learning disabilities is the failure of a child to interact successfully with the curriculum. The mission of education has been, and shall be, the presentation of information to the learner with the outcome observed in behavioral change. The major media through which we work in education are generally called curricula. Haring (1968) has described curriculum in the following manner:

> A curriculum is a plan for the arrangement of information and experiences which educators consider necessary for children to cope successfully with life. This general view of curriculum involves the teacher in arranging the variables of instruction to produce the behavior sought—an approach that encompasses what to teach, how to teach, and how to improve teaching (Bellack, 1969). The child and his own development, as well as the final goals of instruction, are influences on the final design of the curriculum. Consequently, effectively designed curriculum starts with the child at his level of entering behavior and guides him efficiently and effectively toward terminal objectives (p. 1).

A prescription is a specified instructional act, drawn out of or away from the broad curriculum, designed to alter a target behavior identified during the act of describing (diagnosing) behavior.

Diagnosis and prescription in education were defined by Hickey and Hoffman (1973) as

Diagnosis: the process by which the state of the learner at a given moment of time is assessed in relation to certain factors as the basis for determining learning needs.

Prescription: the process by which modifications are made in the activities of learning comprising a generalized learning program in order to meet the specifically identified or diagnosed needs of the learner (p. 35).

Figure 12 denotes the diagnosis and prescriptive process as it is defined by Hickey and Hoffman. Please note that by assessing the five learner aspects listed, a prescriptive program profile as well as a student's diagnostic profile is prepared, both of which lead to a prescriptive decision based on student diagnostic profile, diagnostic placement test, and program prescription profiles. The authors do not provide us with the profile they used, the tests they used, the rules for arriving at a prescription, or the components of a prescriptive package.

La Crosse et al. (1973) described prescriptive teaching as a process for individualizing instruction. Individual differences are specified through diagnosis, and an instructional objective is prepared. Each instructional objective has three parts: (1) It identifies the terminal behavior; (2) it describes the condition under which the behavior is expected to occur; (3) it defines the criteria for acceptable performance.

Bennett (1972) has proposed that the name *prescriptive teaching* be used to note the absence of stigma attached to terms such as "perceptually impaired," "emotionally disturbed," "neurologically impaired," and

Figure 12

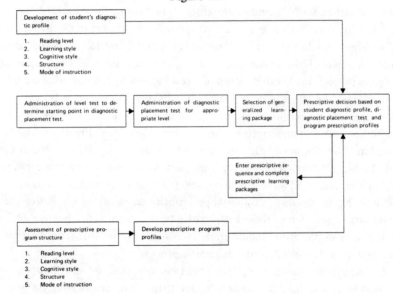

Development of student's diagnostic profile

1. Reading level
2. Learning style
3. Cognitive style
4. Structure
5. Mode of instruction

Administration of level test to determine starting point in diagnostic placement test.

Administration of diagnostic placement test for appropriate level

Selection of generalized learning package

Prescriptive decision based on student diagnostic profile, diagnostic placement test and program prescription profiles

Enter prescriptive sequence and complete prescriptive learning packages

Assessment of prescriptive program structure

1. Reading level
2. Learning style
3. Cognitive style
4. Structure
5. Mode of instruction

Develop prescriptive program profiles

Hickey and Hoffman, *Educational Technology,* 1973, p. 37.

other special class designations. Terms that can be used interchangeably with "prescriptive teaching" are "resource room," "open-end classroom," "learning laboratory," and "educational center."

Zimpelman (1974), in operationalizing a diagnostic-prescriptive system in Louisville public schools, used three levels of screening and diagnosis. These levels were: Level 1—overall screening—compare a child's academic performance to others of his age and grade; Level 2—specific diagnosis—indication of relative strengths and weaknesses through the administration of a test battery by a monitoring technician; Level 3—intensive diagnosis—performed by the reading specialist on individual diagnostic tests.

She defines the diagnostic-prescriptive process in the context of the word *prescribe,* which means to literally write down beforehand, and *prescriptive,* which means to set down directions. The process of the diagnostic system used in Louisville was to diagnose, prescribe, implement, and monitor. An instructional delivery system grid of *what, who,* and *how* was superimposed upon a three-stage process of skill identification, individualized implementation of a class program, and individual teaching relationship.

For the purpose of this discussion of diagnostic-prescriptive teaching, we will ignore the diagnostic aspect. Chapter 3 contains a discussion of those issues which have caused us the greatest difficulty. The reader may wish to review the sections on formal and informal assessment in that chapter to become acquainted with the important issues related to that aspect of the diagnostic process.

It should be obvious that we have not yet developed (and validated) information-processing behavioral models to the point that we can account for learner characteristics as measured from formal tests. Therefore, there has been a general effort to abandon formal tests (Ysseldyke and Salvia, 1974) and to replace them with informal measures of a specific aspect of curricula contexts. The major difficulty with that reasoning is that it does not provide any information on the rules for utilizing a particular method or material. Informal tests are good devices to tell us where to begin a given instructional task and possibly how to use it. Informal tests do not explain what to teach, unless children are locked into assessment or prognostic classes for several weeks where they try several materials. Such an approach would be impossible for all but a few children who fail to respond to other forms of instructional delivery.

Heine and Rahaim (1973) note that the diagnostic aspect leading to teaching requires flexible and continuous probing by the teacher, but it does not require any one particular organizational pattern, setting, form, or style of teaching. Using information from diagnosis, an instructional effort is planned, but that diagnostic effort does not stop when treatment begins. It is their opinion that continuous treatment and diagnosis are the essence of prescriptive teaching. "Prescriptive teaching can be viewed as an alternating teach-test process with the teacher alternating his role between teacher and tester" (p. 1).

First, teachers must know what to look for on which dimensions. Second, they must collect the data systematically by objective and carefully executed observations of characteristic student behavior. Consequently, each teacher must develop a repertoire of informal evaluative techniques in a number of relevant areas. By developing skill in the informal assessment of student behavior teachers will be able to:

1. ascertain areas of strength and weakness in pupils and, in many instances, identify the basis for educational difficulties;

2. gain an understanding of the most efficacious techniques for presenting subject matter to youngsters who exhibit various learning problems;

3. construct curricula in a logical sequence; and

4.   appreciate the degree to which materials should be presented, using one
or a combination of pertinent instructional media.

The primary task of the prescriptive teacher is to develop in the child a sense of competency. The child must have:

1.   a sense of trust about himself and others;
2.   a sense of well-being in the learning situation;
3.   a sense of being able to communicate effectively with others;
4.   a sense of certainty that given behaviors will produce a given response.

Not until the child acquires this sense of competency will he be receptive to any treatment or instructional program.

Frierson (1967) states that the prescriptive educator "must continually view education as applied science rather than a wholly intuitive art. Yet (prescriptive) education will be strongest if the children being served are considered *first* to be children having distinctly human needs, and not merely broken-down learning machines whose needs can be met by following a service manual" (p. 488).

One of the more healthy methods of prescriptive teaching is the use of a specific aspect of the curriculum to accomplish a targeted behavioral objective. Certainly, one of the hoped-for differences between regular education and special education is that regular educators tend to teach from canned curricula. That is, they begin on page one of a basal reading series, and hopefully 180 days later they will be at the end of the series for the year—both textbook and workbook. Lundgren (1972) concluded that the curriculum is defined by the set of text materials commercially purchased by a given school system. Prescriptive teaching is the act of reaching into a given curriculum program and determining if a given aspect is suitable to use in obtaining a desired result.

Utilizing target behaviors as the aim to be accomplished in preparing an instructional objective has given way to several so-called diagnostic-prescriptive process models that elicit what happens next following each stage or step, depending on a yes or no answer to what one is looking to find. None of these so-called process models discloses the context used in the assessment or the level of judgment in establishing whether something is yes or no, successfully passed or not passed; and in general they do not specify the behaviors that a particular process was attempting to target. Moreover, they are unrelated in terminology, in practical application, or in developing the rules they might apply to the reasons for preparing a prescription. The so-called decision models prepared by Cartwright, Cartwright, and Ysseldyke (1973) and Freund (1972) suffer, I believe, from this general overemphasis on form and lack of emphasis on substance. They are devoid of the substance which might lead to a prescription. Most special educators agree that target behaviors can be specified as aims in instructional objectives. What we fail to agree upon are the enabling steps necessary to achieve that objective. Therefore, we remain totally stymied at the process level, unable to attach the content to the question. A prescription is the substantive act of specifying how and what instructional aspect is to be taught. Anytime we define a target behavior and address its achievement by stripping out a small piece of instruction from a canned curriculum, or construct or develop and/or specify an enabling step short of having the child go from "A" to "Z" in that program, whatever it may be, we have indeed prepared a substantive educational prescription. Anytime we base that enabling step, as a sequential act directed at having a child obtain a target behavior as part or parcel of a behavioral objective, we are engaging in the process of prescriptive teaching.

Prescriptive teaching is *not* teaching to one personological aptitude or plugging into a canned curriculum. Those who feel that aptitude-by-treatment-interaction research is synonymous with diagnostic-prescriptive teaching have been too anxious to apply statistical treatment to an inappropriately selected number of target behaviors, probably not reliably measured, and therefore invalidly described.

Such confusion does point out the necessity of working from a taxonomy of learner characteristics, developing the best measures possible that will lend themselves to a decision-tree matrix. A decision-tree matrix, utilizing the same terminology in ascertaining learner characteristics and in describing prescriptions drawn from curriculum, would promote lifting a diagnostic-prescriptive process. The ardent need for a taxonomy that will apply to both learner characteristics and the analysis, storage, and retrieval of instructional materials is vitally needed. Once we have developed a means for consistently describing learner characteristics and classifying instructional components, then a serious search for the rules which will permit us to say what prescription applies most efficiently, and/or most effectively, to a given target behavior (learner characteristic) can begin.

Summary

This chapter attempted to review the current state of the educational intervention act. It examined the interventions, classifying items as (1) academic remedial, (2) perceptual-motor, (3) and (4) language and behavioral management or modification techniques. The final section focused on a current practice of diagnostic-prescriptive teaching. The only safe conclusion is that special education has developed a workable continuum of instructional delivery systems. It has not developed a means of achieving a high state of accountability for the instructional substance being used. Therefore, we lack information as to what material works best with which type of instructional problem. We have not yet learned the rules for preparing instructional prescriptions, and we shall continue to appropriate the curriculum for goodness of fit through a trial and error process. In the absence of needed rules for preparing instruction and faced with the necessity of curricular search, we must justify what we do by answering two critical questions: Are we using the most effective (amount learned) curricula? Are we using the most efficient (time to test learning task) curricula?

LEARNING   OBJECTIVES
Chapter 4

Cognitive Objectives

After carefully reading this chapter, you will be able to:

1) Identify the four major classifications of curriculum used with learning-disabled children.
2) Determine if there is any direct transfer effect between perceptual training and academic learning.
3) Determine the effectiveness of perceptual training in justifying its use. If so, under what conditions and with what children.
4) List the primary similarities and differences in the language training approaches.
5) Describe the difference between psychotherapy and behavior modification.
6) Explain the diagnostic-prescriptive concept, and outline one workable model for implementing such a teaching strategy.

LEARNING   OBJECTIVES
Chapter 4

Affective Objectives

1) How important is the teacher variable in identifying appropriate instructional programs?
2) What are the characteristics of an appropriate instructional program?
3) What are your feelings regarding the research on various instructional programs?
4) Is there a "special curriculum" that can be identified as being distinctive in character from the curriculum in regular education?
5) Is diagnostic-prescriptive teaching a solution to using whole curricula approaches since those approaches are usually drawn from a commercially produced source?

A REVIEW OF INSTRUCTIONAL PRACTICES

Curricula used with the learning-disabled child can be divided into four major types:

1 _____
2 _____
3 _____
4 _____

These major types are by no means rigid, as there is considerable overlapping in all of them. However, each type is characterized by a differing general trend of emphasis. Throughout each type, professionals tended to concern themselves with a specific theory of learning disorder.

Define academic remediation:

_____
_____
_____
_____
_____
_____
_____

READER'S NOTES

[Refer to p. _____]

[Refer to p. _____]

A REVIEW OF INSTRUCTIONAL PRACTICES

Define perceptual motor:

_____
_____
_____
_____
_____

Define language training:

_____
_____
_____
_____
_____

What is behavior modification, and how is it used? Give four examples.
Example 1: _____
_____
_____

Example 2: _____
_____
_____

READER'S NOTES

A REVIEW OF INSTRUCTIONAL PRACTICES

Example 3: _____
_____
_____
_____

Example 4: _____
_____
_____
_____

Academic remediation involves direct work with the child using academic types of teaching material, e.g., direct work on word recognition, phonic skills, sight vocabulary, reading comprehension, math remediation, etc.

Frequently, remediation is regarded as a concentrated effort using standard developmental teaching methodology, in most cases provided through individualized instruction. The adoption of the curriculum and method to a particular child is referred to as clinical teaching and seems to be suitable to the "catch-up-child"; however, it has been found that this approach is not practically suited to the

READER'S NOTES

A REVIEW OF INSTRUCTIONAL PRACTICES

child with learning disabilities. The latter is more successfully treated when radical changes have been effected in the curriculum and methodology.

In discussing variations in strategies for approaching remediation of the learning disabled, several general trends surface:

[Refer to p. _____]

I.   PERCEPTUAL TRAINING
Some characteristics

_____

_____

_____

_____

[Refer to p. _____]

II.   MOTOR, TACTILE, AND KINESTHETIC TRAINING
Some characteristics

_____

_____

_____

_____

READER'S NOTES   **A REVIEW OF INSTRUCTIONAL PRACTICES**

[Refer to p. _____]   III.   **LANGUAGE TRAINING**
                                           Some characteristics

_____

_____

_____

_____

[Refer to p. _____]   IV.   **PSYCHOTHERAPY AND BEHAVIORAL MODIFICATION**
                                           Some characteristics

_____

_____

_____

_____

[Refer to p. _____]   V.   **DIAGNOSTIC PRESCRIPTIVE TEACHING WITH LEARN-
                                           ING DISABILITIES**
                                           Some characteristics

_____

_____

_____

5 An Instructional System for Teachers of Learning-Disabled Children

James H. Reese

Introduction

SYSTEM is defined as "an aggregation or assemblage of objects joined in regular interaction or interdependence" (Webster's Third New International Dictionary, 1966, p. 2322). Applying this definition to our views for teaching children with learning disabilities, we would define an instructional system as the interrelated and interacting teaching components organized to attain satisfactory learning progress.

The proposed instructional system is based on the characteristics common to the various "diagnostic-prescriptive" teaching models reported in the literature (Peters, 1965; Johnson and Myklebust, 1967; Prillaman, 1968; Popham and Baker, 1970; Gerlach and Ely, 1971; Lerner, 1971; and Sabatino, 1970). The basic components of the instructional system are: (1) assessment, (2) formulation of an instructional hypothesis and establishing program goals, (3) establishing and sequencing of specific instructional objectives and selecting appropriate instructional strategies, and (4) evaluation. While in this context the four components may appear to be mutually exclusive, in reality they are not. The components are interrelated, each dependent on the other.

In order to provide successful instructional programming for children with learning disabilities, a teacher must know a child's specific educational strengths and weaknesses as well as the child's present instructional needs for remaining in or returning to the educational mainstream. Such information acts as a roadmap for the teacher in deciding where to begin and what direction to take with a learning-disabled child in terms of outlining an instructional program and preparing and sequencing instructional objectives to achieve the program's goals. Similarly, a teacher cannot select an instructional strategy until an objective has been set. Gerlach and Ely (1971) noted, "A medium of instruction must be selected on the basis of its potential for implementing a stated objective" (p. 281). Each step of the instructional program should be evaluated, thus providing the teacher with the feedback necessary to insure the success of the program.

The instructional system emphasizes an approach which we feel is both logical and self-correcting, contributing to the decision-making process of arriving at usable instructional objectives and strategies for children with learning disabilities. It cannot be overemphasized that the instructional system is not a method but an approach. The uniqueness of a system approach is that it directs the teacher's activities when using any of the many teaching methods (cf. Myers and Hammill, 1969) that are available. This is important, since the Model Learning Disabilities Systems views learning disabilities teachers not as technicians but as professional special educators who must render decisions about what to teach, how to teach it, how long to teach it, and when to implement a new or alternate teaching method.

The term *instructional system* refers to the total educational program for the learning-disabled child and encompasses all activities affecting the child following the screening procedure discussed in Chapter 4. This program includes the four basic components of assessment, formulating an instructional hypothesis and establishing program goals, establishing and sequencing specific instructional objectives and selecting appropriate instructional strategies to achieve these goals, and ongoing evaluation. It also includes the placement decision (self-contained, full-time special class, assessment class, or resource room) and the follow-up activities once the child returns to his regular classroom on a full-time basis.

The relationship between the various steps of the screening and instructional systems is presented graphically in Figure 13. Note that the screening and instructional systems overlap at assessment. While assessment is primarily considered a component of the instructional system, it is also a continuation of the screening system. This overlapping or coupling is natural since the screening and assessment results are combined to provide a total evaluation of the child and render a decision as to what type of placement would be most appropriate.

Assessment

The purpose of assessment is "to expand, probe, verify, and if need be, discard the conclusions" (Hammill, 1971) of the screening procedure while, at the same time, providing the necessary information for program planning. The screening procedure identifies a child as learning disabled and identifies possible problem areas, but does not provide a total evaluation. The intent of assessment, using both formal and informal

Figure 13

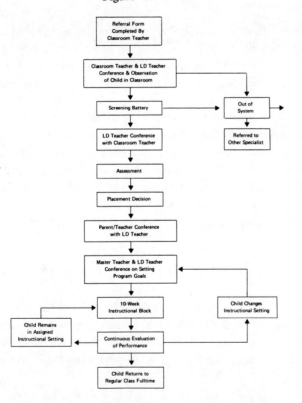

diagnostic procedures, is two-fold: to determine (1) how a child learns, that is, what channel or channels are open and the rate and amount of input the child can adequately manage, and (2) whether the difficulty is primarily at a perceptual, symbolic, or conceptual level (Johnson, 1967; Lerner, 1971). A complete assessment should include the following:

1. review of educational history
2. conferences with previous classroom teachers
3. review of biographical data and medical history
4. review of any previous psychological, clinical, or social agency reports
5. conferences with parents
6. further evaluation, using both standardized instruments and teacher-prepared inventories and tests
7. classroom observations and conferences with the classroom teacher.

The major task of the teacher during the assessment stage is to consolidate and organize all available information on the child and then observe the child in the classroom and conduct any testing necessary for developing an appropriate program of intervention. Observation of the child in the classroom should not be overlooked. Assessment, or diagnosis, is not complete until the teacher sees the problem in large perspective, that is, sees the child's difficulties in the classroom environment. The question of whether or not to conduct further testing is quite simple. If the information available and the observations made provide sufficient guidance for program planning (stating an instructional hypothesis and preparing program goals), then no further testing is necessary. The teacher should, however, make a careful and detailed examination of the child's specific weaknesses in information processing and academic skill development. The guiding rule is that assessment should do more than simply verify that the child is learning disabled; it should indicate what specific behavioral and/or academic areas are in need of management or remediation and provide an idea of what the management or remedial techniques might be.

When using previous diagnostic reports and test information during assessment, the teacher should keep in mind that children are constantly growing (socially, emotionally, physically, mentally) as a result of maturation and experiences both in and out of school. What a child did not know or do last month or six months ago he may know or do now. What worked with a child last month or six months ago may not be practical now. The teacher must be alert to the fact that previous diagnostic reports and test information may be inappropriate or outdated. Similarly, any test of a particular skill/behavior is only a sample of that skill/behavior at a specific time using a specific technique. The teacher must realize that there are many factors that can and will affect the child's performance, such as fear of the testing situation, illness, recent punishment, hunger, fatigue, anger, level of rapport with the examiner, and the reliability and validity of the instrument or instruments. The interpretation of any results must consider the effects of any of these confounding factors. For these reasons, then, assessment is not a once-and-done-with activity, but a continuing, diagnostic-instructional relationship wherein questions, phrased as instructional hypotheses, are raised, and teaching methods tried in order to determine those that work most efficiently and effectively.

Instructional Hypothesis and Program Goals

Assessment provides the learning disabilities teacher with the diagnostic information necessary for stating an instructional hypothesis and defining program goals. The instructional hypothesis simply states the learning disabilities teacher's views on how the child learns (i.e., learning style) according to the interpretation of the screening and assessment results.

Children with learning disabilities are not a homogeneous group. Each child has a preferred means of receiving and processing information from the environment. Some may be "visual learners" who have difficulty processing auditory stimuli, while others may be "auditory learners" who have problems in processing visual stimuli. Some may be able to learn via a single sensory channel, but unable to integrate information from two or more channels. On the other hand, some may have no preferred means of receiving information, demonstrating a generalized "input" problem. Others may only have problems with "output," i.e., expression via oral or written messages (Johnson, 1967). Likewise, children differ in the amount of information they can efficiently process for a given time period and in the rate at which they learn.

The instructional hypothesis states the child's primary problem, his preferred means of receiving and processing information, and the amount and rate of input that can be managed. Since the statement is a hypothesis, it will change as it is proven inadequate during instruction and as the teacher gains more insight into the child's learning habits.

Program goals are those statements outlining the major aims of the child's program. In formulating program goals, three questions should be considered. Should the initial impetus of the instructional program be directed at remediating:

1. a specific academic problem?
2. a specific information processing behavior (e.g., visual or auditory perception, specific language disability)?
3. an overt behavior that interferes with the instructional process?

Instructional Objectives and Instructional Strategies

Once the goals of the instructional system are established, the task then becomes one of establishing and sequencing objectives and selecting relevant strategies. There exists a clear distinction between program goals and instructional objectives. Goals state the major aims of the child's program, while instructional objectives are the enabling steps to goal achievement. A useful instructional objective states: (1) the skill or behavior the teacher wants the child to develop, (2) the amount of time the teacher thinks it will take to develop that skill or behavior, and (3) the degree of success or accuracy the child should demonstrate. Some examples of instructional objectives are:

1.   The child will demonstrate knowledge of the concepts of *when, where, what, why,* and *who* with 90 percent accuracy in ten thirty-minute instructional sessions;

2.   The child will recall four-object sequences with 90 percent accuracy in ten fifteen-minute instructional sessions;

3.   The child will associate the action verbs (running, throwing, jumping, walking, and climbing) with the appropriate actions with 100 percent accuracy in five fifteen-minute instructional sessions;

4.   The child will describe 16 objects (different in shape, size, texture) using only tactile clues with 90 percent accuracy in five thirty-minute instructional sessions.

5.   The child will solve addition problems containing two one-digit numbers with sums of 5 or less with 90 percent accuracy in ten thirty-minute instructional sessions.

The instructional strategy, or prescription, is the statement that describes the teaching method and specifies the material the teacher is using to achieve an instructional objective. Each objective has a well-defined teaching approach. It is the instructional strategy that allows the teacher the most flexibility, permitting: (1) choice from a vast source of commercially available materials or development of teacher-made materials; (2) choice of procedures to achieve the objective; and (3) changes in the prescriptions to obtain the one that is most effective. Some examples of instructional strategies are:

1. Material: *Supportive Reading Skills, Understanding Questions,* Levels A and B (Dexter and Westbrook, Ltd.); teacher-made flashcards (paired)—when-time, who-person, why-reason, where-place, what-thing/person.

Method: Introduce concepts of key question words (when, where, etc.) with flashcards by explaining what each word asks for; practice using oral questions relevant to immediate situation (e.g., Who is wearing a red shirt? When did you eat breakfast? Where are you now?); continue practice using *Understanding Questions.*

2. Material: *Visual Memory Cards,* Levels I and II, and III; *Visual Matching, Memory and Sequencing Exercises,* Book 2; *Visual Sequential Memory Exercises* (Developmental Learning Materials); several small objects—key, block, golf ball, scissors, comb, pencil, pen, eraser, crayon, ring, spoon, fork, paint brush, etc.

Method: Begin with two concrete objects gradually increasing to three and then four; select six objects, group them together, have child look away, then place two objects in front of child and have child look at them for ten seconds; child then looks away as teacher returns

objects to group of six; child then picks and sequences the two objects he saw. Continue
practice using objects and DLM materials until child is able to remember sequence of four
objects.

3.   Material: Magazine pictures depicting children running, walking, throwing, jumping,
and climbing.

Method: Say action verb and demonstrate action; ask child to do it with you—saying verb
and demonstrating action. Next say action verb and ask child to repeat it and demonstrate
action; then demonstrate action and ask child to supply verb. Follow same procedure until
all verbs and actions have been presented. Then have child identify action in pictures and
demonstrate action.

4.   Material: *Sense and Tell* (Scott, Foresman and Company).

Method: Introduce four shapes at a time, permitting child to see and feel each object; assist
child in verbalizing what he sees and feels (e.g., it is round and small, it is square and soft, it
is long and thin, etc.); then have child identify/describe objects using "Mystery Box."

5.   *Moving Up in Numbers,* cards 11–20 (Developmental Learning Materials); counting
sticks; teacher-made worksheets.

Method: Child solves problems using counting sticks—substitutes correct number of sticks
for numbers in problem; gradually diminish concrete support until child can solve problems
without counting sticks.

A major aim of the instructional system is to sequence instructional objectives so that the child realizes
continuous progress toward the program goals. Steenburger (1973) has stated:

The writing of objectives forces the teacher to organize the teaching material into orderly, successive increments. Objectives state the specific criteria of acceptable performance so that goals can be recognized and achieved by the student and performance and growth can be measured (p. 7).

Sequencing of instructional objectives means organizing instructional activities so that the child experiences "orderly, successive increments" in the development of necessary academic skills and appropriate school behaviors. Once the program goals have been stated, the teacher must then analyze the steps necessary to attain each goal. The teacher must ask, "What is the orderly sequence of skills and/or behaviors leading to each goal?" If each goal is to be achieved, the teacher must isolate, describe, and organize the steps that will lead to that goal (Bateman, 1971). The teacher is well advised to accept the notion that learning is cumulative, i.e., skills build on one another. A hit-or-miss sequence of activities may occasionally provide satisfactory achievement of desired goals, but invariably such guesswork results in inconsistent performance.

In the attempt to organize the enabling steps of a goal, the teacher should keep in mind that there may be several different organizational patterns or ladders for that goal (Bateman, 1971). The point of this statement is that the teacher should find the ladder most suitable for the child by determining what enabling behaviors the child has already mastered. This is most easily accomplished by working backwards from the desired terminal behavior (i.e., goal) and locating the child's entry point (i.e., point of initial instruction) on the ladder. The implication is that instruction must begin at the child's level in the hierarchy of skills leading to the goal, thus eliminating the waste of valuable time in teaching skills the child has already mastered.

Evaluation

There are two points of evaluation in the proposed instructional system:
1. an evaluation of each instructional objective
2. an evaluation of pupil progress every ten weeks.

When an instructional objective is stated according to (1) the specific skill or behavior the child should develop, (2) the time period necessary for the acquisition of that skill or behavior, and (3) the degree of success or accuracy the child should demonstrate, then that statement can be evaluated. There are two basic procedures for determining whether the level of success or degree of accuracy has been achieved. The two procedures are: (1) a pre-post, norm-referenced measure of the objective and (2) a criterion-referenced measure of the objective.

A pre-post norm-referenced measure is administered to the child before implementing the instructional strategies for any given objective and at the end of the specified time allotted for that objective. A norm-referenced measure yields a score that is a comparison of that score to some relevant normal distribution; i.e., the score is compared with the test scores of other children. The difficulty in using norm-referenced measures for evaluating instructional objectives is finding a measure that assesses the specific skill/behavior specified by the objective (Gorth and Hambleton, 1972).

A criterion-referenced measure, however, yields a score that is compared with a criterion score defining a particular level of achievement (Shoemaker, 1972). Criterion-referenced measures are "deliberately constructed to yield measurements that are directly interpretable in terms of specified performance standards" (Glaser and Nitko, 1971, p. 653). With criterion-referenced measures, the important statistic is "the raw difference score obtained by subtracting a (child's) examinee's test score from the criterion test score, defining the minimally acceptable level of achievement" (Shoemaker, 1972, p. 215).

For our purposes, a criterion-referenced measure is a daily test of the child's progress toward an objective, the results of which are plotted on a profile. The performance standard of a criterion-referenced measure is stated as a percentage and is usually set at 80–90 percent accuracy, depending on the severity of the child's problem and the nature of the skill or behavior being measured. The performance standard is achieved when the child reaches the desired level of accuracy or success within the specified time period as stated by the objective and maintains that level of performance for at least five consecutive instructional periods.

The value of criterion-referenced measures is that such scores not only provide specific information relative to the performance level of children on specific objectives but also provide ongoing evaluation of the instructional program. In a sense, criterion-referenced measures continue assessment by determining whether or not the child already knows what is to be taught and has learned and remembered what was taught (Gorth and Hambleton, 1972). It must be noted that a particular test score can be both norm-referenced and criterion-referenced; the difference between the two measures is relative to how the test score is interpreted (Shoemaker, 1972).

Figure 14 outlines how the evaluation of an instructional objective "locks together" the components of the instructional system. Note that there are four basic steps necessary for such an evaluation to occur:

1. specify instructional objective (remember this includes skill/behavior, performance standard, and time limit);
2. specify teaching method;

Figure 14
Instructional System

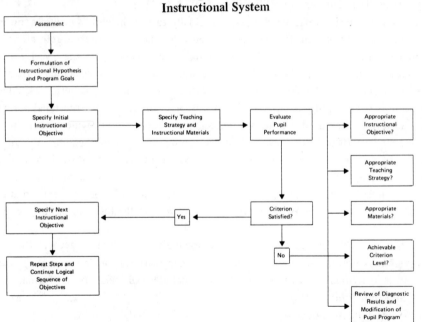

3.   specify material;

4.   evaluate pupil performance.

If the child satisfies the initial instructional objective by achieving the desired level of success, then the instructional hypothesis is retained, and the next logical instructional objective is specified, following the outlined instructional sequence. If the child does not achieve the specified criterion level of success the teacher should answer several questions:

1.   Is the initial instructional objective appropriate?

2.   Is the prescription appropriate?

3.   Is the criterion level of success within the child's limits?

4.   Is there a need for reviewing the assessment information and modifying the initial instructional hypothesis?

The decision as to which element (instructional objective, teaching method, material, criterion of success) needs to be modified is based on the teacher's professional judgment. The only guideline is that if the initial instructional objective is retained with changes occurring only in the prescriptions during the first ten-week block of instruction and satisfactory progress is not achieved, then the assessment results are reviewed and another instructional hypothesis formulated or further diagnosis initiated. As Wedell (1970) has suggested, diagnosis is an ongoing process of hypothesis verification. Evaluation is a continuous process of the instructional system, and if implemented properly, it makes the system self-correcting.

Every ten weeks the teacher reviews the child's program and progress. The intent of this cursory evaluation is to make certain the program is proceeding on target, or in other words, to prevent the teacher from losing sight of the program goals. Also, such an evaluation assists the teacher in predicting when the child might be returning to the regular classroom on a full-time basis with support services. This is important since both the child and the classroom teacher must be prepared for this reentry or change.

A Final Note

It has been stated that the proposed instructional system is self-correcting. Self-correction will occur only if the teacher accepts and applies the principle that diagnosis (assessment) and evaluation are continuous processes of the instructional system. Diagnosis of the child's problem and evaluation of intervention are integral aspects of the on-going instructional activities or learning experiences. If instructional activities are to be tailored to satisfy the needs of an individual child, and if these activities are to be modified or changed as more insight into the child's learning style is gained, or as additional needs become apparent, then the teacher must constantly monitor the child's performance during instructional activities.

Every teacher's dream is to facilitate "peak learning," but because children are constantly changing and the teacher's access to and control over environmental circumstances are limited, peak learning is probably unattainable (Adelman, 1971). But if a teacher follows the procedures outlined in this chapter, we feel he will come as close to establishing the optimal match between child and instructional alternatives as anyone possibly can.

Following are the Individual Profile Record and the Instructional Data Log, two forms which teachers may find useful when following the instructional procedures discussed in this chapter.

APPENDIX   A

MODEL LEARNING DISABILITIES SYSTEMS

INSTRUCTIONAL DATA LOG

PUPIL NAME:_____   I.D. #:_____GRADE:_____

TEACHER: _____   DESCRIPTOR:_____

INSTRUCTIONAL OBJECTIVE	PRESCRIPTION	MIN./SESSION/ # OF SESSIONS	DATES	CRITERION ACHIEVED	PRETEST RESULTS	POSTTEST RESULTS

MODEL LEARNING DISABILITIES SYSTEMS

INDIVIDUAL PROFILE RECORD

PUPIL NAME _____   SEX _____   BIRTHDATE _____   GRADE _____   CLASSROOM TEACHER _____

DISTRICT _____   BUILDING _____   LD TEACHER _____   ID NUMBER _____

	AE	5-2	5-8	6-2	6-8	7-2	7-8	8-2	8-8	9-2	9-8	10-2	10-8	11-2	11-8	
	GE	K	K.5	1.0	1.5	2.0	2.5	3.0	3.5	4.0	4.5	5.0	5.5	6.0	6.5	
PIAT Mathematics																
PIAT Reading Recognition																
PIAT Reading Comprehension																
PIAT Spelling																
Verbal Conceptualization																
Nonverbal Conceptualization																
Visual Discrimination																
Visual-Motor Integration																
Auditory Perception																

I. SCREENING PROFILE (continued)

A. VISUAL ACUITY   B. AUDITORY ACUITY   C. SPECIAL SERVICES

__ Normal   __ Normal   __ Speech Therapist   __ Language Specialist
__ Corrected   __ Corrected   __ Audiologist   __ Guidance Counselor
__ Uncorrected   __ Uncorrected   __ Reading Specialist   __ Mental Health Clinic
                                            __ Social Worker   __ Other–Specify: _____

II. DIAGNOSTIC PROFILE

A. MOTOR DEVELOPMENT   B. VISUAL PERCEPTION   C. AUDITORY PERCEPTION

__ Gross   __ Fine   __ Discrimination   __ Discrimination
__ Left-Right Orientation   __ Memory   __ Memory
__ Body Awareness   __ Figure-Ground   __ Figure-Ground, Localization

II. DIAGNOSTIC PROFILE (continued)

D. LANGUAGE-CONCEPTUALIZATION   **E. READING**   **F. ARITHMETIC**

___ Expressive   ___ Concrete   ___ Letter Recognition   ___ Numerical Meaning
  ___ Vocabulary   ___ Functional   ___ Word Attack   ___ Computation
  ___ Syntax   ___ Abstract   ___ Phonics   ___ Addition ___ Multiplication
___ Receptive   ___ Structural   ___ Subtraction ___ Division
                                                  ___ Vocabulary   ___ Fractions, Decimals, Percentages
                                                  ___ Comprehension   ___ Measurement

G. BEHAVIOR

___ Attention   ___ Social Interaction   Comments: _____
  ___ Short Span   ___ Withdrawn   _____
  ___ Perseveration   ___ Aggressive   _____
___ Activity Level   ___ Sudden Mood Changes   _____
  ___ Hyperactive
  ___ Hypoactive

III. INSTRUCTIONAL HYPOTHESIS

A. INITIAL   Date: _____   B. REVISION NO. ___   Date: _____

_____   _____
_____   _____
_____   _____

C. REVISION NO. ___ Date: _____   D. REVISION NO. ___   Date: _____

_____   _____
_____   _____
_____   _____

IV. PROGRAM GOALS

A. _____   B. _____
_____   _____
_____   _____

C. _____   D. _____
_____   _____
_____   _____

IV. PROGRAM GOALS (continued)

E. _____   F. _____
   _____   _____
   _____   _____

G. _____   H. _____
   _____   _____
   _____   _____

V. SCHOOL AND HOME INFORMATION

A. _____ Class Enrollment   I. _____ Father's Education
B. _____ Grades Repeated   J. _____ Mother's Education
C. _____ Special Services   K. _____ Home Status
D. _____ Number of Siblings   L. _____ Father's Occupation
E. _____ Number of Older Female Siblings   M. _____ Mother's Occupation
F. _____ Number of Younger Female Siblings   N. _____ Parent/Guardian
G. _____ Number of Older Male Siblings   O. _____ Address
H. _____ Number of Younger Male Siblings   _____
                                              P. _____ Home Telephone

CODE

A.   Number of Pupils in Class

B.   K=Kindergarten; 1=First; 2=Second; etc.

C.   1=Speech Therapist; 2=Language Specialist;
3=Audiologist; 4=Guidance Counselor;
5=Remedial Reading Teacher; 6=Social Worker;
7=Mental Health Clinic; 8=Other

D.-H. Number of Brothers and Sisters;
E+F+G+H = D

I.-J. 9=Completed Ninth Grade; 10=Completed Tenth
Grade, etc.; 13=Two Years of College or Trade
School; 14=B.A. or B.S. Degree; 15=Master's
Degree; 16=Ph.D., etc.

K.   1=Home intact—both parents living at home;
2=Parents are separated, living with mother;
3=Parents are separated, living with father;
4=Father deceased, living with mother;
5=Mother deceased, living with father;
6=Father deceased, mother remarried;

CODE (continued)

K.   7=Mother deceased, father remarried;
        8=Living with relatives;
        9=Legal guardians appointed;
        10=Foster home.

L.-M.   List Occupations

N.-O.   Enter Names and Home Address

P.   List Home Telephone Number and an Emergency Number
        in Parentheses.

APPENDIX B

Directions for Final Report of Student Progress

The Final Report of Student Progress is the last step in the evaluation of pupils serviced under the system developed by the Model Program. This final evaluation must be made available to all school personnel who have an interest in the child's educational growth. The Final Report of Student Progress is to be completed at the end of the school year. Copies of the report will be filed in the district and project cumulative folders and be given to the regular class teacher and the building principal. The report must be signed by the learning disabilities teacher completing the form and by whoever receives the report.

When completing the progress report, include the following:
1. ID information
2. Dates of instruction, beginning and ending
3. Description of intervention which asks that the teacher state the areas of instruction.
4. All pre-post test results
5. Recommended assignment in project or regular class and recommended curriculum that should be continued the following year.

The final progress report also asks for a reply from the classroom teacher and principal. The learning disabilities teacher should see that the report includes these replies.

Model Learning Disabilities Systems

Final Report of Student Progress

Student Name: _____ Sex: _____

Birthdate: _____ Grade: _____ School: _____

Teacher: _____ Assignment: _____   3. Recommended for next year:

LD Teacher: _____   Program Assignment: _____

Date Instruction Began: _____   _____

1. Description of Instruction/Management Intervention: _____

_____   Instruction/Management: _____

_____   _____

_____   _____

_____   _____

_____   _____

_____   _____

2. Results of Instructional Program:

Date	Test	Pre-Score	Date	Test	Posttest Score
_____	_____	_____	_____	_____	_____
_____	_____	_____	_____	_____	_____
_____	_____	_____	_____	_____	_____
_____	_____	_____	_____	_____	_____

Classroom Teacher Reply: _____

_____   Report Compiled by:

Principal's Reply: _____

_____   Report Received by:

Directions for Teacher Report of Student Progress

The progress reports are necessary to maintain continuous evaluation of the student's progress and to maintain close contact between the learning disabilities teacher and the regular classroom teacher regarding each student being serviced by the Model Learning Disabilities Systems. Therefore, forms are provided for the learning disabilities teacher to report student progress to the classroom teacher and/or principal. These duplicate progress reports are to be completed and sent on a weekly basis. The forms are in duplicate in order for the classroom teacher to respond, to retain a copy, and then to return the completed form to the learning disabilities teacher. In this way, both teachers are taking a good look at the curriculum area the child is working in and at the progress he is making in that area. The form also facilitates continuous interaction between the learning disabilities teacher and the classroom teacher. The learning disabilities teacher should keep the completed progress report forms in students' respective folders. A form is also provided for the learning disabilities teacher to enter the date that each progress report is sent. This form should also be kept in each student's folder. Using this procedure, ongoing evaluation of pupil progress can be achieved.

MODEL LEARNING DISABILITIES SYSTEMS

To Teacher Report of Student Progress

STUDENT NAME: _____ DATE: _____

TO: _____ MEMO: _____

_____

_____

_____

SIGNED: _____

REPLY: _____

_____

_____

_____

SIGNED: _____

MODEL LEARNING DISABILITIES SYSTEMS

Teacher Report of Student Progress

STUDENT NAME: _____

CLASSROOM TEACHER: _____

Dates of Progress Report:

1. _____	19. _____
2. _____	20. _____
3. _____	21. _____
4. _____	22. _____
5. _____	23. _____
6. _____	24. _____
7. _____	25. _____
8. _____	26. _____
9. _____	27. _____
10. _____	28. _____
11. _____	29. _____
12. _____	30. _____
13. _____	31. _____
14. _____	32. _____
15. _____	33. _____
16. _____	34. _____
17. _____	35. _____
18. _____	36. _____

L E A R N I N G   O B J E C T I V E S
Chapter 5

Cognitive Objectives

At the completion of this chapter you will be able to:

1)   Identify and define the four components of the instructional system.
2)   State the components of an instructional objective and prescription.
3)   Differentiate between a norm-referenced measure and a criterion-referenced measure.
4)   Construct a flowchart of activities in implementing the instructional system.
5)   Identify and define the terms *instructional hypothesis* and *program goal.*

L E A R N I N G   O B J E C T I V E S
Chapter 5

Affective Objectives

After reading the chapter, the author intends that you will:

1) Value the importance of individually designed instructional programs for learning-disabled children.

2) Recognize the importance of a complete educational assessment.

3) Value the importance of evaluating instructional effectiveness.

4) Recognize the value of the instructional system as a road map for guiding teacher activities in planning and implementing instructional programs for learning-disabled children.

READER'S NOTES

The term *instructional system* implies the total educational program of the learning-disabled child, encompassing all activities affecting the child following screening. This includes the four basic components of the instructional system. The four components of the system are:

[Refer to p. _____]
1. _____
2. _____
3. _____
4. _____

It also includes two other activities:

[Refer to p. _____]
1. _____
2. _____

The four components of the instructional system may appear to be mutually exclusive, but when the system is implemented, the com-

[Refer to p. _____]
ponents are _____ . The dependency of the components on one another creates an instructional approach

[Refer to p. _____]
which is both _____ and

_____ .

READER'S NOTES

[Refer to p. _____]

The purpose of assessment is to expand, verify, and if warranted, discard the conclusions of the screening system while at the same time providing the necessary information for program planning. A complete assessment should include:

1. _____
2. _____
3. _____
4. _____
5. _____
6. _____
7. _____

The major task of the teacher during assessment is to _____

[Refer to p. _____]

_____ and _____

all available information on the child. This includes viewing the problem in large perspective, that is, observing the child's difficul-

[Refer to p. _____]

ties in the _____ .

Assessment provides the teacher with the diagnostic information necessary for generating two types of statements:

READER'S NOTES

[Refer to p. _____]   1. _____

[Refer to p. _____]   2. _____

Once these statements have been established, the teacher's task be-

[Refer to p. _____]   comes one of establishing and sequencing _____

_____ and selecting relevant

_____ .

There is a distinction between program goals and instructional objectives. Program goals are defined as:

[Refer to p. _____]   _____

_____

_____

while instructional objectives are defined as:

_____

_____

_____

Usable instructional objectives delineate three specific variables.
These are:

[Refer to p. _____]   1. _____

James H. Reese

READER'S NOTES

[Refer to p. _____]

[Refer to p. _____]

[Refer to p. _____]

2. _____

3. _____

The instructional prescription describes the _____

_____ and specifies the _____

the teacher is using to achieve an instructional objective.

The evaluation component of the proposed instructional system has two purposes:

1. _____

2. _____

The two basic procedures for determining whether the level of success for an instructional objective has been achieved are:

1. _____

2. _____

T = TRUE   F = FALSE

(Rewrite the statements that are false so that they are
true statements. Use space at the left.)

T F   1. Children with learning disabilities are a homogeneous
           group.

T F   2. Previous diagnostic reports and test information pro-
           vide more than sufficient data for program planning.

T F   3. An instructional system is defined as the interrelated
           and interacting teaching components organized so as
           to facilitate satisfactory learning progress.

T F   4. The proposed instructional system is a specific remedial
           instructional method.

T F   5. While assessment is primarily considered a component
           of the instructional system, it is also a continuation of
           the screening system.

T F   6. Assessment always includes the administration of tests.

T F   7. Assessment is primarily intended to identify a child as
           learning disabled.

T F   8. A criterion-referenced measure yields a score that is a comparison of that score to some relevant normal distribution.

T F   9. Assessment can be viewed as a continuing, diagnostic-instructional relationship.

T F   10. The following is a complete instructional objective: The child will solve addition problems with 80 percent accuracy.

T F   11. Instructional hypotheses outline the major aims of the child's instructional program.

T F   12. An instructional prescription states the child's primary problem, his preferred means of receiving and processing information, and the amount and rate of input that he can manage.

T F   13. The following is a complete instructional objective: the child will name the letters of the alphabet in five fifteen-minute instructional sessions.

T F   14. As identified in this chapter, a criterion-referenced measure is a daily test of the child's progress toward an objective.

Definitions

1. Instructional system _____

    _____

    _____

2. Norm-referenced measure _____

    _____

    _____

3. Instructional hypothesis _____

    _____

    _____

4. Instructional objective _____

    _____

    _____

5. Program goal _____

    _____

    _____

6. Instructional prescription _____

    _____

    _____

7. Criterion-referenced measure _____

_____

_____

8. Performance standard _____

_____

_____

9. Sequencing of instructional objectives _____

_____

_____

6 Instructional Materials for Learning-Disabled Children

James H. Reese and Carl R. Schmidt

Introduction

SPECIAL education programs and services for learning-disabled children have rapidly proliferated within the last decade. Parallelling the growth of such programs has been an increased production of special materials for use with handicapped children. Unfortunately, a huge gap has been generated between the need for special materials and a knowledge of what is available. Furthermore, few educators have the time to examine materials critically before purchasing them. The severity of this problem was noted by Kirst and Walker (1971), who estimated that 75 percent of a pupil's in-class time and 90 percent of his homework time were spent using materials, principally textbooks. Yet few schools spend more than 3 percent of their budgets for materials, and few teachers spend more than 1 percent of their time evaluating and selecting materials. This chapter was prepared with that problem in mind and was designed to assist special education directors, supervisors, and teachers in selecting materials for their programs.

The following outline describes what is included in this chapter:

Section 1: Guidelines for Selecting Instructional Materials

Section 2: Descriptor System for Categorizing Materials

Section 3: Commercially-Prepared Instructional Materials for Learning-Disabled Children

Section 4: High Interest-Low Difficulty Reading Materials

Section 5: Teaching Machines—Descriptions of Operation and Accompanying Programs

Section 6: Distributors and Addresses

Guidelines for Selecting Instructional Materials

The MLDS staff has found the following guidelines useful in selecting instructional materials.

1. *Appropriateness*
   A. Face Validity—Does the material look as if it will do what the author/publisher says it will do?
   B. Your Objectives—What are the needs of your children, and for what specific objectives do you intend to use the material? Will the material enable you and the children to achieve the stated objectives?
   C. Difficulty Level—Is the material at the children's performance level?

2. *Motivational Effectiveness*
   A. Is the material stimulating to you, the teacher?
   B. Does the material appear to have student appeal?

3. *Quality*

   A. Is the material durable?

   B. Does the material appear to be sufficient in scope and detail?

   C. Does the material appear to be well sequenced?

   D. Does the material include all the necessary equipment?

   E. Does the material include a teacher's manual? Does the manual provide directions for using the material?

4. *Implementation*

   A. Do you, the teacher, have to attend a special workshop or training session to learn how to use the material?

   B. How much teacher time and effort are required to use the material effectively?

   C. How much adapting of the material will be necessary for use with your children?

   D. Does the material require any special equipment for implementation? Is that equipment available?

5. *Cost and Usage*

   A. Is the price of the material reasonable?

   B. How often will the material be used, and with how many of your children can you use the material?

6. *Evaluation*

   A. Does the material have a built-in system for monitoring pupil progress? If not, can you prepare an evaluation format for the material?

B. Is there any literature examining the material and its effectiveness (e.g., "Programs, Materials and Techniques" in the *Journal of Learning Disabilities,* "Off the Shelf" in *Teaching Exceptional Children*)? Is there a teacher you know who has used the material? What are her comments about the material?

Descriptor System for Categorizing Materials

The MLDS has used the following Descriptor System in categorizing materials. Following the coded list of descriptors is an alphabetical listing of the terms and definitions.

Descriptor System

1.0	*MOTOR*
1.1	GROSS
1.11	Coordination-Balance
1.12	Strength-Endurance
1.2	PERCEPTUAL-MOTOR
1.21	Eye-Hand Coordination
1.22	Directionality
1.3	BODY AWARENESS
2.0	*PERCEPTION*
2.1	VISUAL
2.11	Discrimination

4.14	Vocabulary
4.15	Comprehension
4.2	**SPELLING**
4.3	**WRITING**
4.31	Manuscript
4.32	Cursive
4.4	**ARITHMETIC**
4.41	Numeration
4.42	Computation
4.43	Measurement

Definitions

Auditory Perception. The process of efficiently interpreting and organizing sensory information received by the ears. Materials included under this heading train any of the following subskills: discrimination, memory, sequencing, sound localization, and closure. Auditory perception does *not* refer to auditory acuity or sensing; the ears provide the means for sound input but do not interpret or attach meaning to this information.

Body Awareness. Knowledge of size, shape, functions, and names of body parts. Also includes to some degree the concepts of sense of directionality and laterality.

Computation. Arithmetic operations, i.e., addition, subtraction, multiplication, and division; may also include materials dealing with fractions, decimals, and percentages.

Gross Motor. The coordinated use of large muscle groups. Materials included under this heading assist in the development of balance and coordination for locomotion and also strength, agility, and endurance.

Language. The ability to receive messages (written or oral), organize and interpret (attach meaning to establish relationships and form concepts) those messages, and express ideas, feelings, etc., through clear sequential verbal patterns.

Measurement. Arithmetic concepts and skills regarding the quantification of length, area, volume, speed, time, and money.

Numeration. Arithmetic concepts including rote counting, one-to-one correspondence, sets, symbol identification, cardinal numbers, and place value.

Perceptual-Motor. Coordination of perceptual and motor systems, e.g., coordination, visual perception, and fine motor control in tracing, writing, and drawing.

Phonics. Decoding skills for reading, stressing the relationship of the sounds of language (phonemes) with the corresponding written symbols (graphemes).

Structural Analysis. Decoding skills of reading, stressing the analysis of a word by breaking it down into its parts (root, suffix, prefix).

Tactile Perception. The ability to interpret (attach meaning to) environmental information via the sense of touch. Materials included under this heading stress discrimination of size, shape, and texture by touch.

Visual Perception. The process of efficiently interpreting and organizing sensory information received by the eyes. Materials included under this heading train any of the following subskills: discrimination, memory, sequencing, and figure-ground (see auditory perception).

Word Attack. Skill in decoding familiar printed words.

Word Recognition. Materials included under this heading build a sight vocabulary, i.e., printed words which are (rapidly) recognized without use of word attack techniques.

Commercially-Prepared Instructional Materials for Learning-Disabled Children

Key
Material: Commercial name of the material.
Company: Publisher/distributor of the material.
Grade Level: PS-Preschool, P-Primary, I-Intermediate, JH-Junior High, SH-Senior High; when one of these abbreviations appears in parentheses, it means the material was not prepared for that age group but can be used with that group.

MOTOR

GROSS MOTOR

MATERIAL	COMPANY	GRADE LEVEL
Frostig Move-Grow-Learn	Follett Publishing Co.	PS, P
Dyna-Balance Walking Board	Developmental Learning Materials	PS, P (I)
Weights	Developmental Learning Materials	PS, P, I
Vanguard School Program, Part 1	Teaching Resources	PS, P (I)
Circle Balance Discs	J. A. Preston Corp.	PS, P (I)
Foot Placement Ladder	J. A. Preston Corp.	PS, P (I)
Twister Board	J. A. Preston Corp.	PS, P
Bouncing Tube	J. A. Preston Corp.	PS, P
Jump Rope	J. A. Preston Corp.	PS, P, I
Preschool Climber	J. A. Preston Corp.	PS, P
Climbing Ladder	J. A. Preston Corp.	PS, P
Rope Ladder	J. A. Preston Corp.	PS, P, I
Doorway Chinning Bar	J. A. Preston Corp.	PS, P, I

MOTOR

SENSORY-MOTOR

Eye-hand Coordination

MATERIAL	COMPANY	GRADE LEVEL
Peglace Board	Developmental Learning Materials	PS, P
Lacing Boards	Developmental Learning Materials	PS, P
Large Beads and Strings	Childcraft	PS, P
Colored Beads (small) and Strings	Childcraft	PS, P
Beaded Pegs and Pegboards	Childcraft	PS, P
Peg Sorting Board	Childcraft	PS, P
Pounding Bench	Special Education Materials	PS
Giant Pound-A-Peg with Blocks	Special Education Materials	PS
Threading Block	Special Education Materials	PS
Dubnoff Program 1	Teaching Resources	PS, P
Vanguard School Program, Part 2	Teaching Resources	PS, P
Pathway School Program I	Teaching Resources	PS, P
Fitzhugh PLUS Programs—Perceptual Training (Books 101, 102, 104)	Allied Education Council	P
Perceptual Skills Curriculum Program I: Visual-Motor Skills	Walker Educational Book Corp.	PS, P
Beginning to Learn: Fine Motor Skills	Science Research Associates	PS

MOTOR

BODY AWARENESS

MATERIAL	COMPANY	GRADE LEVEL
Body Awareness	Educational Programmers	PS, P
Body Concept Spirit Masters I and II	Developmental Learning Materials	PS, P
Vanguard School Program, Part I	Teaching Resources	PS, P
Body Position Cards	Teaching Resources	PS, P
Large Body Puzzles	Developmental Learning Materials	PS, P
Position in Space Posters	Developmental Learning Materials	PS, P
People Puzzles	Developmental Learning Materials	PS, P
Perceptual Skills Curriculum Program III: General-Motor Skills	Walker Educational Book Corp.	PS, P
Developing Better Self Awareness	Educational Innovations	PS, P

PERCEPTION

VISUAL

Discrimination

MATERIAL	COMPANY	GRADE LEVEL
TARGET Red	Field Educational Publications	P
Michigan Tracking Program—Visual Tracking	Ann Arbor Publishers	P (I)
Fitzhugh Plus Programs—Perceptual Training (Books 101, 102, 104)	Allied Education Council	P (I)
Erie Program, Parts 1–4	Teaching Resources	P
Detect Visual	Science Research Associates	PS, P
Visual Readiness Skills, Levels 1 and 2	Continental Press	PS, P
Seeing Likenesses and Differences, Levels 1, 2, 3	Continental Press	PS, P
Visual Discrimination, Levels A, B, C	Continental Press	PS, P
Vanguard School Program, Part III	Teaching Resources	P
Visual Discrimination Flip Books, I, II, III	Developmental Learning Materials	PS, P
Beginning to Learn: Perceptual Skills	Science Research Associates	PS, P
Early Childhood Form Constancy Program	JSE Press	PS, P

PERCEPTION

VISUAL

Memory

MATERIAL	COMPANY	GRADE LEVEL
Visual Memory Cards I and II, III, IV	Developmental Learning Materials	PS, P
Memory	Milton Bradley Co.	PS, P
Fitzhugh PLUS Program—Perceptual Training (Books 101, 102, 104)	Allied Education Council	P
Visual Sequential Memory Exercises	Developmental Learning Materials	PS, P
Detect Visual	Science Research Associates	PS, P
Beginning to Learn: Perceptual Skills	Science Research Associates	PS, P
Memory and Sequencing	JSE Press	P

PERCEPTION

VISUAL

Figure-ground

MATERIAL	COMPANY	GRADE LEVEL
Perceptual Activities	Ann Arbor Publishers	PS, P
The Frostig Remediation Program	Follett Publishing Co.	PS, P
Vanguard School Program, Part 4	Teaching Resources	PS, P

PERCEPTION

AUDITORY

Discrimination

MATERIAL	COMPANY	GRADE LEVEL
Sound/Order/Sense	Follett Publishing Co.	P
Auditory Perception Training	Developmental Learning Materials	P (I)
Peabody Language Development Kits, Levels 1–3	American Guidance Service	P (I)
TARGET Red	Field Educational Publications	P (I)
Gateway to Good Reading	Imperial International Learning Corp.	P
Listen and Do—Vowels and Consonants	Houghton-Mifflin	P (I)
TARGET Yellow	Field Educational Publications	P (I)
Perceptual Skills Curriculum, Program II: Auditory-Motor Skills	Walker Educational Book Corp.	PS, P
Auditory Perception Skills, Series II	Tapes Unlimited	P (I)

PERCEPTION

AUDITORY

Memory

MATERIAL	COMPANY	GRADE LEVEL
Auditory Perception Training	Developmental Learning Materials	P (I)
Buzzer Board	Developmental Learning Materials	P (I)
Peabody Language Development Kits, Levels 1–3	American Guidance Service	P (I)
Gateway to Good Reading	Imperial International Learning Corp.	P
Listening Games	Acadia Press	PS, P
Michigan Tracking Program—Symbol Tracking	Ann Arbor Publishers	P (I)
Auditory Perception Skills, Series II	Tapes Unlimited	P (I)

PERCEPTION

AUDITORY

Figure-ground

MATERIAL	COMPANY	GRADE LEVEL
Auditory Perception Skills, Series II	Tapes Unlimited	PS, P
Auditory Perception Training	Developmental Learning Materials	PS, P

PERCEPTION

TACTILE

Discrimination

MATERIAL	COMPANY	GRADE LEVEL
Tactile Board Set	J. A. Preston Corp.	PS, P
Textured Cubes and Spheres	J. A. Preston Corp.	PS, P
Tactile Textures Set	J. A. Preston Corp.	PS, P
Tactile Surface Ball	J. A. Preston Corp.	PS, P
Touch-and-Match Textures	Teaching Resources	PS, P

LANGUAGE

CONCEPTUAL

MATERIAL	COMPANY	GRADE LEVEL
Association Picture Cards I, II, and III	Developmental Learning Materials	P
Motor Expressive Language Picture Cards I and II	Developmental Learning Materials	P
Category Cards	Developmental Learning Materials	P
Sequential Picture Cards I, II, II, and IV	Developmental Learning Materials	P
Logic Cards	Developmental Learning Materials	P
Sort-A-Card Game	Milton Bradley Co.	P (I)
Vegetables and Fruits Poster Cards	Milton Bradley Co.	P
Animals and Their Young Poster Cards	Milton Bradley Co.	P
Peabody Language Development Kits I, II, and III	American Guidance Service	P (I)

LANGUAGE

CONCEPTUAL (continued)

MATERIAL	COMPANY	GRADE LEVEL
Classification Game Kit	J. A. Preston Corp.	P
Opposites, Differences, and Likenesses Kit	J. A. Preston Corp.	P
Cognitive Skills: Sequence Picture Cards	Teaching Resources	P
GOAL: Language Development	Milton Bradley Co.	PS, P
Early Childhood Enrichment Series: Unit 2, Learning to Develop Language Skills	Milton Bradley Co.	PS, P
Language Lotto	Appleton-Century-Crofts	PS, P
Language Concepts	Educational Programmers	P

LANGUAGE

EXPRESSIVE

MATERIAL	COMPANY	GRADE LEVEL
Sequential Picture Cards I, II, III, and IV	Developmental Learning Materials	P
Logic Cards	Developmental Learning Materials	P
Reaction Cards	Developmental Learning Materials	P
Language Expression Circles	Developmental Learning Materials	P
Motor Expressive Language Picture Cards I and II	Developmental Learning Materials	P
Story Cards: Tell What Part Is Missing	Milton Bradley Co.	P
Peabody Language Development Kits I, II, and III	American Guidance Service	P (I)
Opposites Flannel Aid	Milton Bradley Co.	P
Homonym Cards	Developmental Learning Materials	P

LANGUAGE

EXPRESSIVE (continued)

MATERIAL	COMPANY	GRADE LEVEL
Antonym Cards	Developmental Learning Materials	P
Homophone Cards	Developmental Learning Materials	P
Storytelling Posters	Developmental Learning Materials	P (I)
The Many Faces of Children Posters	Developmental Learning Materials	P (I)
The Many Faces of Youth Posters	Developmental Learning Materials	P (I)
Language Development Program	Science Research Associates	P, I
Cognitive Skills: What's Missing	Teaching Resources	P
GOAL: Language Development	Milton Bradley Co.	PS, P
Early Childhood Enrichment Series: Unit 2, Learning to Develop Language Skills	Milton Bradley Co.	PS, P
Language Lotto	Appleton-Century-Crofts	PS, P
Language Concepts	Educational Programmers	P

ACADEMIC

READING

Letter Recognition

MATERIAL	COMPANY	GRADE LEVEL
Detect Tactile	Science Research Associates	PS, P
Alphabet Cards	Developmental Learning Materials	PS, P
Cursive Alphabet Cards	Developmental Learning Materials	P
Letter Names and Sounds	Educational Programmers	P
Giant Alphabet Poster Cards	Milton Bradley Co.	PS, P
Sandpaper Letters	J. A. Preston Corp.	PS, P
Plywood Letters	J. A. Preston Corp.	PS, P
Follow-the-Arrow Letter Formation	J. A. Preston Corp.	P
Groovy Letters	J. A. Preston Corp.	P
Audio Reading Progress Laboratory (Level A)	Educational Progress Corp.	PS, P

ACADEMIC

READING

Letter Recognition (continued)

MATERIAL	COMPANY	GRADE LEVEL
Visual Readiness Skills, Levels 1 and 2	Continental Press	PS, P
Seeing Likenesses and Differences, Levels 1 and 2	Continental Press	PS, P
Alphabet Acrobatics	Behavioral Research Laboratories	PS, P
Sandpaper Alphabet (Lower Case Manuscript, Upper Case Manuscript, Lower Case Cursive, Upper Case Cursive)	Educational Teaching Aids Division	P
Alphabet Paper (Manuscript and Cursive)	Open Court Publishing Co.	P, I
Early Childhood Form Constancy Program	JSE Press	PS, P

ACADEMIC

READING

Word Attack

Phonics

MATERIAL	COMPANY	GRADE LEVEL
TARGET Yellow	Field Educational Publications	P
Cues and Signals Series	Ann Arbor Publishers	P (I)
Visual Aural Discriminations, Book I–V	Ann Arbor Publishers	P (I)
The St. Louis Program	Imperial International Learning Corp.	P (I)
Primary Reading Program	Imperial International Learning Corp.	P
Studio 10 Reading Powerpacs	Imperial International Learning Corp.	I, JH
Minisystems–Primary Reading (Levels B, C, D)	D. C. Heath & Co.	P (I)
Mott Basic Language Skills Programs, Semi-Programmed Series (Books 1301, 1302, 1303, 1304, 1305, 1306)	Allied Education Council	P, I

ACADEMIC

READING

Word Attack

Phonics (continued)

MATERIAL	COMPANY	GRADE LEVEL
Mott Basic Language Skills Programs, Classroom Series (Books 300a, 300b)	Allied Education Council	P, I
Listen and Do—Vowels and Consonants	Houghton-Mifflin	P
Consonant Lotto	Garrard	P
Vowel Lotto	Garrard	P
Phonics We Use Learning Games Kit	Lyons and Carnahan	P
The New Phonics We Use Series	Lyons and Carnahan	P
Durrell-Murphy Phonics Practice Program	Harcourt-Brace-Jovanovich	P, I
First Talking Alphabet	Scott, Foresman and Co.	P
Second Talking Alphabet	Scott, Foresman and Co.	P (I)

ACADEMIC

READING

Word Attack

Phonics (continued)

MATERIAL	COMPANY	GRADE LEVEL
Merrill Phonics Skilltexts/Skilltapes	Charles E. Merrill Publishing Co.	
UNO–A Phonics Game	Kenworthy Educational Service	P (I)
Phonic Word Blend Flip Charts	Kenworthy Educational Service	P (I)
Junior Phonic Rummy	Kenworthy Educational Service	P
Phonic Rummy	Kenworthy Educational Service	P (I)
Initial and Final Consonants	Ideal	P
Blends and Digraphs	Ideal	P, I
Vowels	Ideal	P, I
Vowel Enrichment	Ideal	P, I
Phonic Analysis	Ideal	P, I
The Sound Way to Easy Reading	Bremner-Davis PHONICS	P (I)

ACADEMIC

READING

Word Attack

Phonics (continued)

MATERIAL	COMPANY	GRADE LEVEL
Game Power for Phonics	The Spin-A-Test Co.	P
Sound Wheels	Interstate Printers and Publishers	P
Individualized Phonics	Teachers Publishing Corp.	P, I
Directional Phonics	Teaching Technology Corp.	P, I
Transitional Phonics	Teaching Technology Corp.	I (JH)
Word Recognition and Building Kit	Educational Teaching Aids Division	P, I
Individual Reading Games	Allied Education Council	P, I
Sound Foundations Program (Spelling and Phonics)	Developmental Learning Materials	P, I
Crossword Puzzles for Phonics (Liquid Duplicators)	Mafex Associates	P, I
Speech-to-Print Phonics	Harcourt, Brace, Jovanovich	P, I

ACADEMIC

READING

Word Attack

Structural Analysis

MATERIAL	COMPANY	GRADE LEVEL
Merrill PHONICS Skilltexts/Skilltapes	Charles E. Merrill Publishing Co.	P, I
Mott Basic Language Skills Programs Semi-Programmed Series (Books 1303, 1305, 1306, 1607)	Allied Education Council	P, I
Mott Basic Language Skills Programs Classroom Series (Book 600A)	Allied Education Council	I
Minisystems—Primary Reading (Level D)	D. C. Heath & Co.	P, I
Aural Reading Lab	Imperial International Learning Corp.	JH

ACADEMIC

READING

Word Attack

Structural Analysis (continued)

MATERIAL	COMPANY	GRADE LEVEL
Cues and Signals Series, Cues and Signals IV	Ann Arbor Publishers	P, I
Transitional Phonics	Teaching Technology Corp.	I, JH
The New Phonics We Use	Lyons and Carnahan	I
Individual Reading Games	Allied Education Council	P, I

ACADEMIC

READING

Word Recognition

MATERIAL	COMPANY	GRADE LEVEL
Reading Readiness (Sullivan)	Behavioral Research Laboratories	P
Confused Words	Teaching Technology Corp.	P, I
Confused Word Phrases	Teaching Technology Corp.	P, I
Basic Sight Vocabulary Cards	Garrard Publishing Co.	P, I
Picture-Word Cards	Garrard Publishing Co.	P
Vocab-Tracks	Developmental Learning Materials	P, I
Word-Picture Dominoes	Developmental Learning Materials	P, I
Word Recognition and Building Kit	Educational Teaching Aids Division	P, I
Pairs Word Game	Milton Bradley Co.	P
Picture Word Builder	Milton Bradley Co.	P
Picture Flash Words for Beginners	Milton Bradley Co.	P
Educational Flash Words, Groups 1 and 2	Milton Bradley Co.	P
Word-Matching Game	Open Court Publishing Co.	P

ACADEMIC

READING

Vocabulary

MATERIAL	COMPANY	GRADE LEVEL
Context Vocabulary	Teaching Technology Corp.	P, I
Supportive Reading Skills	Dexter and Westbrook, Limited	P, I
Understanding Questions (A, B, C)		
Understanding Word Groups (A, B, C)		
Specific Skill Series	Barnell Loft, Limited	P, I (JH)
Using the Context		
Picto-Cabulary Series	Barnell Loft, Limited	P, I (JH)
Word Comprehension and Paragraph	Behavioral Research Laboratories	P, I (JH)
Comprehension Exercises		
Mott Basic Language Skills Programs,	Allied Education Council	I, JH
Semi-Programmed Series (Books		
1607, 1608, 1609)		

ACADEMIC

READING

Vocabulary (continued)

MATERIAL	COMPANY	GRADE LEVEL
Mott Basic Language Skills Programs, Classroom Series (Books 300B, 600A)	Allied Education Council	P, I, JH
TARGET Green	Field Educational Publications	I, JH
TARGET Yellow	Field Educational Publications	JH, SH
Picture-Word Cards	Garrard Publishing Co.	P
Aural Reading Lab	Imperial International Learning Corp.	JH
The Macmillan Reading Spectrum: The Spectrum of Skills—Vocabulary Development Booklets	Macmillan Co.	I, JH (SH)
Veri-Tech	Educational Teaching Aids Division	P, I
Vocab-Tracks	Developmental Learning Materials	P, I

ACADEMIC

READING

Comprehension

MATERIAL	COMPANY	GRADE LEVEL
The Cornerstone Readers	Field Educational Publications	I, JH
The Kaleidoscope Readers	Field Educational Publications	JH, SH
Reader's Digest Skill Builders	Reader's Digest Services	P, I, JH, SH
Reading Comprehension in Varied Subject Matter	Educators Publishing Service	I, JH, SH
New Practice Readers	Webster/McGraw-Hill	I, JH, SH
SPECIFIC SKILL SERIES	Barnell Loft, Limited	P, I, JH, SH
Detecting the Sequence		
Getting the Facts		
Drawing Conclusions		
Getting the Main Idea		
Using the Context		

ACADEMIC

READING

Comprehension (continued)

MATERIAL	COMPANY	GRADE LEVEL
Following Directions		
Locating the Answer		
Reading for Concepts	Webster/McGraw-Hill	I, JH, SH
Reading Skill Cards	Webster/McGraw-Hill	I, JH
Understanding Questions A, B, C	Dexter and Westbrook, Limited	P
Understanding Word Groups A, B, C	Dexter and Westbrook, Limited	P
Primary Reading Program	Imperial International Learning Corp.	P
Intermediate Reading Program	Imperial International Learning Corp.	I
Skilpacers	Random House	P, I, JH
Mott Basic Language Skills Program, Comprehension Series (Books 301-304, 601-604)	Allied Educational Council	I, JH

ACADEMIC

READING

Comprehension (continued)

MATERIAL	COMPANY	GRADE LEVEL
Mott Basic Language Skills Programs, Classroom Series (Books 300B; 600A, B; 900A, B)	Allied Educational Council	I, JH, SH
Mott Basic Language Skills Programs, Semi-Programmed Series (Books 1301–1306, 1607–1610)	Allied Educational Council	P, I, JH
Michigan Tracking Program, Word Tracking	Ann Arbor Publishers	P, I, JH
Teenage Tales (Second and Third Editions)	D. C. Heath & Co.	JH, SH
Remedial Reading	The Economy Co.	I, JH, SH

ACADEMIC

READING

Comprehension (continued)

MATERIAL	COMPANY	GRADE LEVEL
Michigan Language Program, Reading Words 3, 4, 5 Word Attack and Comprehension Readers 1–4	Learning Research Associates	P, I, JH
Aural Reading Lab	Imperial International Learning Corp.	JH
Comprehension Readers (Sullivan)	Behavioral Research Laboratories	P, I
Word Comprehension and Paragraph Comprehension Exercises	Behavioral Research Laboratories	P, I (JH)
Comprehension Skills	Teaching Technology Corp.	I, JH
Catching On	Open Court Publishing Co.	P, I
Vocab-Tracks	Developmental Learning Materials	P, I

ACADEMIC

SPELLING

MATERIAL	COMPANY	GRADE LEVEL
Minisystems, On My Own in Spelling (Levels 3, 4, 5)	D. C. Heath & Co.	I, JH
Basic Goals in Spelling (4th Edition)	Webster/McGraw-Hill	P, I, JH
Webstermasters	Webster/McGraw-Hill	P, I
Continuous Progress in Spelling	The Economy Co.	P, I, JH
Our Daily Words	Imperial International Learning Corp.	P, I (JH)
Words and Patterns: The SRA Spelling Series	Science Research Associates	P, I
Word Study I and II: The SRA Spelling Series	Science Research Associates	JH
Spelling Word Power Laboratory Series	Science Research Associates	I, JH
Spelling Learning Games Kit (Kits A, B, C, D, E)	Lyons and Carnahan	P, I

ACADEMIC

SPELLING (continued)

MATERIAL	COMPANY	GRADE LEVEL
A Spelling Workbook for Early Primary Corrective Work (Books I and II)	Educators Publishing Service	P
A Spelling Workbook for Corrective Drill for Elementary Grades	Educators Publishing Service	I
A Spelling Workbook Emphasizing Rules (Rules and Generalizations for Corrective Drill)	Educators Publishing Service	JH, SH
Spelling (Buchanan and Sullivan)	Behavioral Research Laboratories	P, I
Word Recognition and Building Kit	Educational Teaching Aids Division	P, I
Spell/Write	Noble and Noble	P (I)
Sound Foundations Program	Developmental Learning Materials	P, I

ACADEMIC

WRITING

Manuscript

MATERIAL	COMPANY	GRADE LEVEL
Writing Practice Slate, Manuscript	Aero Educational Products	P
Learning to Write, Book I	Educators Publishing Service	P
Dubnoff Program 1, Level 3	Teaching Resources	P
Tracing Paper Designs	Developmental Learning Materials	P
Handwriting 1	Behavioral Research Laboratories	P
Sandpaper Alphabet (Lower Case Manuscript, Upper Case Manuscript)	Educational Teaching Aids Division	P
Alphabet Paper (Manuscript)	Open Court Publishing Co.	P, I

ACADEMIC

WRITING

Cursive

MATERIAL	COMPANY	GRADE LEVEL
Writing Practice Slate, Cursive	Aero Educational Products	P, I
Cursive Writing, Levels 1 and 2	Ann Arbor Publishers	P, I
Cursive Tracking	Ann Arbor Publishers	P, I
Learning to Write, Book II	Educators Publishing Service	P, I
Dubnoff Program 3	Teaching Resources	P, I
Sandpaper Alphabet (Lower Case Cursive, Upper Case Cursive)	Educational Teaching Aids Division	P
Alphabet Paper (Cursive)	Open Court Publishing Co.	P, I

ACADEMIC

ARITHMETIC

Numeration

MATERIAL	COMPANY	GRADE LEVEL
Cues and Signals Series, Number Tracking	Ann Arbor Publishers	P
Mathematics Involvement Program	Science Research Associates	P, I
Primary Math Skills Improvement Program	Imperial International Learning Corp.	P
Minisystems, Elementary School Mathematics (Levels A, B, C)	D. C. Heath & Co.	P
Early Childhood Enrichment Series: Unit 3, Development of Number Readiness	Milton Bradley Co.	P
Inquisitive Games	Science Research Associates	P
Enlarged Place Value Sticks	Ideal	P (I)
Modern Computing Abacus	Ideal	P, I

ACADEMIC

ARITHMETIC

Numeration (continued)

MATERIAL	COMPANY	GRADE LEVEL
Place Value Building Set	Ideal	P (I)
First Arithmetic Game	Garrard Publishing Co.	P
The 10 Game	Garrard Publishing Co.	P
Number Concept Cards	Milton Bradley Co.	P
Math Practice Slates, Set 1	Aero Educational Products	P
Place Value Board	Ideal	I
Unifix Structural Math Materials	Educational Teaching Aids Division	P, I
Fifth Unifix Kit	Educational Teaching Aids Division	P, I
Chip Trading Math Lab Kit	Scott Scientific	P, I
Flip-A-Strip Place Value Chart	Developmental Learning Materials	P, I
Readiness in Math (Sullivan)	Behavioral Research Laboratories	PS, P
Beginner's Math Lab Set No. 2	Educational Teaching Aids Division	P
Pacemaker Arithmetic Program	Fearon Publishers, Lear Siegler	P

ACADEMIC

ARITHMETIC

Computation

MATERIAL	COMPANY	GRADE LEVEL
Guidebook to Mathematics	The Economy Co.	I, JH, SH
The Learning Skills Series: Arithmetic (Books A–D)	Webster/McGraw-Hill	I, JH, SH
Minisystems, Elementary School Mathematics (Levels B, C, D, E, F, G)	D. C. Heath & Co.	P, I (JH)
Systemathix (Studybooks A, B, C, D, E)	W. H. Sadlier	P, I, JH
Individualized Mathematics: Drill and Practice Kits	Random House	I, JH (SH)
Experiencing Mathematics (A–E)	Random House	I, JH (SH)
Say-It Addition	Garrard Publishing Co.	P, I
Say-It Subtraction	Garrard Publishing Co.	P, I
Say-It Multiplication	Garrard Publishing Co.	P, I (JH)
Say-It Division	Garrard Publishing Co.	P, I (JH)

ACADEMIC

ARITHMETIC

Computation (continued)

MATERIAL	COMPANY	GRADE LEVEL
Make One	Garrard Publishing Co.	I (JH)
Math Practice Slates, Sets 1, 2, 3, 4, 5, 6	Aero Educational Products	P, I (JH)
MASTER (Multi-Level Arithmetic Skills Training Education Resource)	Individualized Teaching Material	I, JH
Math Mastery, Introduction to Fraction Concepts, Fractional Number Computation, Adding and Subtracting Whole Numbers, Multiplying and Dividing Whole Numbers	Electronic Learning	P, I, JH
Self-Instructional Number Wheels: Addition-Subtraction, Multiplication-Division	Milton Bradley Co.	P, I

ACADEMIC

ARITHMETIC

Computation (continued)

MATERIAL	COMPANY	GRADE LEVEL
Mathfacts Games, Addition and Subtraction (Levels 1, 2, 3, 4, 5)	Milton Bradley Co.	P, I
Quizmo (Educational Lotto), Add–Subtract	Milton Bradley Co.	P, I
Quizmo (Educational Lotto), Multiply–Divide	Milton Bradley Co.	P, I
Desk Tapes (Number Lines)	Instructo	P
Computapes	Science Research Associates	I, JH (SH)
Chip Trading Math Lab Kit	Scott Scientific	P, I
Moving Up In Numbers	Developmental Learning Materials	P, I
AOT Math Cards, Addition, Subtraction, Multiplication, Division	Developmental Learning Materials	P, I

ACADEMIC

ARITHMETIC

Computation (continued)

MATERIAL	COMPANY	GRADE LEVEL
Fitzhugh PLUS Programs, Number Concepts (Books 203, 204, 206)	Allied Education Council	P, I (JH)
Noonan-Spradley Computational Skills Program	Allied Education Council	P, I (JH)
The Sullivan Mathematics Laboratory	Behavioral Research Laboratories	P, I
Arithmetic Drill	Teaching Technology Corp.	P, I (JH)
Fifth Unifix Kit	Educational Teaching Aids Division	P, I
Beginner's Math Lab Sets 3 and 4	Educational Teaching Aids Division	P, I
Veri-Tech	Educational Teaching Aids Division	P, I
Classroom Learning Labs	Educational Teaching Aids Division	P, I
Pacemaker Arithmetic Program	Fearon Publishers, Lear Siegler	P

ACADEMIC

ARITHMETIC

Measurement

MATERIAL	COMPANY	GRADE LEVEL
Two-Faced Clock Dial	Ideal	PS, P
Time Teacher	Developmental Learning Materials	PS, P
Clock Stamp	Developmental Learning Materials	PS, P, I
Plastic Clock	Developmental Learning Materials	PS, P
Coin Stamps	Developmental Learning Materials	P, I
Educational Toy Money	Milton Bradley Co.	P (I)
Linear Measures	Developmental Learning Materials	P, I
Demonstration Rulers	Ideal	P, I
Liquid Measure	Ideal	P, I
Dry Measure	Ideal	P, I
Comparison Balance	Developmental Learning Materials	P, I
Playstore Scale	Ideal	P, I
Measurement Chart	Ideal	P, I

ACADEMIC

ARITHMETIC

Measurement (continued)

MATERIAL	COMPANY	GRADE LEVEL
It's About Time	Edmark Associates	P, I
Time Wise	HED, Inc.	P, I
Math Explora Tapes (Group 2)	International Teaching Tapes	I (JH)
Time Duplicating Masters, Levels I, II, III	Mafex Associates	P, I
United States Money (Liquid Duplicators), Levels I, II, III	Mafex Associates	P, I
Measurement (Liquid Duplicators), Levels I, II, III	Mafex Associates	P, I
Pay the Cashier Game	Mafex Associates	P, I
Change Maker	Mafex Associates	P, I
Measure-Up	Fearon Publishers, Lear Siegler	P, I
Money Makes Sense	Fearon Publishers, Lear Siegler	P, I
Using Dollars and Sense	Fearon Publishers, Lear Siegler	P, I

High Interest-Low Difficulty Reading Materials
(RL - Reading Level, IL - Interest Level)

Field Educational Publications

> *The Checkered Flag Series*
> RL: 2.4 to 4.5   IL: JH, SH
> *Checkered Flag Classroom Audio-Visual Kits*
> *The Morgan Bay Mysteries*
> RL: 2.0 to 4.5   IL: K, JH (SH)
> *The Wildlife Adventure Series*
> RL: 2.5 to 4.5   IL: I, JH
> *The Deep-Sea Adventure Series*
> RL: 1.5 to 5.0   IL: I, JH (SH)
> *Happenings*
> RL: 4.0 to 5.0   IL: JH, SH

D. C. Heath & Co.

> *Teen-Age Tales*
> RL: 3.0 to 6.0   IL: JH, SH
> *Heath Urban Reading Program*
> RL: 4.0 to 7.5   IL: JH (SH)

Mafex Associates

Inner Ring Books for Reluctant Readers
RL: NA   IL: JH, SH
A Developmental Approach Teaching Aid for Retarded Readers
RL: 2.0 to 7.5   IL: I, JH (SH)

Benefic Press

Space Science Fiction Series
RL: 2.0 to 6.0   IL: I, JH
Racing Wheels Series
RL: 2.0 to 4.0   IL: I, JH
Target Today Series
RL: 2.0 to 6.0   IL: I, JH
World of Adventure Series
RL: 2.0 to 6.0   IL: I, JH
Sports Mystery Series
RL: 2.0 to 4.0   IL: I, JH
Mystery Adventure Series
RL: 2.0 to 6.0   IL: I, JH

Garrard Publishing Company

    Sports Series
        RL: 4.0   IL: I, JH
    Americans All
        RL: 4.0   IL: I, JH

Noble and Noble, Publishers

    Springboards—Motivational Reading Kit
        RL: 4.0 to 6.5   IL: JH, SH
    Falcon Books
        RL: 4.0 to 8.0   IL: JH, SH

Webster/McGraw-Hill

    The Everyreader Series
        RL: not above 4.0   IL: I, JH, SH
    Reading Incentive Series
        RL: 3.0 to 7.5   IL: JH, SH
    Reading Shelf I and II
        RL: 4.0 to 6.5   IL: JH, SH
    City Limits I and II
        RL: 5.0 to 7.5   IL: JH, SH

Allyn and Bacon

    Breakthrough
        RL: 2.0 to 6.5   IL: JH, SH

Fearon Publishers, Lear Siegler

    Adventures in Space
        RL: NA   IL: I, JH (SH)
    Pacemaker Classics
        RL: 2.0 to 2.5   IL: JH, SH (I)
    Pacemaker Story Books
        RL: 2.0 to 2.5   IL: I, JH
    Pacemaker True Adventures
        RL: 2.0 to 2.5   IL: I, JH
    Adventures in Urban Reading
        RL: NA   IL: JH, SH

Teaching Machines
Descriptions of Operation and Accompanying Programs

Key
Name and Company: Commercial name of equipment/programs and publisher/distributor.
Grade Levels: Age group which can use the material.
Cost: Most recent price of the equipment/programs.
Description: How the equipment operates and the programs available for use with the machine.

AUDIO-VISUAL EQUIPMENT, TEACHING MACHINES, AND ACCOMPANYING PROGRAMS

NAME & COMPANY	GRADE LEVELS	COST	DESCRIPTION
Reading Technology MIND	K–12 and through adult remedial	MACHINERY: $345–600 and up PROGRAMS: $350–2,950 per program	MACHINERY: A coordinated audio-visual cassett player/projector. Cassettes have response pauses built-in. Restart button is on player/projector. Headsets available. Reading program set includes consonants, vowels, blends and di-

NAME & COMPANY	GRADE LEVELS	COST	DESCRIPTION
		$5,800 Reading Set	graphs, substitution, diagnoses, syllable division.
Tutorgram Enrichment Reading Corporation of America	Preschool–3	MACHINERY: $29.50 PROGRAMS: $8.50 ea. Blank Cards $6.50/54	MACHINERY: Easel upon which program cards are placed. Child responds to each card by using an electric pointer. If the answer is correct, a buzzer and light are activated. PROGRAMS: Language Arts Readiness (2); Alphabet Recognition and Sequencing; Basic Word Recognition; Common Terms; Basic Mathematics; Consonant Sounds; Primary Science; Vowels; Primary Social Studies; Coin Recognition; Equivalent Coins; Rhyming Elements; Mathematics; Science.

NAME & COMPANY	GRADE LEVELS	COST	DESCRIPTION
Project LIFE/PAL General Electric/ Project LIFE Program	Preschool–4	MACHINERY: $399 PROGRAMS: $30–54 per set; $180–612 per series	MACHINERY: Film strip viewer with automatic advance keyed to multiple-choice response panel. PROGRAM SERIES: Perceptual Training (4 sets); Thinking Activities (12 sets); Programmed Language/Reading (4 levels, 8 sets each, first 3 levels, 4 sets highest level); Supplementary (3 sets).
Hoffman Programs Hoffman Information Systems	K–6		MACHINERY: Film strip viewer and synchronized record player. PROGRAMS: Various, including Mathematics, Reading, Primary Language, and Phonics Survey Tests.
Flex-Ed Flex-Ed Systems	K–3	MACHINERY: $40	MACHINERY: "Easel" upon which worksheets are placed. Child presses

NAME & COMPANY	GRADE LEVELS	COST	DESCRIPTION
		PROGRAMS: $27–60 ea. $225 for entire math or reading set	answer. Correct response activates light and beeper. PROGRAMS: Mathematics (Readiness, plus one set each for grades 1, 2, and 3); Reading (Readiness, Alphabet, plus one set each for grades 1, 2, and 3).
Systems 80 Borg-Warner Co.	Preschool–Adult	MACHINERY: $4.95 or $30/yr. rental to qualified institutions PROGRAMS: $112.50–$162.50 per kit	MACHINERY: Filmstrip viewer and synchronized record player. Automatic advance keyed to multiple-choice response. PROGRAMS: Mathematics (13 kits); Language Concepts (3 kits); Letter Names and Sounds (14 kits); Spelling (7 kits); Improving Reading Skills (6 kits); French and Spanish (4 kits each).
Phono-Viewer 1000	Preschool–3	MACHINERY:	MACHINERY: Synchronized filmstrip

NAME & COMPANY	GRADE LEVELS	COST	DESCRIPTION
General Learning Co.		$59.95 Headphones: $9.95 PROGRAMS: $20/set of 5 or $2.50 ea.	viewer and record player. PROGRAMS: Music Series (4 sets); Stories/Plays/Seasons (7 sets); Art Media (2 sets); Mathematics (4 sets); Language Arts (4 sets); Bible Programs (50 programs).
Audio Flashcard Electronic Futures	Preschool–6 and adaptable	MACHINERY: $200 and up PROGRAMS: $41–676.50 Individual Sets: $25.50–112.75 Blank Cards: $18/150 and $15.50/100	MACHINERY: Tape recorder/playback which "reads" and records on cards approximately 4 in. × 12 in., allowing for recording of student's verbal response. PROGRAMS: Various, including Mathematics (5 programs); Reading Readiness; Phonics (2 programs); Foreign Languages (3 programs); Object Recognition; English.

NAME & COMPANY	GRADE LEVELS	COST	DESCRIPTION
Language Master Bell & Howell	Preschool–adult and adaptable	MACHINERY: $12.95 and up plus accessories PROGRAMS & CARD SETS: $17.95–219.00 Blank Cards: $6.00/100; oversized available	MACHINERY: Tape recorder/playback which "reads" and records on cards approximately 4 in. × 9 in., allowing for recording of verbal student response. PROGRAMS: Various, including Reading (5 programs); English; Speech Therapy; Mathematics; Science; Foreign Languages (5 programs).
Spellbinder Spellbinder	Preschool–3	MACHINERY: $55 PROGRAMS: $55/ea.	MACHINERY: Lower easel upon which problem cards are placed. Correct response card placed in upper easel activates light. PROGRAMS: 4 levels, 8 series, including Reading, Spelling, Mathematics.

NAME & COMPANY	GRADE LEVELS	COST	DESCRIPTION
MAST Programmed Instructor MAST Development Co.	Primary–12 and Adult	MACHINERY: $164.50-$270 and up PROGRAMS: $22-$144	MACHINERY: Filmstrip cartridge viewer with space for student write-in response. Correct answer given after each student response. PROGRAMS: English (11 programs); Mathematics (4 levels, 30 programs total); Science (2 levels, 8 programs total).
Talking Page Prentice-Hall Learning Systems	K–4 and High School	MACHINERY: $289 PROGRAMS: $150/module	MACHINERY: Easel for workpage and synchronized record player. PROGRAMS (Each program may contain several modules): Pre-Reading; Elementary Reading; Mathematics; Career Education.

NAME & COMPANY	GRADE LEVELS	COST	DESCRIPTION
Multiputer Centurion International Industries	1–6	MACHINERY: $249.50	MACHINERY: Desk calculator programmed to present students with addition, subtraction, multiplication, and division problems. Correct response activates "happy face." Incorrect activates "sad face." Records total number of correct responses. Adaptable to restrict problem types.

Distributors and Addresses

Acadia Press, Inc., P.O. Box 1086, Dept. 4, 438 Alder Street, Scranton, Pa., 18501.

Aero Educational Products, St. Charles, Ill., 60174.

Allied Education Council, P.O. Box 78, Galien, Mich., 49113.

Allyn and Bacon, Inc., Rockleigh, N.J., 07647.

American Guidance Service, Publisher's Building, Circle Pines, Minn., 55014.

Ann Arbor Publishers, P.O. Box 388, Worthington, Ohio, 43085.

Appleton-Century-Crofts, Educational Division, Meredith Corporation, 440 Park Avenue South, New York, N.Y., 10016.

Barnell Loft, Ltd., 958 Church Street, Baldwin, N.Y., 11510.

Behavioral Research Laboratories, P.O. Box 577, Palo Alto, Calif., 94302.

Bell and Howell Company, Audio-Visual Products Division, 7100 McCormick Road, Chicago, Ill., 60645.

Benefic Press, 10300 West Roosevelt Road, Westchester, Ill., 60153.

Borg-Warner Company, Borg-Warner Educational Systems, 600 West University Drive, Arlington Heights, Ill., 60004.

Bremner-Davis Phonics, 161 Green Bay Road, Wilmette, Ill., 60091.

Centurion International Industries, Audio-Visual Marketing Company, 2549 Middlefield Road, Redwood City, Calif., 94063.

Childcraft Education Corporation, 964 Third Street, New York, N.Y., 10022.

Continental Press, Elizabethtown, Pa., 17022.

Developmental Learning Materials, 7440 Natchez Avenue, Niles, Ill., 60648.

Dexter and Westbrook, Ltd., 958 Church Street, Baldwin, N.Y., 11510.

Economy Company (The), Drawer A, 5811 West Minnesota, Indianapolis, Ind., 46241.

Edmark Associates, 655 South Orcas Street, Seattle, Wash., 98108.

Educational Innovations, Inc., 416 West Pascagoula, P.O. Box 3171, Jackson, Miss., 39207.

Educational Programmers, Inc., P.O. Box 332, Roseburg, Ore., 97470.

Educational Teaching Aids Division, A. Daigger and Company, 159 West Kinzie Street, Chicago, Ill., 60610.

Educators Publishing Service, 75 Moulton Street, Cambridge, Mass., 02138

Electronic Futures, 202 Lake Miriam Drive, Lakeland, Fla., 33803.

Electronic Learning, Inc., Glen Cove, N.Y., 11542.

Enrichment Reading Corporation of America, Iron Ridge, Wis., 53035.

Fearon Publishers, Lear Siegler, Inc., Education Division, 6 Davis Drive, Belmont, Calif., 94002.

Field Educational Publications, Inc., 3430 Sunset Avenue, Ocean City, N.J., 07712

Flex-Ed Systems, Inc., P.O. Box 8306, Jackson, Miss., 39204.

Follett Publishing Company, 1010 West Washington Boulevard, Chicago, Ill., 60607.

Garrard Publishing Company, Champaign, Ill., 61820.

General Electric/Project LIFE Program, Instructional Industries, Executive Park, Ballston, N.Y., 12019.

General Learning Company, Morristown, N.J., 07960.

Harcourt-Brace-Jovanovich, Inc., 757 Third Avenue, New York, N.Y., 10017.

D. C. Heath and Company, 125 Spring Street, Lexington, Mass., 02173.

HED, Inc., P.O. Box 1, Fort Collins, Colo., 80521.

Hoffman Information Systems, 5623 Peck Road, Arcadia, Calif., 91006.

Houghton-Mifflin, Hopewell-Pennington Road, Hopewell, N.J., 08525.

Ideal School Supply Company, 11000 South Lavergne Avenue, Oak Lawn, Ill., 60453.

Imperial International Learning Corporation, Box 548, Kankakee, Ill., 60901.

Individualized Teaching Material, Box 6741, St. Petersburg Beach, Fla., 33736.

Instructo Corporation, Paoli, Pa., 19301.

International Teaching Tapes, Inc., Educational Development Corporation Building, P.O. Drawer 865, Lakeland, Fla., 33803.

Interstate Printers and Publishers, Inc., 19–27 North Jackson Street, Danville, Ill., 61832.

JSE Press, 3515 Woodhaven Road, Philadelphia, Pa., 19154.

Kenworthy Educational Service, Inc., P.O. Box 3031, Buffalo, N.Y., 14205.

Learning Research Associates, 1501 Broadway, New York, N.Y., 10036.

Lyons and Carnahan, 407 East 25th Street, Chicago, Ill., 60616.

Macmillan Company, School Service Department, Riverside, N.J., 08075.

Mafex Associates, Inc., 111 Barron Avenue, Johnstown, Pa., 15906.

MAST Development Company, Educational Systems Division, 2212 East Twelfth Street, Davenport, Iowa, 52803.

Charles E. Merrill Publishing Company, 1300 Alum Creek Drive, Columbus, Ohio, 43216.

Milton Bradley Company, Springfield, Mass., 01101.

MIND, 1133 Avenue of the Americas, New York, N.Y., 10036.

Noble and Noble, Publishers, Inc., 750 Third Avenue, New York, N.Y., 10017.

Open Court Publishing Company, Box 599, LaSalle, Ill., 61301.

Prentice-Hall Learning Systems, c/o Instructional Electronic Systems, 321 Century Plaza, Lansdale, Pa., 19446.

J. A. Preston Corporation, 71 Fifth Avenue, New York, N.Y., 10003.

Random House, School Division, 201 East 50th Street, New York, N.Y., 10022.

Reader's Digest Services, Educational Division, Pleasantville, N.Y., 10570.

W. H. Sadlier, Inc., 11 Park Place, New York, N.Y., 10007.

Science Research Associates, 259 East Erie Street, Chicago, Ill., 60611.

Scott, Foresman and Company, 2000 East Lake Avenue, Glenview, Ill., 60025.

Scott Scientific, Inc., Box 2121, Fort Collins, Colo., 80521.

Special Education Materials, Inc., 484 South Broadway, Yonkers, N.Y., 10705.

Spellbinder, Inc., 33 Bradford Street, Concord, Mass., 01742.

Spin-A-Test Company, P.O. Box 823, Pleasanton, Calif., 94566.

Tapes Unlimited, 13001 Puritan Avenue, Detroit, Mich., 48227.

Teachers Publishing Corporation, Macmillan Company, School Division, Department SNY, Riverside, N.J., 08075.

Teaching Resources Corporation, 100 Bolyston Street, Boston, Mass., 02116.

Teaching Technology Corporation, P.O. Box 3278, 7471 Greenbush Avenue, North Hollywood, Calif., 91609.

Walker Educational Book Corporation, 720 Fifth Avenue, New York, N.Y., 10019.

Webster/McGraw-Hill, 1221 Avenue of the Americas, New York, N.Y., 10020.

7   Secondary Programming
Sidney R. Miller

Introduction

UNLIKE the already much-discussed elementary level student, the learning-disabled adolescent has been until recently ignored and miseducated. There are several reasons for the benign neglect of the youth aged 12 through 20. This neglect has occurred because the secondary level youth is more complex and thus a more difficult individual to teach. Such a young person, if he has reached junior or senior high with educational handicaps, has been experiencing school failure for several years. These problems have been compounded by the physiological, biological, and cognitive development of the adolescent. As has been noted by numerous researchers (Erikson, 1968; Bruner, 1966; Ausubel, 1957; and Piaget, 1969), the adolescent is experiencing significant and cognitive changes beginning around 11 years of age. These changes continue until the adolescent is approximately 17.

Belatedly, secondary programs for the learning-disabled adolescent have been receiving attention (Brolin and Thomas, 1971; Glueck, 1953; and Younie and Clark, 1969) since the court decisions of the early 1970s (Mills vs. the Board of Education, 1972; Diana vs. State Board of Education, 1970), resulting in special education legislation in such states as Maine, California, and Illinois. These court decisions and legislative acts have resulted in broadened public school responsibilities toward the exceptional student between 3 and 21 years of age.

As of 1972, only one-fourth to one-third of all special programs in the United States were directed to the adolescent student (Martin, 1972). It was further observed that only around 20 percent of handicapped children leaving schools in the next four years would be fully employed and seek higher education. Of the remaining students, 40 percent would be underemployed, and 26 percent would be unemployed. Martin recommended the development of programs in which job skills rather than the conventional curriculum would be taught. Yet a survey of special educators indicated that few individuals working with adolescents believed they possessed the competencies to instruct the student in anything but the conventional mathematics and language skills (Brolin, 1973).

Characteristics of the Learning-Disabled Adolescent

In studying adolescent youth with learning problems, Walters and Krenzler (1970) noted that school dropouts tended to exhibit two to eight factors associated with poor school performance. The eight factors are: age, intelligence, grade, reading and arithmetic achievement, socioeconomic level, absenteeism, school participation, and grade point average. The research has emphasized that problems in any one of the above factors was not an accurate indicator of a potential dropout. In comparing the variables, Walters and Krenzler found arithmetic scores, age, intelligence, and father's occupation were good predictive combinations for a dropout. The investigators noted that students with poor arithmetic scores, who were older than their grade-level peers and whose fathers were on the lower-level occupation scale, were more likely to leave school early. McCandless (1970) reports that 14 percent of all dropouts were at or above the 64th percentile in intelligence test scores. In other words, they were in the top 36 percent of the national population intellectually. This finding agrees with others (Quay, 1965; Roman, 1957; and Glueck and Glueck, 1950), who note that around 75 percent of dropouts and delinquents have reading disabilities and are not necessarily intellectually retarded.

Following this up, Sabatino (1974) indicated that many of the neglected adolescents in our schools with average or above average intelligence should be considered learning disabled. For secondary schools to adopt this definition and move in the direction of developing resource room programs for the adolescent would mark a significant break with the past, though it would be compatible with contemporary educational findings and trends. Until now public educators have dealt with the troubled adolescent as either retarded, lazy, or turned-off, and have placed him into "maintenance" classrooms or vocational programs, where the primary thrust kept him out of the popular mainstream of intellectual, academic, social, and career development. As a result, many of the secondary school learning-disabled students now either have an aversion to evaluation or lack the skills and information to deal with testing situations (Clarke and Waters, 1972). Wade and Shertzer (1970) found that counseling such students reduced their level of anxiety. The investigators concluded that lack of personal direction generated the anxiety; when counseling was provided, enabling students to formulate career goals, the anxiety level was diminished, and performance increased in testing situations and in the classroom.

The fact that a significant portion of secondary school dropouts, delinquents, and low achievers have normal or above normal intelligence and are often retarded readers gives credence to Sabatino's plea (1974) that such youth be treated as severe learning-disabled youth. As of now, the primary diagnostic instruments are generally inadequate and inappropriate. Sabatino advocated that diagnostic instruments be more educationally relevant to the adolescent and less directed at the problem. He emphasized that the student is educationally, not emotionally, impaired. Any emotional overlay arises from the crisis of school failure and significant social, physical, and intellectual change.

Management Procedures

The lack of clear definitions and well-enunciated programs and instructional strategies has resulted in efforts at delineating behavioral data so that the educator can gain insights when interacting with the learning-disabled adolescent. In working with the secondary student the most common approaches have been either counseling or behavior modification, both of which have some demonstrated short-term effects but little long term value.

Jersild (1957), in defining parameters affecting deviant adolescent behavior, contended that a majority of adolescent behavior disorders are merely exaggerated manifestations of emotional instability. Since then Erikson (1968), Mussen, Conger, and Kagan (1969), and Piaget (1969) have all noted that adolescence is an inherent crisis period in each individual's development. It is a period in which an individual is beginning to experiment with such abstract notions as democracy, freedom, identity, and equality. This phenomenon, combined with the learning-disabled adolescent's inability to compete academically, results in the exclusion from interaction by "avant-garde" social groups; and the tendency of school personnel to counsel the student into programs that the community and peers consider to be at the lower end of the preparatory scale only accentuates the crisis between childhood and adulthood (Reagor, 1973). In looking at alternative approaches, Anadam and Williams (1971) found in working with eighth grade students that teacher-student consultative models of classroom management were more effective than the more traditional teacher-curriculum model. Wagner (1972) concluded that many disaffected secondary students feel alienated, believing the curriculum to be irrelevant since it fails to appeal to their individual interests and needs.

Behavioral Strategies

The literature points to the consultative model as the most popular and effective with adolescent youths with learning handicaps. The need to establish a personal identity and the requirement of society that an individual between 13 and 18 begin to establish career goals result in a need for the adolescent to participate in professional-life decisions. Thus, both personal and societal demands require that the student become an integral part of the educational goals and objectives.

Sabatino contends that the traditional psychiatric-psychological therapeutic model has failed to meet the needs of such youth (1974). Further, he contends that there is evidence that such corrective techniques may be harmful in an adolescent's emotional and educational maturation. It is for this reason that the literature and efforts in behavioral strategies have been expanding. Several studies have been conducted with adolescents (Atthowe and Krasner, 1965; Steffy, 1966; Slack and Schwitzgebel, 1960; and Meichenbaum, Bowers, and Ross, 1968). Many of these programs have resulted in behavioral changes. Slack and Schwitzgebel (1960), using food and money, were able to reduce the chronic disruptive behavior of ghetto area boys. Cohen et al. (1966) has demonstrated the effectiveness of food and money in positively altering behavior among adolescents in academic environments. Two studies (Smith and Riebock, 1971; and Pendrak, 1974) demonstrated the effectiveness of performance-contracting with adolescent students in reading. Both studies reported that overt behavior and reading performance improved through the use of contracting. Wagner (1972), noting that the disadvantaged often feel disenfranchised by the educational setting, recommends behavioral changes in the schools. Among these modifications were making the curriculum relevant, teaching to the student's strengths, having teacher-parent conferences near the student's home, and providing the student with close and continual behavioral and educational monitoring.

Academic Instruction

Further studies have been completed on the relationship between reading and adolescent problems. Alsop (1973) and Staats and Butterfield (1965) discussed programming for reading disabilities in youths. Staats and Butterfield (1965) showed the validity of diminishing reinforcement techniques in the teaching of reading to a 14-year-old delinquent male with a second-grade reading level. The subject was able to increase his reading level 2.8 grades. His behavior in school also improved. Earlier, Dorney (1967) demonstrated the modification of attitudes of adolescents through the use of reading instruction, and Raygor's (1970) study suggests that results on the Cooperative English Test enhance the prediction of potentially troubled adolescents. Fendrick and Bond (1936) discussed adolescence and reading as did other early studies (Kvaraceus, 1964; Glueck and Glueck, 1934, 1950, 1953). The Illinois Curriculum Program *Counteracting School Dropouts* (1967) shows that a number of Illinois schools use special education programs geared to diminishing the soaring dropout rates. Developmental and/or remedial reading courses, vocational classes, and work-study programs were among those receiving the highest ratings as far as effectiveness and actual use.

The U.S. Department of Health, Education, and Welfare (1973) publication "Positive Approaches to Dropout Prevention" discusses many projects around the country using various means to decrease dropouts. Among them are the use of expanded career education programs, teacher awareness/training programs, and changes in counseling services. A Counseling Learning Center was established in St. Louis (Project Stay), whose purpose was to work with pupils referred as potential dropouts and provide technical *preventive* assistance to teachers in the regular classroom. Other programs relating delinquency to specific learning disabilities are Clossen (1971), Dimitz (1957), Frease (1972), Graubard (1967), Kelgard (1968), Schlichter and Ratcliff (1971), and Walle (1972). The efficacy of these programs has not as yet been determined.

Educational Schema

The effectiveness of any educational program can often be best measured by the consistency of personnel and the clarity of its procedures (Harris and Sipay, 1971). The program that possesses clearly defined procedures for screening, diagnosis, placement, management/instruction, and evaluation will be able to reach more students in a limited period of time and provide them with the essential assistance. It is paramount, once a student is referred to the special education diagnostician, that there be a prescribed diagnostic-assessment

Figure 15

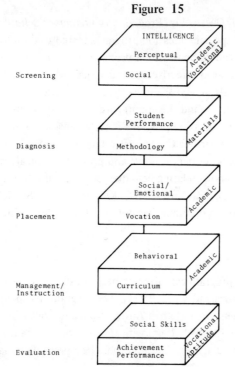

battery which evaluates intellectual functioning, aptitude levels, and performance competency. This information will enable the diagnostician to prepare a proper instructional program. But the assessment of academic skills should be only one component of the screening process. When developing adolescent programs, the career needs of the student must also be considered and surveyed.

Some school systems and institutions are still using educational diagnostic instruments whose ceilings are too low for use with adolescents. The Illinois Test of Psycholinguistic Abilities (ITPA) ceilings are: auditory reception—10 years, 2 months; visual reception—10 years, 10 months; auditory association—10 years, 11 months; visual association—10 years, 3 months; verbal expression—10 years, 11 months; manual expression—10 years, 4 months; grammatical closure—10 years, 4 months; visual closure—10 years, 6 months; auditory sequential memory—10 years, 3 months; visual sequential memory—10 years, 5 months; auditory closure—10 years; and sound blending—8 years, 7 months. The Frostig Test of Visual Perception ceilings are: eye-motor coordination—10 years; figure-ground discrimination—8 years, 3 months; form constancy—9 years; position in space—8 years, 9 months; and spatial relations—8 years, 6 months. Group achievement instruments such as the Wide Range Achievement Test (WRAT) or, used as a group test, the California Achievement Test, the Stanford Achievement Test, and the Metropolitan Achievement Test can be used to assess specific educational components, but they should not be used in isolation to establish intelligence, aptitude, and performance ability in designated materials. Each of these instruments falls short individually. The ITPA, Frostig, and Wepman tests have norms that are inadequate and inappropriate. The four achievement tests are wholly and substantially paper and pencil tests. In addition, psychologists and diagnostic teachers often fail to conduct item analysis of the test results, which would reap greater instructional information than would cumulative grade-equivalent scores. To assess effectively the learning competencies, styles, and knowledge of the adolescent, educators must employ instruments that not only establish operational levels of the student but also illuminate levels of academic and intellectual strengths and weakness (preference). The current evaluation battery is almost totally dependent on the paper and pencil (visual motor) competencies and fails to evaluate the auditory modality.

The recommended procedure for more accurate and informative test protocol would be to assess first the achievement performance of students using instruments that measure both oral and written performance. In addition, a test must be used that assesses modality of learning, basic aptitudes, intelligence, and competence in specific instructional materials.

Figure 16 illustrates the competencies and the instruments recommended for a thorough screening of adolescents. The battery not only would enable the diagnostician to determine achievement level in two separate modalities of learning, it would enable one to establish career goals and competencies, which are essential components and concerns of the adolescent.

Diagnostic Data

Once the process is completed, the diagnostician must seek to establish the student's academic, social, and vocational preferences. Learning-disabled adolescents, like younger children, have strengths and weaknesses. Some can read aloud and orally discuss the story and its characters much more effectively than if they were asked to read silently and then write responses to formal questions. Others are unable to read aloud and would prefer the silent reading, written response approach. With others some combination of the two must be

Figure 16

ACHIEVEMENT

	Reading	Mathematics	Language
Visual	word attack (Metropolitan)	reasoning (Key math)	spelling (Wide Range Ach. Test)
Oral	word attack (Spache)	reasoning (Key math)	
Visual	comprehension (Metropolitan)		composition an(teacher prepared and grade exercise)
Oral	comprehension (Spache)		

INFORMATION PROCESSING DATA

Perceptual - motor	Manipulative
Beery-Butenica NGATB	Minnesota-Rate of Manipulation Test

DIFFERENTIATED INTELLIGENCE TEST

Wechsler Intelligence Scale for Children
or, Wechsler Intelligence Adult Scale

VOCATIONAL ASSESSMENT

NGATB Teacher Interview

employed. The diagnostic process must also consider the potential instructional methodology and the materials appropriate to the student's strengths and preferences and compatible with the suggested methodology. Teachers should not feel tied to the initial diagnostic findings. Interaction with the student often provides added information that will contribute to more accurate diagnostic-assessment findings. Teachers should be continually evaluating the student's strengths/weaknesses, and the methods and materials selected.

Specifically, the diagnostician must clearly profile the six behavioral characteristics.

1. What learning strengths and weaknesses does the learning-disabled adolescent possess?
2. What are the student's personal and instructional preferences?
3. Where do the gaps exist in each individual diagnostic-assessment profile?
4. What are the behavior characteristics of each student that inhibit learning?
5. What model of teacher could most effectively interact with each of the students?
6. What are the student's personal goals—academically, vocationally, and socially?

Placement Alternatives

Once the diagnostic-assessment process has been completed, the diagnostician should, in concert with the school counselor, make an appropriate placement. This is a difficult process, and many factors must be considered. Not only must the student's academic needs be considered, but also his social/emotional and vocational needs must be determined. There are at least eight possible alternative placements the teacher and counselor could make for each student. They are:

a.   remaining in a regular classroom and receiving special assistance from an itinerant special education instructor;

b.   remaining in a regular classroom and receiving special assistance from an itinerant teacher and then going to a vocational site;

c.   moving to another room with a teacher who could more effectively relate to the student;

d.   remaining in the regular classroom and receiving peer tutoring;

e.   remaining in the regular classroom, receiving peer tutoring, and attending, part-time, a vocational center;

f.   leaving the room for short periods each day and receiving resource room teacher assistance;

g.   moving to a self-contained classroom to receive assistance in those academic areas which are low, and then participating in regular classes where he can succeed;

h.   remaining full-time in a self-contained special education room;

i.   spending a portion of time each day in a self-contained classroom, the remaining time to be spent at a job site;

j.   attending a career education site that not only provides instruction in reading, mathematics, and language, but also prepares the individual in a specific vocational area.

The above alternatives should not be considered in the light of "good" and "bad." Rather each alternative must be evaluated on the basis of which is most appropriate to the individual student's needs. If the concept of individualized instruction is going to move from the rhetorical to the performance arena, the schools and the diagnostic teachers must initiate the concept of differential placement. The literature well illustrates the fact that there is no one best strategy to assist the adolescent experiencing educational, personal, and social deviance.

Instructional Approach

Once the diagnosis and placement are completed, the diagnostician must determine the instructional approach to be used. There are three basic strategies that can be employed. The placement decision must be made only after all the potential possibilities have been considered and the most relevant solution determined. This decision must be ratified by the student and his parents.

The management/instructional decisions must rely on the diagnostic findings and the placement decisions. A compatible behavioral management/instructional decision will facilitate appropriate, relevant learning.

The teacher can choose among three instructional strategies:

1. the fixed curriculum with predesignated materials and teacher established goals;

2. a curriculum with specified and alternative goals that allows the student to select a portion of the curriculum goals and objectives, instructional materials, and contingencies. This approach involves a trade-off between the school's need to educate and the student's need for relevant information and materials.

3. an open curriculum in which the adolescent is free to state all the goals and all the materials.

The second choice is the most realistic for the learning-disabled adolescent, who research demonstrates is highly anxious, is uncertain of his future, and has experienced long periods of failure (Wade and Shertzer, 1970). Such individuals are likely to be turned off to school and learning and to approach new school experiences with doubt and anxiety. Such students also need to be personally involved. The student should believe he has a stake in the outcome (Ariel, 1972). Thus, blending the fixed curriculum with the open curriculum can result in a rich program, one which not only provides the student with the essential skills and information but also is highly motivating. Here too, the final decision must be made only after consultation with the adolescent student.

The student has already been subjected to traditional programming, in which the teacher establishes the direction and possesses all the answers and the student has no alternatives. This approach has failed, as evidenced by the student's referral to the learning disability diagnostician along with other students who are considered dropouts, truants, delinquents, or reading retardates.

Materials Selection

Once the instructional strategies have been determined, the materials can be selected. Here too, there are a wide variety of tactics and materials which can be used. They include:

1. *High Interest-Low Vocabulary Readers.* This type of educational approach

capitalizes on the student's personal and social interests. It requires the classroom to have a variety of reading programs that cover a breadth of topics.

2.   *Student's Own Language Program.* This program involves the instructor eliciting from the student the types of vocabulary he or she would like to learn. These vocabulary words are then used in sentences that the student reads. The use of this approach should be specifically geared to getting the student eventually into the reading of standard high-interest reading material.

3.   *Linguistic Reading Approach.* This approach is a highly structured sight-sound system of reading, in which the student is taught visual and auditory patterns that are invariant.

4.   *Language Experience.* This programmed system uses provocative materials already devised by a publisher and/or the instructor to stimulate discussion, followed by reading and writing skill development.

5.   *Mathematics.* Besides the conventional teaching of computations, quantity, distance, and value, mathematics can be used to teach abstract concepts which are integral to reading, language, and math processes.

Among the reading programs that could be used with the adolescent are:

1.   *Student's Own Language Program*
     Based on Sylvia Ashton-Warner's "Teacher"

2.   *High Interest Look-Say Programs*
     Dan Frontier Series
     Fearon's "Pacemaker Series"

Behavioral Laboratories "Readers"
D. C. Heath & Co. "Teen-Age Tales"
LMI Literature Samplers
Globe Publishing Stories for Teenagers
Field Editor's Checker Flag Series
3. *Linguistic Reading Approach*
SRA Reading Laboratory
Stanchfield Reading Series
Merrill Linguistics Reader
4. *Language Experience Programs*
Encyclopaedia Britannica Language Experience Program
5. *Mathematics*
Greater Cleveland Math Program (great emphasis on concept formation)
McGraw-Hill's Webster Mathematics Series (considerable overlearning prescribed)
6. *Skill Builders*
The Reader's Digest Skill Builders
The New Practice Readers
Basic Reading Skills for High School

The above reading programs should not be considered panaceas. They are relevant instructional materials when applied appropriately; they can assist the student to achieve the essential learning skills and information while appealing to his social developmental needs.

Environmental Structure

Whether the diagnosis and instruction take place in a class or a resource room the teacher must design an environmental structure that appeals to the needs of all the personalities using the facility. This means that materials, study areas, resources, discussion centers, and instructional centers must be assessed in the room design. In addition, sound, light, and space are factors that ultimately must be considered if the ecological design is going to work. The following is a design of a recommended ecological setting.

The intent of the room design is to facilitate structured teacher-student interpretation and also to provide areas for independent study. The horseshoe-shaped table will enable the teacher to work with up to seven students in concert or individually on any of the specific academic or career areas. This design enables the teacher to be at the elbow of all students and reduces her need to move hastily around the room. Besides the central instructional center, the room will have five special interest areas—social studies area, library and career information center, science centers, and instructional and listening materials centers. The areas are structured so that the teacher can visually monitor each of the areas, while allowing students to use them as part of their independent study responsibilities. Shelves and dividers should separate the various areas so that chosen areas of independent study are well defined and simultaneously provide the student a degree of privacy. Well-structured rooms, in which all materials are properly shelved and where all individuals understand and appreciate the rules of usage, provide and promote effective and purposeful learning.

Figure 17

MODEL ROOM

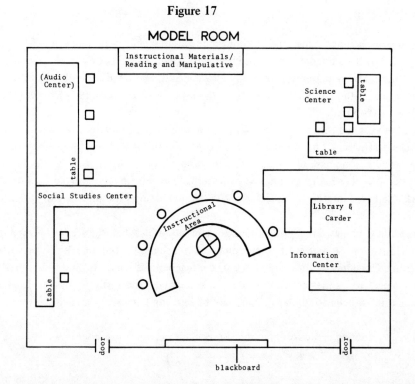

Management Tactics

Instructional approaches and materials without appropriate behavioral management tactics are ultimately doomed when applied to the adolescent student who has experienced years of school frustration. An effective secondary teacher should be acquainted with the theories of Skinner (1968), Bandura (1969), and Lazarus (1971). The application of these theories is contained in programs of Hewett (1968), Peter (1965), Kunzelmann et al. (1970), and Smith (1970).

Each of the theories and programs acknowledges the necessity of moving from concrete reinforcement to more abstract social reinforcers. The literature also supports the thesis that reinforcement procedures must consider not only the production phase of learning but also time factors. Too frequently educators have reinforced the completion of a task—referred to as frequency measure. They have not supported the length of time the student will work at a task (duration measure), nor have they measured the intensity of the student's involvement in an activity.

In working with an adolescent, baseline behavior (the point at which the student is operating in the academic areas) and classroom conduct must be pinpointed so teacher and student know where they are and where they are going. Once this has been determined, the teacher and student can develop meaningful and realistic goals and objectives as they relate to reading, mathematics, social studies, career development, and the language arts. This type of behavioral management can be best implemented through the use of performance contracting.

Performance contracting is the forming of an agreement between a teacher and a student. In the agreement the student acknowledges that for a specified quantity and quality of performance he will receive a reward (either money, tokens, food, or free time). Before the performance contract is initiated the diagnostic-assessment process must be completed. From this data the teacher can establish baseline expectations (the level of performance) for the student. Among the types of instruments used in diagnostic-assessment process are intelligence, aptitude, achievement, and criterion measurement tests. Each of these instruments enables the instructor to identify more aptly the student's skills and interests.

Once the baseline data have been determined, the teacher, in conjunction with the student, establishes realistic goals and objectives. If the student is unable or unready to reach work in consultation with the teacher, she alone establishes the goals and objectives. In addition, once realistic objectives are established, contingencies for completion of the specific quantity at a specified level of quality are determined.

When the student has reached the point of being able to work in concert with the teacher, the teacher must consult the student about objectives and contingencies. It is the designated purpose of performance contracting that the agreement be a joint and not a unilateral decision.

Once every two to three weeks a review of the goals, objectives, methods, and materials must be evaluated to determine whether the program is on track and on time. Often student and teacher, once the goals and objectives have been pinpointed, neglect to determine whether the original conclusions were appropriate, relevant, and effective. If they fail to meet the test of appropriateness, relevancy, and effectiveness, then they must be redrawn. Evaluation and reevaluation are essential components of any program.

Among the contingencies that can be used are food, money, chips, verbal praise, a pat-on-the-back, time off, other curriculum opportunities, and desired job or work stations.

Figure 18

Learning Contract

From: Date _____

To: Date _____

Parties to agreement:

_____
Teacher's Signature

_____
Student's Signature

The two parties agree that the following performance contract will take effect immediately following the signing of this document by the contractor (the teacher) and the contractee (student). The student agrees to perform the following tasks and the teacher agrees to recognize the performance.

Figure 18 (continued)

Areas and Tasks	Material Used and Amount to be Completed	Level of Performance	Contingency in Recognition of Performance
Reading 1. 2.			
Mathematics 1. 2.			
Language Arts 1. 2.			
Career Preparation 1. 2.			
Vocational Development 1. 2.			
Social Behavior 1. 2.			

Reinforcers, like the remainder of the program, must be continuously evaluated to measure their effectiveness. The reevaluation process must again include the use of criterion tests that measure academic development, performance charts that measure overt behavior, and student-teacher conferences that pinpoint personal attitudes as they relate to achievement, general behavior, and self-image.

Summary

The new legislation and litigation are compelling school personnel interacting with educationally handicapped youth to reassess the characteristics and needs of these students. For too long, the educationally handicapped adolescent has been given minimal attention by school administrators, teachers, curriculum developers, and researchers. Only now are the schools beginning to recognize that youth functioning far below normal expectation academically are not necessarily retarded, lazy, or turned-off and that they require innovative instructional programs and strategies if learning is to occur. All adolescent youth have initial difficulty because of the biological, physiological, and cognitive maturation that begins to occur around the ages of 12 to 13. These changes are compounded by new expectations by the schools and the community, which demand more of the adolescent than they do of children aged 10 to 11, but deny the youth the prerogatives of adulthood.

The literature demonstrates that many of the youth having trouble in the school setting are capable of learning and establishing career goals, and it also demonstrates that specific types of contingencies—food, money, time out, time off—do contribute to behavioral change. This same literature also demonstrates that diagnostic assessment procedures used in evaluating youth are often inappropriate and inadequate. For too long, special educators and school psychologists have depended upon instrumentation which tops out at the elementary level, i.e., Frostig, ITPA, and Wepman. There is a documented need for a new set of tools to become part of the arsenal in the diagnostic/assessment of learning-disabled youth. This test battery must include career and personality oriented instruments, as well as the conventional academic-aptitude measures.

Another deficit in secondary programmatic designs has been the poor choice of instructional materials and the questionable use of materials that are available. Experience and history have demonstrated that traditional basal readers that provide appropriate reading-level vocabulary and skills fail to offer appropriate motivational subject matter for the adolescent. Youth asked to read such material often become hostile and resist instruction. For secondary youth, the material must be high-interest, low-vocabulary, geared to teaching specific skills, and presented in a manner which encourages and promotes the pursuit of learning, whether the areas be language arts, mathematics, social studies, and/or career planning and development.

Parallel to the instructional improvement of each student in recent years is a movement toward individual learning contracts. The premise is that mutually agreed upon goals and objectives result in a more positive attitude toward learning on the part of the student and greater acceptance of individual needs on the part of the teacher. This phenomenon is now moving into the secondary public schools' instructional design but has not reached the level of acceptance found at the elementary level. For such youth, there is a unique need to develop performance contracts with well-delineated instructional objectives and contingencies. Without enabling such youth to share in their academic program development, there is minimal expectation that they will accept or participate in any type of instructional program.

A state-of-the-art review demonstrates that secondary programs need an overhaul, emphasizing realistic comprehension of adolescent needs and demanding more appropriate and relevant aptitude assessment, instruction, and contingencies. The contemporary models under which secondary learning disability programs are serviced need dramatic revision and alteration. Without radical change the secondary educationally handicapped youth will be left to wander aimlessly through the educational labyrinth, which has until now used elementary level methods and materials on learning-disabled adolescents.

L E A R N I N G   O B J E C T I V E S
Chapter 7

Cognitive Objectives

After carefully reading this chapter, you will be able to:

1) Describe the characteristics of secondary learning-disabled youth.
2) List the management procedures proven to be most effective with adolescent youth.
3) Recognize the types of academic instructional strategies which alter behavior.
4) Select the diagnostic instruments most effective in assessing these youth.
5) Know the parameters of programming for secondary students and the alternatives available to teacher and student.
6) Describe the types of instructional materials available and the environment that should be provided in either a resource or self-contained environment.

L E A R N I N G   O B J E C T I V E S
Chapter 7

Affective Objectives

After reading this chapter, the author intends that you will:

1) Distinguish between the underlying factors that contribute to the crisis of adolescence and the observable behavior associated with learning-disabled youth.
2) Recognize that secondary students' needs vary significantly from the needs of elementary level students in programming and instruction.
3) Identify the developmental differences between students 5 through 12 and those older than 12.
4) Acknowledge that the developmental phenomena require educators to provide alternative strategies for secondary learning-disabled students.
5) Understand that many high school dropouts are not delinquent or retarded but are learning-disabled youth who require unique educational experiences.

READER'S NOTES

PRIMER FOR SECONDARY PROGRAMS

Recent events have prompted the emergence of secondary programs for learning-disabled youth. These events were:

[Refer to p. _____]

1. _____
2. _____
3. _____

Findings by several authorities have prompted educators to conclude that many educationally handicapped secondary youth are learning disabled. The findings were:

[Refer to p. _____]

1. _____
2. _____
3. _____
4. _____
5. _____

In your own words, describe two of the behavioral strategies available to educators of secondary youth and summarize the overall findings of the literature pertaining to behavioral management.

PRIMER FOR SECONDARY PROGRAMS

Describe two strategies   Summarize findings

_____   _____

_____   _____

_____   _____

_____   _____

_____   _____

_____   _____

_____   _____

_____   _____

_____   _____

_____   _____

In designing a program, the teacher must insure that the instruction
meets the youth's _____ needs,
_____ milieu, and
_____ goals.

[Refer to p. ____]
[Refer to p. ____]
[Refer to p. ____]

READER'S NOTES

[Refer to p. _____]

PRIMER FOR SECONDARY PROGRAMS

Diagnostic instruments used on adolescent youth in the past fail along one significant variable. This variable is _____
_____ .

There are five levels of concern in educating the adolescent youth. They are:

1. _____
2. _____
3. _____
4. _____
5. _____

The authors stated six behavioral characteristics of youth that must be considered in designing an effective program. List the six in order and discuss why they are important.

[Refer to p. _____]

1. _____
_____
_____
_____
_____

READER'S NOTES

PRIMER FOR SECONDARY PROGRAMS

2. _____
_____
_____
_____
3. _____
_____
_____
_____
4. _____
_____
_____
_____
_____
5. _____
_____
_____
_____
_____

PRIMER FOR SECONDARY PROGRAMS

6. _____

_____

_____

Placement, like diagnosis, must be differentiated. Discuss the reasons
for the placement alternatives.

[Refer to p. _____]   _____

_____

_____

_____

_____

What should the goals of the teacher be in selecting materials for
learning-disabled youth?

[Refer to p. _____]   _____

_____

_____

_____

PRIMER FOR SECONDARY PROGRAMS

In establishing a room environment, there are specific goals that a
teacher must move toward. They are:

[Refer to p. _____]

1. _____

2. _____

3. _____

One basic management strategy is recommended in working with
learning-disabled youth. Describe the strategy and the possible contingencies.

Strategy   Contingencies

_____   1. _____

_____   _____

_____   2. _____

_____   _____

_____   3. _____

_____   _____

_____   4. _____

_____   _____

_____   5. _____

_____   _____

8 A Suggested Guide to Inservice Programs
Debora G. Boeck

Introduction

INSERVICE education is designed to facilitate the ongoing development of professionals by providing systematic instruction within an educational environment (Letson, 1971). School systems are responsible for providing and evaluating educational programs and therefore should provide inservice activities based on the evaluation of these programs. In planning inservice activities, the total school staff should be considered. For example, teachers should assist in the development of inservice programs, since the teaching role is the most vital staff responsibility. Letson (1971) lists the following as commonly accepted procedures for establishing and implementing local inservice programs: a) inservice programs should be planned to meet the needs of the staff, school, or district; b) objectives should be clearly stated; c) inservice activities should meet the needs of these specific objectives; d) inservice activities should always take into account changing curriculum and teaching methodology.

Continuing inservice within the schools is supported by much of the professional literature. Bryen (1973) reported that specialized programs and specially trained teachers are in short supply, and, therefore, regular class teachers can typically expect to have several exceptional children each year. Moreover, recent trends in education, such as mainstreaming, have led to an increase in the number of exceptional children in the classroom.

As a result of these trends in education, researchers have investigated the effects of integrating exceptional children into regular classrooms (Adelman, 1972; Budoff, 1972; Yates, 1973). These authors conclude that in order for mainstreaming to be successful, continuing inservice training is necessary.

Many inservice techniques are currently being explored. Overline (1972) reported that nineteen of these have been summarized by the National Education Association:

1. classes and courses
2. institutes
3. conferences
4. workshops
5. staff meetings
6. committees
7. professional readings
8. individual conferences
9. visitations and demonstrations
10. field trips

11. travel
12. camping
13. work experiences
14. teacher exchanges
15. research
16. writing
17. association work
18. cultural experiences
19. community organizations

Yates (1973) conducted a study to determine the effectiveness of inservice training to increase regular classroom teachers' special education information base and to alter their perceptions of integrating handicapped children into regular classrooms. The author noted that preservice education programs do not require special education courses for regular education teachers, but in order to successfully integrate exceptional children into regular classrooms, inservice programs are necessary.

Thirty regular classroom teachers served as the experimental group, and ten served as the control group. Five instruments were used for pre- and posttest data for both groups: Dogmatism Scale Form E, Critical Thinking Appraisal, Special Education Information Questionnaire, Adjective Self Description, and Classroom Integration Inventory. Results demonstrated a significant difference for the experimental group in test scores related to special education information. The experimental group also showed a significant difference on specific subtests of the Classroom Integration Inventory. Yates concluded that inservice education does increase teachers' special education information base and does modify their perceptions of integrating exceptional children.

In experimenting with the use of special teachers as change-agents, Adelman (1972) and his colleagues suggest using special teachers as inservice specialists to work with regular classroom teachers. These special teachers serve as advocates of the rights and needs of children with learning problems and provide information concerning these children.

Overline (1972) investigated the effects of an inservice program in learning disabilities. A four-day inservice workshop was designed to make a positive change in elementary classroom teachers' attitudes and instructional activities related to learning-disabled children. The research sample consisted of 64 (36 experimental, 28 control) elementary school teachers.

Experimental teachers scored significantly higher on the Minnesota Teacher Attitude Inventory and showed significant improvement in the ability to individualize instruction. Overline concluded that inservice is effective in changing teacher attitudes and that behavioral observations are effective in evaluating inservice programs. The change of attitudes cannot, however, be assumed to be the cause of actual behavior changes.

Implementing a new program in a school district requires that all personnel have a basic understanding of special education principles and that administrators, supervisors, teachers, and other specialists understand their role in relation to the new program. Most importantly, an inservice program must be provided for the regular classroom teachers, who, in conjunction with the learning disabilities specialist, bear the major responsibility for the learning-disabled child.

The regular classroom teachers need to understand the mainstreaming concept, what

the benefits are for the child and to teachers when programmatic instructional
procedures are offered through special education resource teachers and strategists
(Sabatino and Boeck, 1973, p. 113).

Rappaport and McNary (1970) state that inservice training for both new and experienced teachers
should be directed toward meaningful observation of the child for the purpose of making an assessment of
skills necessary to perform the tasks required. Furthermore, inservice should assist the teacher in developing
effective communication and positive emotional responses that will be conducive to the child's learning.
To have a successful inservice, it is necessary to approach the training from a teacher's standpoint; in this
way, the teacher's understanding and knowledge of children with learning disorders is increased.

The Model Learning Disabilities Systems makes use of inservice training as one important means of
program implementation. This inservice is provided for administrators, resource personnel, learning
disabilities and regular classroom teachers, and the community. Such services are invaluable as a means of
developing community awareness and facilitating program implementation.

In a preceding chapter the focus was on the principles and use of a management system for the
program area of learning disabilities. The primary reason for using a systems approach is to assist a school
system and community in viewing a total learning disabilities program as more than the sum of its parts.
As was previously stated in Chapter 2, frequently a learning disabilities program is a school administration's
response to community or teacher pressures to do something. What may develop is a partial learning
disabilities program representing selected aspects of a total program. Far too frequently the program
becomes a catch-all operation representing only a token effort. The conviction of the Model Learning
Disabilities Systems (MLDS) staff is that a program representing less than a total commitment to a learning

disabilities program is not a wise administrative decision. The all or nothing attitude of the MLDS staff is the result of observations, over a period of time, of schools that attempted to initiate or shore up a sagging special education program by implementing a single learning disabilities class. Such attempts were inevitably too restricted to serve the broad spectrum of learning-disabled children.

The next logical question may be how to alter and bring to awareness the goals for a total learning disabilities program. The finest of programs must be explained to the people who support it (the community). It must also be explained to those actively involved in its implementation (other professional educators). It is taking too much for granted to assume that a good program will automatically "sell" itself. Instead, the wise consumer wants and needs factual information. The purpose of this chapter is to demonstrate one means of organizing and presenting information to prepare the community and school to receive and work with a total learning disabilities program. The principal components of a learning disabilities program must be identified and planned in such a manner as to allow administrators, supervisors, teachers, and other professionals to participate fully and allow children to enter, exit, and participate fully or in part in the program. In addition, there must be an identifiable beginning, middle, and ending specified in the program objective. To achieve such a flow of program activities, the dissemination of information to community and staff that leads to interpretation and further planning is critical. A graphic representation of suggested inservice activities that aid in the dissemination of information is presented in Figure 19. The four levels of inservice are described below:

1. *Administrative inservice* is synonymous with program planning and comprises the initial steps necessary to establish a total learning disabilities program within a school system.

Figure 19

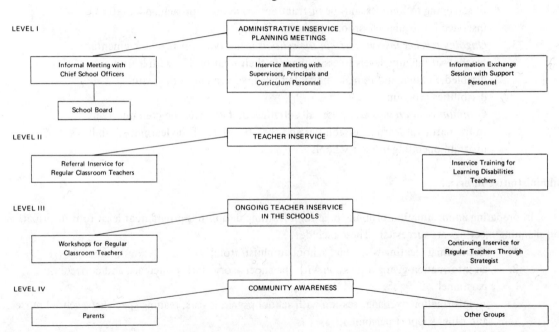

LEVEL I   ADMINISTRATIVE INSERVICE PLANNING MEETINGS

Informal Meeting with Chief School Officers

Inservice Meeting with Supervisors, Principals and Curriculum Personnel

Information Exchange Session with Support Personnel

School Board

LEVEL II   TEACHER INSERVICE

Referral Inservice for Regular Classroom Teachers

Inservice Training for Learning Disabilities Teachers

LEVEL III   ONGOING TEACHER INSERVICE IN THE SCHOOLS

Workshops for Regular Classroom Teachers

Continuing Inservice for Regular Teachers Through Strategist

LEVEL IV   COMMUNITY AWARENESS

Parents

Other Groups

2. *Teacher inservice* involves training for learning disabilities teachers in the use
    of screening techniques and the instructional systems approach and a referral
    inservice for regular classroom teachers.

3. *Ongoing teacher inservice within the schools* is inservice for regular elementary
    teachers at building levels to assist them in their relationship with learning-
    disabled children and to make possible their involvement in the learning
    disabilities program.

4. *Community awareness* comprises all activities that educate the community as
    to the nature of learning disabilities and the objectives of the learning disabilities
    program operating in their schools.

Administrative Inservice

In preparing an information-planning base for a learning disabilities program, at least four information
and planning meetings are suggested. These include:

1. an informal meeting with chief school administrators;

2. an information-giving discussion with the supervisory staff, principals, and curriculum
    personnel;

3. an information-exchange session with school psychologists, reading specialists, school nurses,
    and other support personnel;

      4.   an information-giving and instructional session for regular classroom teachers.
Each of these inservice meetings should be coordinated with the district's staff. Arrangements for time, place, and facilities have to be made and should be made at the convenience of supervisory personnel. These information/planning meetings, with the exception of the session for regular classroom teachers, should be held before the beginning of the school year to lay the groundwork for the new program. The session directed toward regular classroom teachers should take place during the first week of school.

      It is not enough merely to provide information and exchange ideas during these sessions; the dictrict's personnel must understand the purpose of the learning disabilities program and be willing to assist the program's staff in meeting set objectives. The information considered in each of these inservice activities is outlined below.

1.   Informal meeting with chief school administrators:

      In planning and implementing a learning disabilities program, meetings with administrators and supervisors are critical not only to bring everyone to a common informational level but to set objectives and select personnel to be responsible for specific objectives. A cooperative effort between special and regular education administrators is suggested to provide direct supervision of the learning disabilities program, to provide channels of communication for learning disabilities personnel, and to identify specific personnel job descriptions for management by objectives.

    1.1   Administrative decisions are necessary in the following areas:

        1.1a   objectives of program for this school system

        1.1b   the need for such a program, including the projected number of children who will be identified

       1.1c   community awareness/readiness and how to achieve it

       1.1d   principal and teaching staff awareness and readiness to work with such a program and how this is to be facilitated

  1.2   Preparation for board action

       1.2a   specification of objectives for this school system

       1.2b   budget, including cost-reimbursement figures

       1.2c   rationale for this program (priority)

       1.2d   long-range planning for future of learning disabilities program

  1.3   Immediate organizational problems

       1.3a   location of program in the administrative structures

       1.3b   divisions of program, number of special education resource teachers, strategists, assessment class, and self-contained teachers necessary

       1.3c   location of resource rooms, assessment classrooms, and self-contained classrooms in the various buildings

       1.3d   transportation responsibilities and arrangements, lunches, etc.

       1.3e   personnel support from existing staff, i.e., school psychologists, speech therapists, social workers, and others

2.   Information dissemination and discussion with supervisory staff, principals, and curriculum personnel:

    The purpose of this inservice meeting is to facilitate communication and interaction between the learning disabilities program and the elementary education program. Most learning-disabled children are in the regular class; therefore, the learning disabilities teachers must work closely with elementary supervisory staff to provide a total program for children with academic problems. At the same time it is necessary to coordinate the efforts of the elementary supervisors and principals with the goals of the learning disabilities program operating in their schools.

2.1   Update these personnel on their roles in the learning disabilities program

    2.1a   responsibility of principals to provide space in buildings for resource teachers

    2.1b   preparation of times suitable for resource or itinerant teachers to be in specific buildings

2.2   Evaluate learning disabilities teachers

2.3   Develop method whereby principals and/or supervisors can be kept abreast of services provided to children in their area(s)

2.4   Discuss interactions between these personnel and learning disabilities teachers

3.   Information exchange session with school psychologists, reading specialists, school nurses, and other support personnel:

The services provided by school psychologists and other support personnel are valuable in identifying and evaluating children for inclusion in the learning disabilities program. These services, however, must be brought to awareness and discussed to be made beneficial for all involved. Discussions should be conducted to insure the most efficient integration of all services.

3.1   Discuss referral process

    3.1a   referrals by learning disabilities teachers to other services or agencies

3.1b   referrals by school psychologists and others to learning disabilities program
3.2   Discuss exchange of information (records, etc.) or children to assist each other in diagnosis

Teacher Inservice

4.   Inservice of regular classroom teachers:
   The regular classroom teacher plays an important role in selecting the population of children who
are serviced by the learning disabilities teachers. The bulk of referrals come from regular classroom
teachers; therefore, to have a solid base for referral decisions, classroom teachers must receive inservice
training. Initial inservices should provide teachers with information on learning disabilities to assure
the appropriateness of referrals to the program. Inservice for classroom teachers should be conducted
by the learning disabilities teachers at the building level.
4.1   Define *learning disabilities,* with examples of children within the school system
4.2   Discuss the effects of labeling and the self-fulfilling prophecy
4.3   Outline referral procedure (who is to be referred)
4.4   Provide job descriptions of the learning disabilities teachers, with separate discussions for the
           special education resource room teacher, self-contained class teacher, and strategist
4.5   Discuss disabilities teachers' screening and assessment procedures (formal and informal
           instruments and what they measure)
4.6   Discuss the use of the behavioral and task analysis descriptors as observed in the screening and

assessment profiles

4.7   Give some very brief examples of learning disabilities teaching strategies as they occur in the special class and resource room

The philosophy underlying the teacher inservice that should be shared with the classroom teachers concerns two major points:

a)   The major goal of the program is to keep the children in or as near the regular class structure as possible, with aid from special education personnel.

b)   It is necessary to maintain a close working relationship between special educators and regular classroom personnel to achieve a balanced special-regular education curriculum continuum or instructional flow through the elementary school. Thus the program draws from two disciplines—regular and special education.

5.   Inservice of learning disabilities teachers

To implement a resource room program effectively, continuous inservice training of the teaching staff is imperative (Reger, 1973). The inservice for learning disabilities teachers is a workshop designed to orient and instruct them in using the MLDS systems approach. This requires understanding the various task areas under the system, the responsibility they have in each task area, and the activities required to carry out the specific responsibilities. The learning disabilities teachers must receive preservice training in the following areas:

5.1   Screening and Diagnosis (see Chapter 3)

     5.1a   use of test criteria to operationalize learning disabilities definition

5.1b   referral process
5.1c   basic psychometric considerations
5.1d   administration of tests (practice administering tests under observation)
5.1e   scoring of tests (under school psychologist's supervision)
5.1f   reporting process
5.1g   follow-up procedures

5.2   Intervention (see Chapter 5)
5.2a   instructional assessment techniques
5.2b   teaching methods
5.2c   instructional materials (selection and use)
5.2d   instructional objectives and prescriptions
5.2e   evaluation of child's progress

5.3   Coordination of existing services (see Chapters 1, 3, and 9)
5.3a   support team
5.3b   community agencies

Inservice for new learning disabilities teachers extends over a one-week period before the beginning of the school year. Duration of inservice training must be flexible, dependent on the educational level and background of the learning disabilities teachers hired. For example, if a district decides to use existing personnel for the learning disabilities program, more time may be needed to cover the background of learning disabilities, definitions, characteristics, etc. The MLDS recommends that master's level special education teachers with learning disabilities background be hired for the learning disabilities staff when possible.

6.   **On-going Teacher Inservice Within the Schools**

In discussing the practical problems of establishing a resource room program to service exceptional children, Hammill and Wiederholt (1972) mention school staff preparation as a basic problem. It appears that regular classroom teachers are often reluctant to integrate exceptional children into their program, presumably due to a lack of skills and materials necessary to teach such children. In many schools, the task of alleviating teacher concerns has been accomplished through inservice. Hammill and Wiederholt state that regular classroom teachers can develop the necessary skills and information base by receiving inservice training related to areas of exceptionality.

Ongoing inservice within the schools can be achieved in at least two ways:

6.1   Learning disabilities resource teachers can inititate inservice training for regular classroom teacher by offering workshops during the school year. The major objectives of the learning disabilities workshops are to:

A.   develop a better understanding of the learning disabilities program operating in the school system, thereby increasing effective communication among learning disabilities specialists and regular class teachers;

B.   develop teachers' knowledge of learning-disabled children to

increase the appropriateness of referrals made to learning disabilities
specialists;

C.   demonstrate informal assessment techniques to assist teachers in identifying
and diagnosing strengths and weaknesses of learning-disabled children;

D.   demonstrate materials and methods to assist teachers in implementing
recommendations made by learning disabilities specialists or school
psychologists.

An outline of suggested information for presentation follows:

Session 1

6.1a   overview of learning disabilities program operating in the schools

6.1b   definition of learning disabilities

6.1c   prevalence of learning-disabled children in school population

6.1d   characteristics of learning-disabled children

Session 2

6.1e   informal assessment of learning-disabled children

    6.1e1   teacher checklists

    6.1e2   observations of children's behavior

    6.1e3   informal teacher-made tests

Session 3

6.1f   methods and materials for remediation (emphasizing product not process)

	6.1f1	reading materials and methods
	6.1f2	math materials
	6.1f3	language materials and training methods

Session 4

6.1g		methods and materials for remediation (emphasizing process not product)
	6.1g1	visual perceptual materials
	6.1g2	auditory perceptual materials
	6.1g3	behavior modification techniques

6.2   Learning disabilities strategists inservice regular classroom teachers as they work together to meet the needs of individual children. This can be achieved by:

6.2a		reporting screening and diagnostic information to the teacher
	6.2a1	present profiles
	6.2a2	explain grade equivalent scores, mental ages, and percentile scores in relation to each test
	6.2a3	review past educational history and medical history
6.2b		setting program objectives in conjunction with regular class curriculum
6.2c		assisting teacher in writing behavioral objectives
6.2d		demonstrating materials and methods used to meet specific objectives
6.2e		evaluating child's performance with regular classroom teacher
	6.2e1	review daily progress profile

6.2e2   review pre- and posttest objectives

6.2f   follow-up on child after strategist work is completed

Community Awareness

An aspect of inservice education which is too often overlooked is community awareness. It is critically important that the community understand the nature of learning disabilities and the objectives to be met through the program. With this knowledge, the community, especially parents of school age children, will understand the benefits of the program and support the program's underlying concept of mainstreaming.

A list of the possible ways to disseminate information to the community is presented.

7.1   Establish community advisory committee to help study the learning disabilities problem and possible programs

7.2   Present programs and lectures at meetings for the **PTA** and school council study groups, etc., and at service clubs, coffee clubs, etc.

7.3   Disseminate information through local **TV** and radio—news releases and talk shows, local newspaper releases, etc. News articles may deal with:

7.3a   national problems and trends

7.3b   local needs

7.3c   definition and etiology

7.3d   possible alternatives

7.3e   the proposed program

7.4   Organize parent groups to assist program implementation and public information (see Chapter 9)

7.5   Encourage community visitation and continued publicity once the program is established

Evaluation of Inservice Programs

In discussing the role of the public schools, Clements (1969) stated that public schools should have a continuous inservice training program for all school personnel and continuous evaluation and research within the schools.

Although inservice programs are widely implemented in school districts across the nation, little is known about the effectiveness of inservice education. The importance of evaluating inservice training programs has been emphasized by many authors (Haven, 1954; Herrick, 1957; Aaron, 1965; Carsetti, 1969; Schild, 1969). Inservice programs have been evaluated by both direct and indirect methods. The following evaluation methods have been utilized: questionnaires, interviews, opinion inventories, assessment of pupil achievement, and teacher attitude and behavior change (Overline, 1971). The most effective evaluations seem to be those which use objective measures to demonstrate change, either in teacher or child attitude and performance.

Boeck (1975) studied the effectiveness of an inservice in increasing regular classroom teachers' knowledge of learning disabilities. The inservice program consisted of 4 workshops (administered one hour a week over a 4-week period) that provided information on the identification, assessment, and remediation of learning disabilities. The control and experimental groups were pre- and posttested using the Learning Disabilities Information Inventory. Significant differences were found between the experimental group who received inservice training and the control group who did not receive inservice training ($p < .05$).

A principal component of any evaluation is to determine program effectiveness and constitute changes in future developments. One method of evaluating inservice programs used by the MLDS is the measurement of teacher knowledge before and after inservice training (pre and post). The Learning Disabilities Information Inventory (Appendix A) is designed to evaluate teacher knowledge of learning disabilities and can be used as an instrument to measure the effectiveness of the inservice program.

Appendix

LEARNING DISABILITIES INFORMATION INVENTORY

Directions: Answer each multiple-choice item by circling the most appropriate answer. Complete every multiple-choice item, as you will not be penalized for incorrect answers. The true-false items are scored right minus wrong; therefore if you do not know the answer, leave it blank.

MULTIPLE CHOICE

1.   The term *learning-disabled* includes children who have learning problems which are primarily the result of
    a)   emotional disturbance
    b)   developmental aphasia
    c)   visual, hearing, or motor sensory handicaps
    d)   environmental disadvantage

2.   Children who have specific learning disabilities
    a)   achieve at grade level
    b)   achieve above their estimated level of potential
    c)   achieve at their estimated level of potential
    d)   achieve significantly below their estimated level of potential

3.   Which of the following is a characteristic of learning-disabled children?
      a)   integrity of symbolic processes
      b)   visual, auditory, or proprioceptive sensory handicaps
      c)   integrity of mediational processes
      d)   echolalia

4.   A child with an auditory memory disorder may be unable to
      a)   complete a written copying task in a given time period
      b)   remember directions given orally
      c)   discriminate among geometric designs
      d)   remember a series of pictures shown him

5.   A deficit in expressive language may manifest itself in
      a)   the inability to use proper syntax
      b)   the inability to follow the line of conversation
      c)   the inability to understand written directions
      d)   the inability to recognize concrete relationships

6.   A method of teaching visual discrimination in sequential stages is
      a)   to train letter, letter cluster, and word discrimination
      b)   to train geometric shape, word, and letter cluster discrimination
      c)   to begin with word form straphic training
      d)   to train complex designs, geometric shapes, and words

7.   Which of the following materials is designed to train visual-motor skills?
    a)   Continental Press-Visual Discrimination Masters
    b)   Dubnoff School Program I
    c)   Size and Shape Cards by DLM
    d)   Match and Check by Scott Foresman

8.   A procedure for increasing a child's "raising hand to speak" behavior is to
    a)   verbally reprimand him each time he speaks out of turn
    b)   increase the number of situations in which children raise their hands to speak (such as group discussions)
    c)   reward other children for raising their hands to speak
    d)   call attention to his inappropriate behavior

9.   Exposing a series of letters for ten seconds and asking the child to reproduce them in writing in the identical order is an activity for training
    a)   visual acuity
    b)   visual memory skills
    c)   auditory sequencing skills
    d)   haptic perception

10.   Which of the following materials is designed to train visual discrimination problem-solving skills?
    a)   Same or Different Proportion Cards by DLM
    b)   Colored Beads and Bead Patterns by Teaching Resources
    c)   Teacher-made Camouflage Pictures
    d)   Large Parquetry by DLM

11.   A child with a deficit in auditory perception would benefit most from a
      a)   visual-motor approach
      b)   perceptual integration approach
      c)   auditory-visual approach
      d)   multisensory approach

12.   The term aphasia is defined as
      a)   impairment in the ability to read
      b)   impairment in spontaneous writing
      c)   impairment in the ability to use or understand oral language
      d)   impairment in the ability to calculate or manipulate number symbols

13.   The incidence figure(s) most commonly used in establishing the percent of learning disabilities is
      a)   under 10 percent
      b)   10-20 percent
      c)   20-30 percent
      d)   over 30 percent

14.   Haptic perception refers to
      a)   information received through touch, body movements, and muscle feeling
      b)   information received through touch via the fingers and skin surfaces
      c)   information received through bodily feelings of muscular contraction, tension, and relaxation
      d)   information received through visual and auditory modalities

15. You have a learning-disabled child in your classroom. In teaching reading skills you would
    a)   begin remediation at his grade level
    b)   begin remediation at his level of difficulty
    c)   begin remediation at the level where the child has already mastered the skills necessary to perform at that level
    d)   begin remediation at his level of potential

TRUE or FALSE

1. Children who are learning-disabled frequently have minimal brain damage.   T   F

2. Hypoactivity is not a behavior exhibited by learning-disabled children.   T   F

3. Learning-disabled children do not exhibit disorders in more than one academic area.   T   F

4. Learning-disabled children almost always appear inattentive.   T   F

5. A child who has difficulty copying from the chalkboard may have a visual perceptual problem.   T   F

6. Children with visual perceptual problems frequently show reading improvement when correctly fitted with glasses.   T   F

7.   Tracing shapes and letters is a method for training visual-motor abilities as
     well as for teaching the alphabet.   T   F

8.   Word configuration training asks the child to look at each letter in isolation.   T   F

9.   Auditory and tactile reinforcements are recommended aids in training
     visual memory.   T   F

10. In linguistic readers vocabulary is controlled through phonetic and visual
     regularity.   T   F

L E A R N I N G   O B J E C T I V E S
Chapter 8

Cognitive Objectives

After carefully reading this chapter, you will be able to:

1)   Explain the "all or nothing" attitude of the MLDS staff when initiating a learning disabilities program within a school system.

2)   Identify the four major types of inservice programs suggested by the MLDS to aid in the dissemination of information.

3)   Identify the four information and planning meetings for preparing an initial information planning base.

4)   Utilize the Learning Disabilities Information Inventory as a pre- and post-evaluative instrument in determining competency gain at the completion of a teacher inservice program.

L E A R N I N G   O B J E C T I V E S
Chapter 8

Affective Objectives

After reading this chapter, the author intends that you will:

1)   Be aware of the MLDS strategy to provide the needed information to both professional staff and community in developing a learning disabilities program.
2)   Value the principles of inservice education.

READER'S NOTES

INSERVICE PRIMER

The primary reason for utilizing a systems approach in developing a learning disabilities program is to enable both the school system and community to view the program in its whole. When school administrators respond to community or teacher pressures for initiation of a learning disabilities program, it far too frequently treats the program as a "catch-all." From field experience the MLDS staff has acquired an:

(attitude) _____

[Refer to p. _____ in manual.]

_____

towards such haphazard implementation methodology. This less than total commitment to a learning disabilities program is considered inappropriate in the light of the number of children who will benefit from such a program in its fullest form.

To clarify commitment of a school system to the initiation of a learning disabilities program, the reader should attempt to predict and classify the following variables into either a successful

READER'S NOTES

[Refer to p. _____ .]

INSERVICE PRIMER

or unsuccessful implementation "mode."

The organization and dissemination of needed information to prepare both the community and school for implementation of the learning disabilities program is of the utmost importance. The principal components of the learning disabilities program must be presented in such a way that the professional staff can participate fully in implementation and have the opportunity to enter, exit, and participate fully or in part in the program. In addition, there must be an identifiable beginning, middle, and ending specified in the program. To achieve flow of the program and to disseminate information to the community and professional staff vitally needed for interpretation and further planning, the **MLDS** suggests four types of inservice programs:

1. _____
2. _____
3. _____
4. _____

READER'S NOTES

[Refer to p. _____ .]

INSERVICE PRIMER

In preparing an information planning base for a learning disabilities program, at least four strategy meetings are needed; they are:

1. _____

_____

2. _____

_____

3. _____

_____

4. _____

_____

A further explanation of the total **MLDS** learning disabilities implementation strategy can be found in the following learning activity.

Place the title of the approach which fits the randomly selected variables in the box provided. The purpose of this activity is to

READER'S NOTES   **INSERVICE PRIMER**

expose you, the reader, to a total strategy of implementation. Keep in mind that not all variables of a specific strategy will be listed; the reader will have to review this chapter to guarantee his knowledge of the specific variables the MLDS staff suggests under each strategic approach.

PLACE TITLE OF APPROACH   VARIABLES IN EACH APPROACH
IN APPROPRIATE SPACE

-objectives of program for this school
 system
-the need for such a program
-the way to achieve community awareness
-preparation for board action
-immediate organizational problems

READER'S NOTES   **INSERVICE PRIMER**

-the updating of personnel on their roles
 in the learning disabilities program
-responsibility of principals to provide
 space
-evaluation of learning disabilities teachers
 by district supervisor

[Refer to p. _____ .]

-discussion of referral process
-referrals by learning disabilities teacher
 to other agency
-discussion of exchange of information
 (records, etc.) or children to assist each
 other in diagnosis

-definition of learning disabilities children
 with examples of children within the
 school system
-referral procedure—who is referred
-discussion on the use of the behavioral
 characteristics

READER'S NOTES   **INSERVICE PRIMER**

-use of test criteria to operationalize
learning disabilities definition
[Refer to p. _____ .]   -referral process
-intervention
-coordination of existing services

- (example) Learning Disabilities Workshops
[Refer to p. _____ .]   (Sessions I-IV)

-establishing a community advisory
committee
[Refer to p. _____ .]   -disseminating information through local
TV and radio
-local needs

READER'S NOTES	INSERVICE PRIMER

INSERVICE PRIMER

OVERVIEW REVIEW

[Refer to p. ———— .]

School systems are responsible for providing and evaluating educational programs and therefore should provide ——— activities based on the evaluation of these programs. Letson (1971) lists the following as commonly accepted procedures for establishing and implementing local inservice programs:

[Refer to p. ———— .]

a. _____
b. _____
c. _____
d. _____

Each inservice meeting should be coordinated with the district's staff. These information planning meetings, with the exception of the session for ————————————————————————————— ,

[Refer to p. ———— .]

should be held before the beginning of the school year. The session directed toward ———————————————————————————— ———————————————————— should take place during the first

[Refer to p. ———— .]

week of school.

READER'S NOTES   **INSERVICE PRIMER**

It is not enough merely to provide information and exchange
ideas during these sessions; the district's personnel must
understand the purpose of the _____

[Refer to p. _____.]   _____ and be willing to assist the

program's staff in _____

[Refer to p. _____.]   _____

The purpose of the meeting with chief school officers is to provide a cooperative effort between _____

[Refer to p. _____.]   and _____ education administrators

to provide _____

_____

_____

The purpose of meeting with the supervisory staff, principals,
and curriculum personnel is to _____

_____

_____

[Refer to p. _____.]   _____

Discussions with the support staff of schools are vital to insure

READER'S NOTES

[Refer to p. _____ .]

[Refer to p. _____ .]

INSERVICE PRIMER

the most efficient _____
_____ services. The classroom plays an impor-
tant role in selecting the population of children who are serviced
by the learning disabilities program. The _____
of _____ (s) come from regular classroom
teachers; therefore, teachers must receive inservice training. The
philosophy underlying the teacher inservice which should be
shared with the classroom teachers concerns these two points:

a. _____

_____

b. _____

_____

The inservice for learning disabilities teachers is a workshop
designed to orient and instruct them in using the MLDS systems approach. This requires:

1. _____

_____

READER'S NOTES

[Refer to p. _____ .]

INSERVICE PRIMER

2. _____

_____

3. _____

_____

Ongoing inservice can provide vitality and needed input into the learning disabilities program. This strategy can be achieved in two ways:

1. _____

_____

_____

or

2. _____

_____

_____

[Refer to p. _____ .]

[Refer to p. _____ .]

An aspect of inservice education which is too often overlooked is community awareness. It is critically important that the

READER'S NOTES

INSERVICE PRIMER

community understand the nature of learning disabilities
and the objectives to be met through the program. List both
the MLDS suggestions as well as your own to meet this awareness need by the community.

Awareness Strategies

1. _____

2. _____

3. _____

4. _____

5. _____

6. _____

READER'S NOTES

[Refer to p. _____ .]

[Refer to p. _____ .]

[Refer to p. _____ .]

[Refer to p. _____ .]

INSERVICE PRIMER

Definitions
Learning Disabilities Information Inventory
_____
_____
_____

"Mainstreaming Concept"
_____
_____
_____

Support Personnel
_____
_____
_____

Ongoing Inservice
_____
_____
_____

9   Parent and Community Involvement

Carl R. Schmidt and Glen G. Foster

Introduction

As a means of strengthening special education programs the parents of exceptional children and organized community groups should be given a responsible voice in educational policy formation and planning activities (Council on Exceptional Children Policy Statement, 1971, p. 47).

ONE of the most extensive movements in public education is the change occurring in the role relationship of parents to school. Texts published twenty years ago (e.g., Frank, 1950; Grant, 1920) recommended passive parent participation in the educational system (e.g., joining the PTA, providing rides for field trips). Publications of ten years ago (e.g., Mok, 1965) recommended that parents become better informed of educational policies and their child's status. Five years ago a trend toward parent counseling and a recognition of parental concerns in the education of their children became evident (Gordon, 1970). Today parents and the entire community are often viewed as activists and directly aid in the tutoring and therapeutic process. Oberst (1973) points out, "Parents are more knowledgeable and are actively seeking help for their children" (p. 428).

It is recommended that the total community become involved in school programs and policy decisions. Reed (1973) states:

> Community control of schools is inextricably linked to community growth and development. It can lead to community pride, to community ownership, to community power, and to individual power as reflected in the ability of individuals to choose from among an array of educational, social, economic, and political options (p. 363).

Traditionally the child-parent, child-community, and child-school relationships have been regarded as independent of each other. A more integrative view of the situation would see the child as benefiting from the coordinated efforts of all three, as is represented in Figure 20. Here the concern of the parents, school, and community all overlap in the service of children. This chapter presents information relating to the theory and practice of coordinating the energies of parents, school, and community to serve learning-disabled children in the most efficient way.

Figure 21 demonstrates achievement gains which are typical of the progress found in many parent-peer programs. Keel and Harrison (1971) utilized parents and older peers in teaching kindergarten and first-grade children the names and sounds of specific letters, and the combining of these sounds into word or nonsense syllable units. The results show a dramatic improvement in the skills of the tutored children.

Figure 20

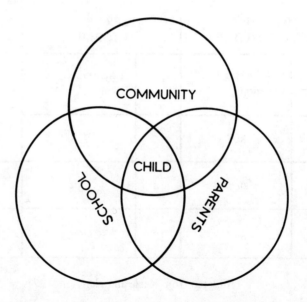

Figure 21

CRITERION ACHIEVEMENT BY TREATMENT GROUP

	PARENT TUTORED		PEER TUTORED		CONTROL	
	N	% Achieving Criterion	N	% Achieving Criterion	N	% Achieving Criterion
Letter Naming	20	80%	14	93%	20	35%
Letter = Sound Association	18	94%	14	93%	20	0%
Sound Blending	14	86%	13	70%	20	0%

Adapted from Keele and Harrison, 1971.

It is asserted that the target child (or children) is not the sole beneficiary of parent and community involvement. Stanford (1973) discusses at length the beneficial interrelationships that may occur as a result of parent and community involvement. One example given relates to the benefits of hiring parents as teacher aides within a classroom. Figure 22 graphically demonstrates the complexity of the results this simple step can have.

Stanford approaches the analysis through five chains—community understanding, program adaptation, direct and indirect parent self-image, and home environment change. All of these may filter down to benefit not only a single child but also all of the children within that school system, parent programs, teachers, and community involved, due to the child's enhanced ability to function within and serve that community. It is possible to extrapolate this example to include peers and community volunteers.

It should be recognized that academic and cognitive development are only two facets of a child's total life experience. The manner in which a child views himself in relation to his peers, his parents, and his community can have a crucial effect on a child's educational performance. If a child has a low self-image and expects to fail (or is expected to fail) that child is more likely to fail (Palardy, 1969; Foster, Ysseldyke, and Reese, 1974). Parents and community must be informed about the problems of the learning-disabled child and, whenever possible, be included as agents to insure a facilitative home, social, and community environment.

Interest in the incorporation of parents and community in the education of learning-disabled children was largely initiated by parents. Parents who were dissatisfied with the services their children were receiving provided the necessary impetus to stimulate research, legislation, and expansion of services (Perry, 1974).

Another compelling reason for including parents and community in a learning disabilities program is the

Figure 22

PARENTS AS PARAPROFESSIONAL EMPLOYEES IN THE SCHOOL PROGRAM

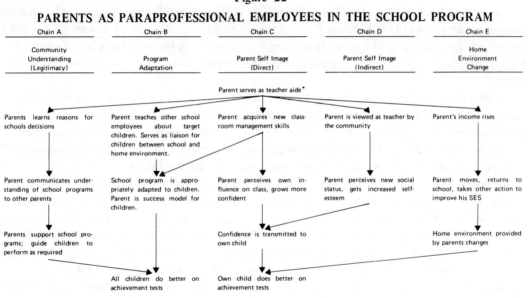

Chain A	Chain B	Chain C	Chain D	Chain E
Community Understanding (Legitimacy)	Program Adaptation	Parent Self Image (Direct)	Parent Self Image (Indirect)	Home Environment Change

Parent serves as teacher aide*

Parents learns reasons for schools decisions

Parent teaches other school employees about target children. Serves as liaison for children between school and home environment.

Parent acquires new classroom management skills

Parent is viewed as teacher by the community

Parent's income rises

Parent communicates understanding of school programs to other parents

School program is appropriately adapted to children. Parent is success model for children.

Parent perceives own influence on class, grows more confident

Parent perceives new social status, gets increased self-esteem

Parent moves, returns to school, takes other action to improve his SES

Parents support school programs; guide children to perform as required

Confidence is transmitted to own child

Home environment provided by parents changes

All children do better on achievement tests

Own child does better on achievement tests

*If parent were employed as school-home coordinator, Chain A would be elaborated.

Stanford Research Institute, *Parent Involvement in Compensatory Education Program,* Research Memorandum 20, 1973, p. 34

lack of professional personnel trained in the field (Jenkins, Mayhall, Peshka, and Jenkins, 1974). Learning disabilities per se are a fairly recent educational concern. Therefore, the number of children needing services is far greater than the capacity of professionals trained to meet these needs (Jenkins, Mayhall, Peshka, and Jenkins, 1974). Parents, peers, and community organizations have shown a will and ability to serve in various capacities to alleviate this imbalance (Sabatino and Abbott, 1974; Middendorf, 1970; Slater, 1971-72).

It can be demonstrated that there is a desire on the part of parents to improve the education of their learning-disabled children, a need to coordinate the child's social-emotional environment with his academic program, and a need for auxiliary personnel. Therefore, it is recommended that parents, peers, and community be included as integral parts of the education of the learning-disabled child.

It is possible to incorporate the parents of learning-disabled children in a number of ways:

1. as auxiliary agents via parent and community groups.
2. as sources of information via interviews, checklists, etc.
3. as recipients of therapy designed to improve the parent-child relationship and home environment.
4. as therapeutic agents for their children, to improve the children's self-image and the parent-child relationship.
5. as tutors.

Limitations

It should be noted that not all professionals agree that parental involvement is advantageous or even desirable (Wilson, 1972). Worden and Snyder (1971) found that tutoring can be "an unsuccessful and unpleasant experience" with older children having known neurological impairment.

Neifort and Gayton (1973) outline several factors which can lead to program failure:

1. *Lack of paternal support*—if one parent has a negative opinion of the program, or minimizes the child's disability, this attitude can erode the other parent's and the child's confidence and minimize the effects of training.

2. *Family power struggle*—if the family has a disruptive set of relationships, a training program can become a battleground and foster an unhealthy climate for learning.

3. *Multiple problem family*—if a family is faced with serious marital, financial, and/or health problems, it is unlikely they will be able to put forth a whole-hearted effort in a home training program.

4. *Large families*—if a parent finds it necessary to take one child to scouts, another to piano lessons, etc., or if a simple problem of overcrowding exists, it is unlikely that the parent will be able to devote sufficient time and/or energy to a home tutorial program.

Parent Groups

> Our ability to provide programs for learning disabled children is directly related to the amount of community support we have. . . . when parents form an organization and speak to local, state, and national governing bodies they speak from a position of strength—a position directly related to the number of people they have in that audience (Brutten, Richardson, Mangel, 1973, p. 198).

Parent groups initially emerged in the 1950-60s as a result of parental dissatisfaction with existing learning disabilities services. Perry (1974) has pointed out that, initially, many local parent organizations were concerned with such issues as raising the level of financial assistance to parents of learning-disabled children and initiating programs where none existed. Parents who could afford it financially were forced to send their children to private schools at the time, since many public schools were unable to provide necessary services. These local groups also provided emotional and, if necessary, legal support to parents having difficulties persuading school districts to retain their learning-disabled children within the public schools.

The primary functions presently served by local parent groups are:

1. Encouraging formation of learning disabilities programs within local school districts;
2. Increasing the parents' knowledge of their children's problems and methods of helping them via outside speakers;
3. Acting as a collective voice when talking with the school district, legislature, etc.;
4. Maintaining libraries containing books and films relating to learning disabilities;

5.   Providing an open forum for discussion of common problems;
6.   Creating "hotline" services for parents in extreme or immediate distress regarding their children, enabling them to contract another member for assistance or moral support;
7.   Raising funds to provide scholarships for teachers going into the field of learning disabilities;
8.   Providing supplementary programs for learning-disabled children, e.g., weekend youth groups designed to build self-confidence through talk ("rap") sessions, field trips, cooking classes, shopping techniques, etc., or summer day camps;
9.   Publicizing the plight of the learning-disabled child to encourage a facilitative environment for the child and to increase the chances of early identification. This publicity is effected through seminars, workshops, conferences, and radio and television coverage.

State and National Parent Groups

Between 1950 and 1960, the local groups organized into larger groups by state. Some of the earlier statewide organizations were the Illinois Fund for Perceptually Handicapped Children, the New York Association for Brain-Injured Children, and the California Association for Neurologically Handicapped Children (CANHC). In 1963, the conference on exploration into problems of the perceptually handicapped child served as a vehicle for the organization of the state groups into the national Association for Children with Learning Disabilities (ACLD). The general acceptance of the term *learning disabilities* can be traced to topics discussed at this meeting. This organization has facilitated the establishment of local chapters by serving as a rallying point. Perry (1974) states that a single article in a national magazine or one letter to a syndicated newspaper column such as "Dear Abby" can precipitate tens of thousands of inquiries to ACLD headquarters. These inquiries come from concerned parents, teachers, and friends of learning-disabled children. Generally, the inquiries are referred to state, and then local, chapters of ACLD, who then contact the individual. National ACLD headquarters is located at:

> 5225 Grace Street
> Pittsburgh, PA 15236
> Telephone: 412-881-1191

ACLD is composed of 27,000 parent volunteers in 48 states, and one full-time national director. One of its prime concerns is publicity directed at eliciting community acceptance of the learning-disabled population and encouraging early identification of learning-disabled children.

At the state and national level, the ACLD has worked to make the public aware of the learning disabilities problem by sponsoring seminars and workshops and publishing educational materials such as the films "Why Billy Can't Learn" and "Anyone Can."

Community Involvement

The ACLD is also coordinating its efforts with the Kiwanis Clubs and with the General Federation of Women's Clubs (GFWC). These types of organizations have much to offer in volunteer services, funds, and human relations.

The stated goals of these community organizations include:

1.   Disseminating information regarding learning disabilities;
2.   Providing leadership training services to volunteer groups;
3.   Developing skills, coordination, political astuteness, and effectiveness of community groups;
4.   Providing direct services to learning-disabled children, including tutorial and recreational programs;
5.   Investigating existing and needed programs in local school districts;
6.   Conducting and coordinating seminars and workshops;
7.   Encouraging teacher awareness to affect early identification and remediation techniques;
8.   Sponsoring full scholarships for teachers taking courses in learning disabilities.

Besides civic organizations, ACLD also utilizes and coordinates professional assistance on its advisory board at state, local, and national levels. At the national level, the board is composed of prominent individuals from the fields of learning disabilities, e.g., Kirk, Cruickshank, Getman, McCarthy, Frostig, and others. Statewide and locally, the advisory boards may be composed of competent local practitioners in psychology, psychiatry, pediatrics, education, law, and other related fields. Typically, the parents provide direct services to aid their learning-disabled children and to help the advisory boards determine the direction of these services.

Legislation and Educational Policies Influenced by Parent Groups

One of the more concrete indices of the effectiveness of the ACLD and other parent and community action groups is the legislation and educational policies regarding learning disabilities that have been influenced by them. At the local level, parent groups have been directly responsible for the establishment of over half of the programs serving learning-disabled children in the country (Clark and Richards, 1968).

Other accomplishments include increasing federal and state financial reimbursements to parents forced to educate their children in private schools, encouraging school district inservice days to educate teachers in the field about learning disabilities, influencing the specific inclusion of "learning disabilities" in the federal education for the handicapped act, making presentations to the White House Council for Children and Youth, securing permission from colleges to allow learning-disabled students to use tape recorders instead of taking notes in class, and allowing learning-disabled entrants to take college board examinations orally.

Those involved in implementing a new program to service children identified as learning disabled may have to contend with pressures from many sources. Administrators and school board members frequently deal with community pressure groups whose concerns vary from lowering taxes to establishing programs for individually handicapped children. As the role of parents, parent groups, and community agencies in education continues to increase in emphasis and effectiveness, the school district is faced with the responsibility of organizing a plan to involve these groups, as well as school personnel, in the development and implementation of needed programs, based on a review of local problems and possible alternatives. It is critically important that teamwork exist between the home, the community, and the schools in developing, implementing, and evaluating programs for children who have learning difficulties.

A main concern of most school administrators is to establish an efficient and effective service that will be well received, understood, and supported by the community. When these efforts meet with resistance, even by parents of the children to be served, program disenchantment can occur for all those involved. Misinformation, fears, and the social stigma often associated with special education placement may cause a great deal of parent resistance. To minimize this type of reaction, the school district would probably benefit from developing an open, honest, and effective public information dissemination plan. Most resistance and fear can be eliminated by providing the community with the facts and problems that have led to the need for learning disabilities programs. This can be accomplished through mass media coverage, contact with community groups, and/or presentations to groups such as the PTA.

Parents and Peers within the Schools

Aside from parent groups working as independent, auxiliary agents, parents can also act as integral parts of the school program. The most direct area of involvement is tutoring. As mentioned earlier, parents are being considered as direct educational agents, especially in preschool and elementary education. This has been prompted by the lack of sufficient professional manpower, financial cutbacks, and other such limitations.

Several investigations of parent effectiveness as tutors have been conducted. Sabatino and Abbott (1974) and Middendorf (1970) trained mothers of disadvantaged children and/or children showing slow visual perceptual development in the use of the Frostig Developmental Program in Visual Perception (DPVP). Both studies demonstrated that mothers can be effective in improving their children's visual perception.

Slater (1971-72) showed that kindergarten learning-disabled children whose mothers were trained to tutor them in auditory discrimination, gross and fine motor coordination, visual motor coordination, and verbal skills improved in these areas more than children whose mothers were not trained.

It has been found that using parents as tutors has not only improved the target academic area but also improved the general social atmosphere at home, improved lines of parent/child and parent/teacher communication, and improved feelings of parent and child self-worth (Sabatino and Abbott, 1974; Slater, 1971-72; Buckner, 1972).

It is occasionally impractical to enlist the services of parents within the school structure. The need for additional personnel is nevertheless present. A reasonable solution to this dilemma is to enlist other students as tutors. The reinforcement capabilities of peers have been well established (Patterson and Anderson, 1964; Hartup, 1964; Drass and Jones, 1971), as has their effectiveness as tutors.

As a direct investigation of alternative solutions to the problem of too few resource-room personnel and too many children in need of help, Jenkins, Mayhall, Peschka, and Jenkins (1974) compared the effectiveness of individual peer tutoring, self instruction, and group instruction. On measures of word recognition, spelling, oral reading, and multiplication, peer tutoring seemed to have the most positive effect. Stander (1972) found similar results using remedial reading students as tutors. As Jenkins et al. (1974) point out, however, it would be difficult to justify taking tutors out of the classroom if they did not demonstrate increased learning as well.

Research indicates that tutors may benefit from the experience as well (Jenkins et al., 1974; Stander, 1972), but there is no universal agreement on this point. Snapp (1972) conducted a study investigating effectiveness of fifth and sixth graders as tutors of disadvantaged first and second graders. He reports high motivation for the tutees but low motivation on the part of the tutors, who were not given rewards. The study indicates that while there were gains, they were too minimal to warrant recommendation of a peer-tutoring program. The MLDS staff has found that tutorial programs can be most helpful. The following describes what we have found to be important factors in instituting such programs.

Instituting Parental and Peer Tutorial Program

It is recommended that the following points be considered in establishing a parent tutoring program:
1. Presenting the parents with an overview of child development and learning theory, stressing areas of particular interest (e.g., perceptual development and its relation to reading);
2. Discussing with the parents the importance of social-emotional factors;
3. Demonstrating learning difficulties to parents from their child's point of view, to aid the parents in acquiring empathy towards their child (e.g., use of a mirror writing device or difficult pattern from the Frostig DPVP);
4. Training the parents in the use of the specific materials, either via manual instructions or adapted version (materials should be selected to optimize ease of administration and feedback objectivity);

5. Recommending procedures for:
    a. establishing realistic goals and daily objectives
    b. arranging a regular work area and time
    c. establishing rewards for work
    d. establishing methods of objective evaluation;
6. Discussing with parents the importance of a positive attitude and reinforcement;
7. Discussing specific problems;
8. Providing ongoing support to parents in areas of tutor techniques, and, if necessary, emotional support.

The training of peer tutors utilizes many of the same techniques as the training of parent tutors, but the procedure is different enough to warrant a separate listing of points to consider.

Points to consider in setting up a peer tutoring program:

1. Material selection—materials should be designed to optimize ease of administration and objective feedback;
2. Age-personality matches—it is usually beneficial to arrange for the tutor to be older than the "student" and essential that they be of compatible personality types;
3. Scheduling;
4. Tutor training—the tutor must be able to handle the materials and be able to provide immediate social reinforcement when appropriate (training a tutor is usually very simple since, in most cases, he/she has been tutored by the resource teacher);

5.   Supervision;
6.   A method of reinforcing the peer tutor (often the "privilege" of teaching another child is sufficient reward).

It is felt that a responsibly executed program of tutor training is one of the most viable means for expanding services to the learning-disabled child. Further, it appears that the serendipitous returns alone in terms of encouraging parental involvement and/or raising the self-image and academic performance of peer tutors make a tutor training program worthwhile.

Assisting Parents in Restructuring the Home Environment

Parents' most pervasive influence is naturally in the home situation, where most of the child's time is spent and where the child establishes emotional stability and feelings of self-worth. In accordance with the federal definition of learning disabilities, the MLDS adopts the policy that learning disabilities are not primarily a function of emotional disturbance. Nevertheless, a learning-disabled child has a great likelihood of developing and exhibiting "disturbing" behaviors, especially in a classroom situation [e.g., easy distractability, hyperactivity, etc. (Brutten, et al., 1973)]. It is important to distinguish between the emotionally disturbed child, whose treatment must be primarily directed at ameliorating the emotional difficulty, and the learning-disabled child. Effective treatment of learning disabilities is directed towards generating success experiences and developing weak information-processing channels through closely systematized presentations of academic materials.

In the case of the learning-disabled child, disturbing behaviors can be the result of consistent failures exhibited in the skill areas and may not be the cause of the failure. A complete program aimed at helping the learning-disabled child cannot ignore the child's emotional state of being and cannot ignore the vital part parents play. Hobbs (1964) has stated that the only way to improve substantially the mental health of our adult population a generation from now is to devote at least 75 percent of mental health resources toward helping children now. Such immediate help can be especially important for the learning-disabled child, who is often burdened with severe failure experiences in addition to the usual difficulties associated with natural development.

Guerney (1964) has suggested that parents, if they could be trained in the essentials of the therapeutic role, would conceivably be more effective than professionals as therapeutic agents. This viewpoint was developed because (a) the parents have meaningful emotional significance to the child, (b) anxieties learned in the presence of, or by the influence of, parental attitude could most effectively be unlearned, or extinguished, under similar conditions, and (c) interpersonal misexpectations could be efficiently corrected if appropriate delineations were made clear to the child by the parent himself as to what is, and what is not, appropriate behavior according to time, place, and circumstance.

The parents of the learning-disabled child may be especially in need of therapeutic assistance. In investigating the possibility that parents of learning-disabled children react in unique, perhaps detrimental, ways towards their children, Brodie (1967) reports that many mothers of learning-disabled children are more secretive in communicating with their child. Furthermore, they tend to have lower expectations for him/her as a learner. Wetter (1971) concludes that these parents may be rejecting their learning-disabled child. In an extensive report by Owen, Adams, Forrest, Stoly, and Fischer (1971), it is stated that parents of learning-disabled children perceive their child as demonstrating more undesirable behavior than other children, as having inadequate language capabilities, and as being more impulsive. It appears that parents of learning-disabled children exert more pressure on and appear less affectionate towards their learning-disabled children.

Two basic approaches to training parents as therapists appear in the literature: child-centered approaches (e.g., the filial technique) and behavioristic approaches (e.g., contingency management). It is felt that both methods can be effective, depending on the preferences, needs, and philosophical points of view of the psychologist and parents involved.

Filial Technique

Filial therapy, as developed by Guerney and Guerney (1966), uses parents as counselors, instituting play therapy sessions with their children. The success of a filial support program depends heavily upon the motivation of the parents involved. Parents whose children are involved in the learning disabilities program are contacted and the goals and nature of the program are explained. It must be stressed at this meeting that a great deal of potential effort is involved but that rewards of such efforts can be very great. Interested parents are organized into small groups (no larger than eight persons) who meet regularly with the psychologist(s) who serve as instructor(s).

Inservice sessions are held once weekly for about three hours. These sessions must be scheduled for an undetermined length of time and should be held until the parents agree that they are no longer useful as instructional vehicles. During these sessions the parents must learn: (a) to be empathic with the child—to make every effort to understand how the child is viewing himself and his world at the moment and what his feelings are at the moment; (b) to be fully understanding and accepting of the child, i.e., his feelings and thoughts, whatever their nature; (c) to leave the directions that the play sessions take (within certain clearly defined limits) completely to the child; (d) to convey this understanding and acceptance to the child; and (e) to follow the basic procedures for conducting a play session. The therapist, after teaching the parents the fundamentals involved, conducts two or three play sessions. When ready, the parents follow suit with practice sessions observed by the therapist and the other parents within the group. Videotape equipment is useful in facilitating the didactic process and can act as an aid to the discussions that follow. As the parents feel comfortable with the techniques involved, they should begin conducting play sessions with their children at home.

The specific procedures covered during these sessions include: (a) materials used; (b) facilities required; (c) time of sessions; (d) setting of limits; and (e) roles of parents and children during the sessions. The observed sessions and group meetings provide opportunities to discuss problems which develop, as well as an opportunity for supportive interaction between the parents. The filial technique can be a useful adjunct to any complete program of services to learning-disabled children.

Contingency Management Approach

A second approach to parent-involved therapy techniques is to train parents or children (peers) in the use of contingency management techniques. Contingency management is a systematic way of looking at cause-effect relationships and can be used as a method of promoting effects which are beneficial to all concerned. All of us are constantly being rewarded or punished (reinforced) for our actions, but often these reinforcements occur in unplanned ways, thereby making possible the reinforcement of undersirable behaviors. If the reinforcements can be controlled, desirable behaviors can be maximized. The individual who is the object of the systematized reinforcements can be fully aware of "what's going on," and the method can still be effective. This can, in fact, increase the effectiveness of the method and is recommended for ethical reasons. (Most employees are constantly aware of the reinforcement schedule they are on—e.g., $3.50 per hour—and this is used to promote high energy output.)

Perhaps the simplest application of contingency management is described by Sluter and Hawkins (1972). In their program, parents simply gave their children monetary rewards contingent upon weekly report-card grades (e.g., A = 10¢, B = 5¢, C = 1¢, etc.). All other sources of money for the children were cut off. The reinforced group showed a marked improvement over the matched control group.

Ryback, Rohrer, Hibler, Replogle, and Surwit (1970-71) discuss several programs in which parents were trained in the use of contingency management techniques in order to teach their children reading at home. In this and other programs reviewed, support was found for the use of parents as tutors of learning-disabled children using contingency management techniques. McKenzie, Clark, Wolf, Kothera, and Benson (1968) report similar results.

Implementing a Contingency Management Training Program

The following points should be covered in training parents in the use of behavior therapy:

I.   Basic Principles
    A.   Positive Reinforcement—Do it. If it feels good, you will do it again.
    B.   Negative Reinforcement—Do it. If it stops the pain, you will do it again.
    C.   Punishment—Do it. If it hurts, you won't do it again.
        [While punishment is a basic principle, it has been shown to be ineffective and to have infinitely more complex and unpredictable effects on behavior than the other reinforcement options.]
    D.   Extinction—Do it. If it doesn't get you anywhere, you will eventually stop doing it.
    E.   Be consistent.
II.   Ethical Considerations
    A.   Behavior Therapy is a tool, not a philosophical position.
    B.   Whenever possible all parties concerned should be aware of contingencies
        1.   Write "job contracts" (e.g., George will do ten single column addition problems in five minutes with 90 percent accuracy, after which he can go out to play)
            a.   state desired behavior
            b.   state time and efficiency requirements
            c.   state reinforcers

      2.   Avoid conflict and/or promote desired outcomes by making public all important cause-effect relationships (e.g., "Do you mind the radio playing while you study?")

  C.   Choose goal behaviors

      1.   Develop empathy for the child

      2.   Remember that most parents always prevail

      3.   Develop methods for equal arbitration

III.   Reinforcers

It should be stressed that this is a most crucial part of any contingency management program. The reinforcement must be satisfactory to the child and must be appropriate for the amount of work to be done, or the entire system becomes unworkable.

  A.   Types

      1.   Primary (e.g., food, sleep, pain, etc.)

      2.   Secondary (tokens, money, etc.)

      3.   Social

  B.   Schedules

      1.   Fixed ratio (Junior get ten cents for sweeping the stairs twice.)

      2.   Variable ratio (Mom occasionally takes Sarah to the movies after Sarah cleans her room.)

      3.   Time contingencies

         a.   Belinda gets dessert if she finishes dinner in 20 minutes.

         b.   Stacy can watch an extra half-hour of television if he does not suck his thumb for two hours.

4.   Multiple or conflicting schedules (Does Eric want an "A" from his teacher or approval from his friends?)

IV.   Case Histories and/or Discussion of Specific Problems

(Krumboltz and Krumboltz [1972] provide some excellent examples and analyses of case histories.)

Many sources report that training parents in therapeutic techniques not only improves the academic achievement of the target learning-disabled child but also improves the whole family atmosphere. The parents tend to be more understanding and accepting of their learning-disabled child and to recognize their importance in their child's development (Barsch, 1961; Myers, 1971-72; Bricklin, 1970). In addition, Edgerly (1971) reports that the academic achievement of the siblings of the target population also increased in most cases.

It should be emphasized that counseling programs for the learning disabled and their families as described above must be implemented by a specialist familiar with these techniques. An area interested in the establishment of such a program must first contact such a resource person, possibly through a university clinical psychology program, a mental health clinic, or the Model Learning Disabilities Systems (Brutten et al. present a comprehensive listing of these services). The purpose here is to point out that such programs can be a useful adjunct to any special pupil service and that, given parent motivation and appropriate personnel, such a program is possible.

Parents as Consultants

Parents are in a unique position to provide educationally relevant information regarding their child. Orton (1970) suggests some of the following areas of interest in which a parent may be most informative:

1. Mother's prenatal health and child's subsequent general health;
2. Rate of development (at what age the child first walked, talked, etc.);
3. Child's social/emotional state of being;
4. Child's areas of interest;
5. Family situation (number and age of family members, home atmosphere, etc.);
6. Parental expectations for the child.

Ideally, both parents should be contacted for an interview, which may be conducted in the child's home. This would be a means of talking to the parents in a setting most comfortable and relaxing to them and would increase the chances of talking to both parents together. It would also allow the interviewer to obtain a "feel" for the home atmosphere beyond its vital statistics, while creating less formal and more open lines of communication.

In conclusion, it is apparent that a symbiotic relationship can and should exist between a learning disabilities program and the community which it serves. Parents, peers, and community members can provide vital services to any learning disabilities program, such as defining the needs of their learning-disabled children, disseminating information concerning the field, and providing direct services for the children involved. The

MLDS has found its contacts with parents, peers, and community to be a rewarding and an indispensable part of the systems approach to learning disabilities.

Acknowledgments

The authors would like to extend special thanks to Onnolee Perry, President of the Pennsylvania Association for Children with Learning Disabilities, for generously sharing her time and knowledge with us in preparing the sections of this chapter dealing with parent groups, and the Association for Children with Learning Disabilities.

LEARNING   OBJECTIVES
Chapter 9

Cognitive Objectives

After carefully reading this chapter, you will be able to:

1)   Identify strategies for incorporating the parents of learning-disabled children into the educational process.
2)   Determine the limitations of such parental involvement in the educational process of their children.
3)   Recognize the functions presently served by local parental groups in the area of special education.
4)   State the functions of the ACLD (Association for Children with Learning Disabilities) and list the joint goals of this organization and community organizations (e.g., Kiwanis Club).
5)   List the points to be considered in establishing a parent tutoring program.
6)   Describe filial therapy.
7)   Explain the Contingency Management Approach and list the points that should be covered when training parents in this therapy technique.
8)   Identify six areas of interest in which the parent can be most informative in regards to learning-disabled children.

LEARNING OBJECTIVES
Chapter 9

Affective Objectives

After reading this chapter, the author intends that you will:

1) Recognize the importance of an informed public (parents and community) in dealing with the problems of the learning-disabled child.

2) Become aware of the growing activism among parents of learning-disabled children.

3) Associate effective public information dissemination planning with elimination of resistance to learning disabilities programs.

4) Judge the assets of parental tutoring.

5) Recognize the vital influences of the home environment on the learning-disabled child.

6) Value the principle of public involvement (parents/community) in learning disabilities programs.

PARENT & COMMUNITY PRIMER

An educational program that fails to meet the needs of the
community leaves much to be desired in terms of effectiveness.
Programs failing to take into consideration the multi-faceted
life of a young child tend to divorce themselves from reality and
consequently fail both child and the community they were intended to serve. The manner in which a child views himself in
relation to his peers, parents, and community can have a crucial
effect on a child's educational performance. Parents and
community must be informed about the problems of the
learning-disabled child, and where at all possible, be included
as agents to insure a facilitative home, social, and community
environment.

It is possible to incorporate the parents of learning-disabled
children in a number of ways:

1. _____

2. _____

[Refer to p. _____ in the manual.]

READER'S NOTES   **PARENT & COMMUNITY PRIMER**

3. _____

4. _____

5. _____

It should be noted that not all professionals share the attitude
of parental involvement as an advantageous strategy. Neifort
and Gayton (1973) outlined several factors in this chapter which
can lead to program failure:

1. _____

2. _____

3. _____

4. _____

A rising activisim among parental groups concerned with up-
grading on local, state, and national levels services provided to
learning-disabled children grew drastically in the 50s and 60s.
The primary functions served by local parent groups are:

1. _____

2. _____

3. _____

[Refer to p. _____ .]

[Refer to p. _____ .]

READER'S NOTES

PARENT & COMMUNITY PRIMER

4. _____

5. _____

6. _____

7. _____

8. _____

9. _____

The impetus for this movement has begun to focus on the national level with the creation of the Association for Children with Learning Disabilities (ACLD). Some primary functions of this national organization are:

1. _____

2. _____

3. _____

4. _____

5. _____

6. _____

7. _____

8. _____

[Refer to p. _____ .]

READER'S NOTES

[Refer to p. _____ .]

PARENT & COMMUNITY PRIMER

For a variety of reasons (mentioned throughout this chapter) parental tutorial programs have been initiated within schools. Instituting this type of program requires careful consideration. The following criteria have been offered by the MLDS staff in establishing such a program.

They are:

_____
_____
_____
_____

In training parents as therapists, there appear to be two basic approaches:

1. _____
2. _____

In the following "compare and contrast block," review either in your mind or by referring back to the appropriate pages, and

READER'S   NOTES

PARENT   &   COMMUNITY   PRIMER

list the philosophy of each approach and your perception of
their similarities and differences.

COMPARE   AND   CONTRAST

Philosophy of   Philosophy of

_____

_____

_____

_____

_____

_____

_____

_____

[Refer to p. _____.]

Parents are in a unique position to aid professionals in a consultative fashion. Orton (1970) suggests several areas in which

READER'S NOTES

[Refer to p. _____ .]

PARENT & COMMUNITY PRIMER

parents can be of a great aid to learning disabilities specialists:

1. _____
2. _____
3. _____
4. _____
5. _____
6. _____

DEFINITIONS

Parental activists: _____
_____

ACLD: _____
_____

Filial inservice sessions: _____
_____

Symbiotic relationship: _____
_____

10 Program and Teacher Evaluation

David G. Carter, *et alia*

Introduction

IN the past, educators have considered the evaluation process to be primarily student evaluation. The public's discontent with the educative process has, however, forced educators into an era of accountability. The public's demand for quality education has compelled American educators to provide hard evidence that existing educational programs and services are, in fact, beneficial.

Accountability is not a problem just for regular educators; the demand for accountability in special education is especially acute. Learning disabilities present a unique set of problems to the evaluation dilemma; disabled children are difficult to categorize or label, and they may cycle through three or more different programs in a given year.

The purpose of this chapter is to provide special educators with guidelines for determining the effectiveness of learning disabilities programs. Part 1 discusses overall program evaluation. Part 2 discusses teacher evaluation, and Part 3 presents a simplified evaluation process for teachers to self-critique their instructional activities.

This chapter deviates from the rest of the text simply because no one system of evaluation is adequate for all program operations. Therefore, in Part 1, three different types of program evaluation are offered to the reader. Their similarities and differences are amplified, and it is left for the receiver to decide which one, or which aspects of them all, can be used. Parts 2 and 3 return to more operationally defined, recommended plans of action.

Part 1: Performance-Based Program Evaluation
David G. Carter

As mentioned earlier, the need for program evaluation is the result of public demand for "proof" that educational services to children are effective and beneficial. Initial efforts in program evaluation focused on theory and on the development of evaluation models with limited implementation. The following discussion hopefully will encourage special educators to lift program evaluation from theory into practice.

Programmatic Evaluation

Evaluation has been defined as "the process of delineating, obtaining, and providing useful information for judging decision alternatives" (Stufflebeam, 1971, p. 40). Program evaluation is more than "cosmetic cardiac," or judging the success or failure of a program on the enthusiasm of students, parents, and teachers. Program evaluation demands that actions be based on systematically collected and analyzed information.

Educators who attempt to provide an effective school program must base their actions on a process of sound educational decision-making which depends upon:

1. clear identification of goals;
2. selection of reasonable means to attain those goals;
3. continuous surveillance of the operation and ongoing activities of one's program;
4. periodic determination of the degree of success of the program.

The CIPP Model

A classification scheme of strategies for evaluating educational change has been developed by Stufflebeam (1971). He identifies four types of evaluation: Context, Input, Process, and Product (CIPP). The classification scheme is shown in Figure 23.

The supervisor's first task is to develop criteria for judging the evaluation activity. The supervisor must be cognizant of these criteria (Stufflebeam, 1971, p. 38):

1. Objectivity
2. Importance
3. Timeliness (Is the information available when needed?)
4. Internal validity
5. Pervasiveness (Does the information reach all who need it?)
6. Credibility (Is the information trusted by those who must use it?)
7. External validity (Is the information generalizable to similar situations?)
8. Reliability
9. Relevance
10. Scope
11. Efficiency

The above criteria are valuable, for they assure the person using the information that it has practical utility and was collected in a scientific manner.

Once the criteria are developed, the supervisor is ready to begin the actual evaluation of the learning disabilities program. The first major objective is to determine needed changes in the program, unmet needs of the students, and reasons why those needs have not been met. These tasks may be accomplished by critically analyzing the following sources:

1. Instructional materials
2. Standardized tests
3. Pupil attendance records
4. Attitudinal surveys
5. Teacher observations
6. Diagnostic tests
7. Dropout data
8. Teacher appraisal files

Regardless of the evaluation model utilized, the person(s) evaluating an educational program will need a plan outlining the steps to be implemented. Stufflebeam (1969) conceptualizes such a plan as follows:

Evaluation Design

A. *Focusing the Evaluation*
   1. Identify the major level(s) of decision-making to be served, e.g., local, state, or national.
   2. Project the decision situations to be served and describe each one in terms of its locus, focus, criticality, timing, and composition of alternatives for each level of decision-making.

      3.   Define criteria for each decision situation by specifying variables for measurement and standards for use in the judgment of alternatives.

      4.   Define policies within which the evaluator must operate.

B.   *Collection of Information*

      1.   Specify the source of the information to be collected.

      2.   Specify the instruments and methods for collecting the needed information.

      3.   Specify the sampling procedure to be employed.

      4.   Specify the conditions and schedule for information collection.

C.   *Organization of Information*

      1.   Provide a format for the information which is to be collected.

      2.   Designate a means for performing the analysis.

D.   *Analysis of Information*

      1.   Select the analytical procedures to be employed.

      2.   Designate a means for performing the analysis.

E.   *Reporting of Information*

      1.   Define the audiences for the evaluation reports.

      2.   Specify means for providing information to the audience.

      3.   Specify the format for evaluation reports and/or reporting sessions.

      4.   Schedule the reporting of information.

F.   *Administration of the Evaluation*

      1.   Summarize the evaluation schedule.

      2.   Define staff and resource requirements and plans for meeting these requirements.

3.   Specify means for meeting policy requirements for conduct of the evaluation.
4.   Evaluate the potential of the evaluation design for providing information which is valid, reliable, credible, timely, and pervasive.
5.   Specify and schedule means for periodic updating of the evaluation design.
6.   Provide a budget for the total evaluation program.

(Daniel Stufflebeam, "Evaluation as Enlightenment for Decision-Making." Paper delivered at Association for Supervision and Curriculum Development, Sarasota, Florida, 19 January 1969, p. 48).

When these steps have been completed, the supervisor should have a clear understanding of the program's problems. Now the supervisor is ready with staff involvement, and he is ready to develop goals and objectives in accordance with the identified problems and needs. But what are the factors that the supervisor should keep in mind when establishing objectives? According to Tyler (1974), these factors are: cultural needs, student knowledge and ability, state of knowledge, school philosophy of education, and selection and statement of objectives that are consistent with learning theory.

It is important to emphasize the need to penetrate the surface concerns or symptoms and sense the causative problems. For example, the environment might be defined as a rural elementary school. The content evaluation reveals that learning-disabled children are not learning to read at a level expected of them, and it might further indicate that a particular problem or problems—inadequate instructional materials, absenteeism, lack of familiarity with learning disabilities program, etc.—were the cause of this failure. What the supervisor has been doing thus far is *context evaluation*.

Once the supervisor is aware of the problems and the objectives for the program, the next task is to

Figure 23

THE CIPP EVALUATION MODEL: THE STRATEGIES

	Context Evaluation	Input Evaluation	Process Evaluation	Product Evaluation
OBJECTIVE	To define the operation context, to identify and assess needs in the context, and to identify and delineate problems underlying the needs.	To identify and assess system capabilities, available input strategies, and designs for implementing the strategies.	To identify or predict, in process, defects in the procedural design or its implementation, and to maintain a record of procedural events and activities.	To relate outcome information to objectives and to context, input, and process information.
METHOD	By describing individually and in relevant perspectives the major subsystems of the context; by comparing actual and intended inputs and outputs of the subsystems; and by analyzing possible causes of discrepancies between actualities and intentions.	By describing and analyzing available human and material resources, solution strategies, and procedural designs for relevance, feasibility and economy in the course of action to be taken.	By monitoring the activity's potential procedural barriers and remaining alert to unanticipated ones.	By defining operationally and measuring criteria associated with the objectives, by comparing these measurements with predetermined standards or comparative bases, and by interpreting the outcome in terms of recorded input and process information.
RELATION TO DECISION MAKING IN THE CHANGE PROCESS	For deciding upon the setting to be served, the goals associated with meeting needs and the objectives associated with solving problems, i.e., for planning needed changes.	For selecting sources of support, solution strategies, and procedural designs, i.e., for programing change activities.	For implementing and refining the program design and procedure, i.e., for effecting process control.	For deciding to continue, terminate, modify or refocus a change activity, and for linking the activity to other major phases of the change process, i.e., for evolving change activities.

A Classification Scheme of Strategies for Evaluation
of Educational Change

Reprinted from a paper delivered by Daniel Stufflebeam, "Evaluation as Enlightenment for Decision-Making," at Sarasota, Florida: Association for Supervision and Curriculum Development, 19 January 1969, p. 31.

determine how to utilize available resources to meet the state goals and objectives. This is *input evaluation,*
and it involves the supervisor in identifying and assessing:
1.   school district capabilities
2.   alternative strategies for meeting the goals and objectives of the program
3.   designs which may be appropriate to implement selected strategy (Stufflebeam, 1971, pp. 222-23).
Ultimately, alternative designs are delineated in terms of resources, time, and budget requirements. Further,
they are assessed for relevance to the stated objectives, their potential procedural obstacles, the significance of
not overcoming these obstacles, and the probability and expense of overcoming them. Essentially, the supervisor collects information in order to decide whether additional resources will be needed to reach the goals and
objectives. This information will also help one to decide which strategy should be used, e.g., the adoption of
existing instructional materials or the development of new materials. These decisions may require changes in
scheduling, staffing, and budget allocation.

After a strategy has been selected, the next step is to begin *process evaluation.* This type of evaluation
provides the supervisor with needed continuous feedback on the program's effectiveness. The objective is to
detect, eliminate, or predict defects in the implementation of the strategy. The supervisor's overall responsibility
is to take corrective steps to eliminate sources of potential failure so that the resources, staff, time, etc. continue
toward the stated objectives. It may be necessary to revise some of the objectives based on findings identified
during this stage in order to avoid following the correct procedure in the wrong direction.

For example, when a school system changes from self-contained learning disabilities classes at the
junior high level to teachers functioning in learning centers, how well-informed are the persons responsible

for the new arrangements? Too often a decision becomes final because continuous feedback on the program effectiveness does not occur. It is important for the supervisor to remember that process evaluation should occur in each type of evaluation.

The last step is *product evaluation*. Its purpose is to determine whether the objectives of the programs were met. If the objectives were not satisfied, product evaluation should provide the supervisor with insight into the reasons for failure. Once the information is collected, it is compared with that obtained from context and process evaluation in order to determine the changes that have been made by the program and the factors that were probably responsible for the changes.

Evaluation Models of Stake and Scriven

Stake's Model (1967) is more detailed than CIPP. It is probably better to look at the major concepts of this model before portraying the complete paradigm (Figure 24). According to Stake, three sources of information should be tapped in an educational curriculum evaluation:

(a) Antecedents: any condition existing prior to teaching and learning that may relate to outcomes (students' aptitude and interest).

(b) Transaction*: countless encounters of students with teachers, other students, and so on.

---

*Transactions are dynamic, whereas antecedents and outcomes are relatively static.

(c)   Outcomes: consequences of educating—immediate and long range, cognitive and affective, personal and community-wide.

Stake identifies two types of evaluation acts (basic activities):

(a)   Judgmental (deciding which set of standards to heed)

   (1)   absolute—comparison of descriptive data of one program with established set of standards of excellence

   (2)   relative—comparison of one program with another

(b)   Descriptive (e.g., Tyler's National Assessment Program)

   (1)   intents—planned-for environmental conditions, demonstrations, coverage of certain subject matter, as well as intended student behavior

   (2)   observations—description cited earlier in this paper (cf. Stake's three sources of information)

There are two ways to process descriptive evaluation:

(a)   finding *congruence* between intents and observations

(b)   finding *contingencies* (or connections, dependencies) among Antecedents, Transactions, and Observations

   (1)   Logical Contingencies (LC): a logical connection between an event and its purpose

   (2)   Observation Contingencies (or EC—empirical): empirically verified connection between an event and its purpose.

The Scriven Evaluation Model (1967) is analogous to CIPP since it poses a taxonomy of types of

Figure 24

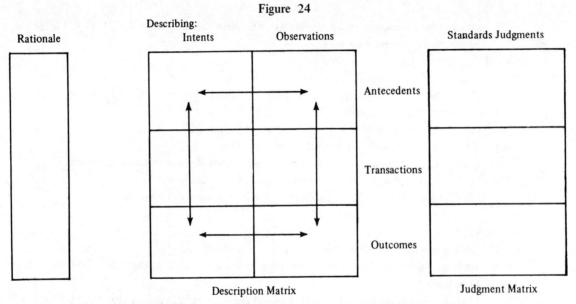

A Layout of Statements and Data to be Collected by the Evaluation Program

(Reprinted with permission from an article by Robert E. Stake in *Teachers College Record*, April 1967, 529.)

evaluation strategies. Both approaches seem to be grand in nature; that is, they suggest large general categories in which various types of "sub-evaluation" designs might operate. Scriven makes a distinction between evaluation goals and evaluation roles: the former attempt to answer certain types of questions with regard to educational instruments (e.g., the degree to which one instrument performs better than another). Evaluation roles, on the other hand, can be variable; an evaluator can (1) contribute to process development of curriculum or self-improvement of a teacher or (2) focus primarily on determination of the overall quality of an educational instrument.

Scriven (1967) identifies four types of evaluation:

(1) Formative: used to improve curriculum during its development; permits intelligent changes to be made

(2) Summative: final evaluation of teaching instrument

(3) Intrinsic: appraisal of the teaching instrument itself, usually in the abstract (e.g., content, goals, teacher attitudes)

(4) Pay-off: study of the effects of the educational instruments on the student. For example, it yields results capable of defending a decision to adopt or not to adopt a particular curriculum innovation.

Summary

Three strategies of evaluation have been discussed. It should be noted, however, that one need not necessarily be constrained within the boundaries of any one of the models presented. The best evaluation design is one constructed of elements from different techniques that meet the purposes for evaluation established by a school system. In fact, Stufflebeam has suggested such a possibility.

Each situation is unique and must be met with ingenuity and expertise. It is hoped that the information presented here will assist the special education supervisor in developing or selecting an appropriate evaluation model for the supervisor's particular situation.

Part 2:
Teacher Appraisal: The Performance Objective Approach
David G. Carter and James H. Reese

Administrators and school board members generally have had difficulty in efficiently evaluating the professional performance of teachers. The ramifications of this inability are particularly evident in California, where legislative action has already taken place to remedy the situation. In 1971, lawmakers enacted Senate Bill 696, which, in essence, created a statewide system of accountability. Briefly stated, the law provides: ". . . that every permanent teacher in the public schools and community colleges of California be evaluated at least once every two years" (Schulman and Trudwell, 1972, p. 32). Legislative action does not negate the need for an effective process for appraising teacher performance, but it can provide the necessary catalytic activity for moving "educational accountability" from its present abstract context to one which is concretely understood by the supervisor and teacher.

Performance Appraisal of Special Education Teachers

One of the recurring issues in the performance appraisal of special education teachers is to whom they are responsible. Traditionally, special education teachers are hired through a special education department in a school district or intermediate unit (regional administrative structure). They are then assigned to a building. The "who" to whom they are responsible is usually an odd arrangement and generally an unwritten rule. Technically, in terms of teaching competencies, they are evaluated by special education supervisors. Their survival, however, usually rests on public relations skills. The word "survival" is emphasized because most special education teachers are evaluated in terms of their relationships with building staff, community, parents, and children rather than on professional skills alone. This is a sad commentary, but we feel it is a true one.

The unresolved question is the identification of "how and who" among special education program director, special education supervisor, basic education supervisors, and building principal in the supervision and appraisal of the special education teacher's performance. More important is a determination of the expectations of each of these people for the special education teacher working in one building in a self-contained class or for the special education resource teacher working in several buildings.

Virginia's Department of Education (1972) has described several models for appraising teacher performance (Appendix A). Using such a format for developing a teacher appraisal model, the Model Learning Disabilities Systems (MLDS) proposes the organizational structure outlined in Figure 25. Within this structure, the special education supervisor is primarily responsible for the appraisal of the special education teacher's performance. This supervisor follows the procedures of informal and formal appraisal, using information from the building principal and basic education supervisor to assist in establishing objectives for improving teacher performance. It must be emphasized, however, that the information from the basic education supervisor and the principal *does not* take the place of actual observation of the teaching process. The special education supervisor, because of his assumed expertise in the area of special education, is the only person who can fully assist the teacher in identifying and working toward the accomplishment of objectives that are content-oriented. The role of the basic education supervisor and building principal is to provide the special

Figure 25
Organizational Structure

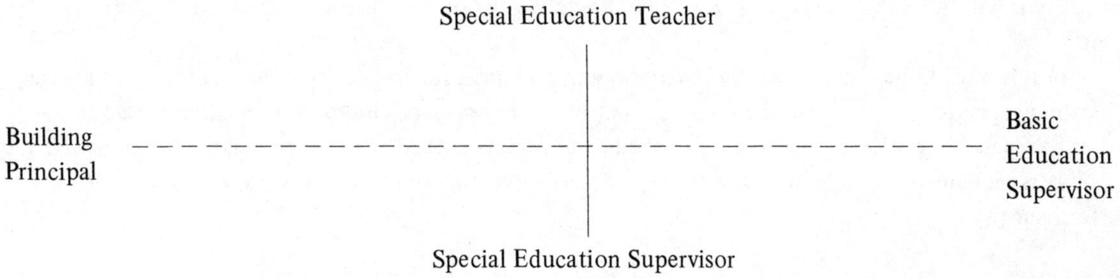

Special Education Teacher

Building
Principal

Basic
Education
Supervisor

Special Education Supervisor

— — — — Dotted line indicates consultative role

———— Solid line indicates total involvement in
the appraisal process

education supervisor with information on (1) the teacher's relationships with fellow staff members, (2) the teacher's observation of building regulations, and (3) the teacher's cooperation with fellow staff members in day-to-day activities. When the basic education supervisor and/or building principal feels that the teacher's difficulty is with teaching process or content, he should discuss the problem with the special education supervisor.

In this model, the basic education supervisor and building principal support the efforts of the special education supervisor. They assist the teacher in improving performance but do nothing that would detract from the teacher's relationship with the special education supervisor. It may be necessary from time to time for all personnel involved to hold a conference to discuss problems and progress relative to the teacher's performance.

Guidelines for Supervisors

Following are some guidelines which Redfern (1972) has suggested for principals, which are also applicable to supervisors or any personnel involved in teacher appraisal:

1. Avoid the "boss complex." Help the teacher feel that the principal doesn't consider himself foremost as a member of the "administrative hierarchy."
2. Clarify the role of the principal and teacher in the evaluation setting.
3. Seek to establish that both the teacher and the principal should be primarily concerned with the educational welfare of the pupils rather than their own self-interest.

4. Be conscious that the evaluator's (principal) personality as well as that of the evaluatee (teacher)—good or bad—will have an influence upon achievable results in the conference.

5. Strive for unity in leadership effort and action among all administrators in the building.

6. Be willing to let the teacher express his feelings in the conference without risk of censure or reprisal even if they are markedly different from those of the evaluator.

7. Provide for privacy.

8. Safeguard the confidential nature of any matter requiring it.

9. Avoid asking for opinions on the spot; allow time for consideration.

10. Strive for a climate of mutual respect.

11. Be prepared to take as well as to give.

12. Be honestly committed to the concept that teacher, principal, and supervisor are members of a team working for the best interests of a good educational program.

13. Take the initiative in encouraging the teacher to make constructive criticisms.

14. Provide the opportunity for the discussion of school problems.

15. Invite suggestions; when they are made, try to do something about them.

16. Don't give the teacher the brush-off when problems are presented.

17. Try to be aware of what the teacher is doing in his classes.

18. Don't talk too much; don't let the teacher talk too little.

The Appraisal Process

The goal throughout the appraisal process must be the improvement of performance and the promotion of professional development. Since supervisors share in their teachers' success or failure, evaluative efforts should be viewed as cooperative endeavors. The appraisal process should assist the teacher and supervisor to:

1. develop a clearer understanding of job expectancies;
2. establish long- and short-term objectives;
3. plan and work for the accomplishment of the above;
4. appraise job performance more accurately.

The appraisal process should be simple and comprehensible. Complicated procedures and voluminous paperwork do not help facilitate the program. According to Koontz (1971), all appraisal programs should satisfy a few basic requirements, and he suggests that the appraisal program should:

1. measure the right things
2. be operational
3. be objective
4. be acceptable
5. be constructive (p. 14).

Criteria Development

School officials cannot make a valid decision on a teacher's performance without initially defining the criteria for "good" teaching. "Each criterion is a standard for judging and the total criteria of teacher effectiveness should be derived from the goals of the educational system" (McNeil, 1971, p. 25). When the criteria are vague, school officials have no recourse but to base their appraisal of a teacher's professional competency on subjective feelings or the number of complaints and/or commendations received from parents and fellow staff members. Standards for good teaching will vary because each school system is unique. Therefore, the criteria should be recorded, and they should be (1) stated in precise, measurable terms, (2) relevant, and (3) used as the yardstick of excellence.

The foregoing will serve as a guide for the supervisor in determining indicators of effective teaching behavior. Of course, there must be agreement on the policies, procedures, and instruments to be used in the appraisal process, and the instruments must be as objective as possible.

Once the criteria have been established, a school district has some additional tasks that should be understood by the teachers prior to the implementation of the appraisal process. Teachers should not only be familiar with the criteria for good teaching but also be aware of the procedures to be followed in judging performance. Procedural statements should identify the "how, when, and where" of the appraisal process. It is suggested that the supervisor review the procedures with all teachers at a faculty meeting prior to the opening of school. The topics to be discussed at this meeting are shown in Figure 26.

Figure 26
Steps for Appraisal of Teacher Performance

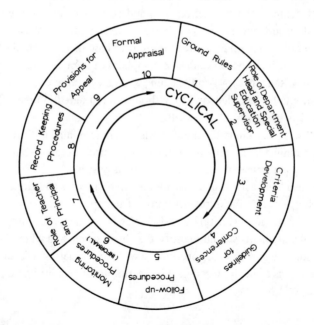

Informal Appraisal

To assist supervisors in avoiding capricious, arbitrary, and subjective discriminatory actions—such as nonreward or dismissal of teachers without providing due process—the appraisal procedure is divided into two parts, informal and formal. The informal phase consists of appraising teacher performance and assisting in overcoming areas of deficiency. Informal appraisal includes at least two observations each semester. These observations range from brief "pop in" visits to thirty-minute stays.

An important aspect of the informal phase is the early involvement of the teacher in the appraisal process. A staff orientation should take place during the first three weeks of the school term or, if possible, prior to the starting date of classes. It should serve to familiarize teachers, principals, and supervisors with the school's expectations of teacher competencies. The introductory session is recommended for teachers new to the school system. The following steps briefly outline the procedure involved in teacher orientation:

1. Notification of date of initial classroom observation
2. Initial observation of teacher by principal/special education supervisor
   a. Content of lesson
   b. Lesson objectives
   c. Level of questioning, i.e., knowledge, application, and evaluation
   d. Degree of student-teacher interaction
   e. Utilization of instructional methods and techniques

Initial Observation

The traditional role of the supervisor is to observe the teaching process. In this role, the supervisor must answer some basic questions:
1. Was the teacher prepared to teach?
2. Did the teacher arouse and maintain pupil interest?
3. Did the teacher's questions generate pupil interest and participation?
4. Did the teacher select appropriate instructional materials, and were the materials used effectively?
5. Did the teacher's verbal and nonverbal expressions reinforce desired pupil behavior?
6. Did the teacher provide activities for practicing and applying the skills taught?
7. Were there satisfactory interpersonal relationships between individual pupils, the teacher, and the group during the teaching-learning situation?

The purpose of the initial observation is to provide the supervisor with an accurate picture of the teacher's strengths and weaknesses so that the supervisor and teacher can work together to improve the teacher's performance. In observing, the supervisor must be attuned to the unique characteristics of the teacher's environment (encompassing general atmosphere of the building, the physical aspects of the building and classroom, the teacher's disposition toward placement) and strive not to be overinterpretative. The supervisor must strive to be objective and should have an objectively structured instrument for recording information concerning the teaching process (Appendix B).

Initial Conference

After the initial observation, a conference should be held. During this conference the teacher and supervisor play mutually supportive roles. The teacher's role is to:

1.   understand problems which affect performance;
2.   recognize the needs for growth and development;
3.   examine the job and determine what must be done to improve results.

The supervisor must:

1.   assure the teacher of assistance in accomplishing future objectives;
2.   open and maintain lines of communication;
3.   identify the teacher's strengths and weaknesses.

At the completion of the conference, the supervisor should make a written record of the proceedings. This record should note the teacher's strengths and weaknesses and suggest a program for improving the identified weaknesses. The supervisor should always give the teacher a copy of the original record. It is advisable that the teacher be asked to sign the written material. It must be emphasized that the teacher's signature does not indicate agreement with what has been written but merely that the material has been read. Such records serve a dual purpose: first, they remind the teacher and supervisor of their respective commitments made during the conference; second, a written record serves to protect the teacher's constitutional rights.

The initial conference between teacher and supervisor reveals areas which need to be improved. These improvements are stated as long- or short-term objectives, depending on the time required to achieve them. To this end, the teacher and supervisor must agree on a timetable for objective fulfillment.

Follow-Up Activities

The follow-up or monitoring activities require the supervisor to:
1. undertake periodic teacher observations;
2. provide the necessary supportive resources;
3. schedule future conferences to discuss teacher progress and make plans for subsequent follow-up activities.

The follow-up activities conform to the same format as the initial observation and conference. The primary purpose of these activities is to improve the teacher's performance by keeping the activities on target toward the established objectives and to provide necessary support to achieve those goals. The supervisor should always keep in mind first, that it may be necessary to revise some of the original objectives, since establishing objectives is a continuous process toward improving teacher performance, and second, that he must always proceed at the teacher's level of understanding. Additional objectives are established only as original goals are reached.

Two further points must be emphasized. First, a teacher's performance depends as much on the teaching situation as on personal attributes. Job satisfaction is positive reinforcement. Immediately the cry will be raised that "a teacher should be able to teach anywhere," but one can respond that, although teachers and pupils may have many things in common, they have individual teaching and learning styles. Can a given teacher be successful in every setting? We believe not. For example, a teacher may be appraised as excellent in a given situation; however, this attainment may be due to the level of administrative support, community expectations, organization of the school, and uniqueness of the pupils. The teacher's personality may also have played some role. Place that teacher in a situation where these variables no longer exist, and the teacher's performance may be adversely affected. Situational aspects, therefore, should be taken into consideration by the personnel appraising teacher performance. The second point is that the supervisor should use conferences as a means of reinforcing the teacher's strengths. The supervisor may play a Pygmalion-like role in helping the teacher's strengths. The supervisor should remember that high expectations tend to generate increased productivity. The key to improving the performance of teachers and other school personnel may be found in Eliza Doolittle's words:

> You see, really and truly, apart from the things anyone can pick up (the dressing and the proper way of speaking, and so on), the difference between a lady and a flower girl is not how she behaves, but how she's treated. I shall always be a flower girl to Professor Higgins, because he always treats me as a flower girl and always will, but I know I can be a lady to you because you treat me as a lady, and always will. (Shaw, 1967, p. 95)

Formal Appraisal

The formal process is viewed as being terminal, since it finalizes the teacher's progress for the year. There are generally two or more thirty-minute observations each year that do not require advance scheduling;

conferences should follow each observation. A synthesis of both the teacher's and the supervisor's perceptions should be forwarded to the appropriate personnel for inclusion in the teacher's personnel folder. Comments obtained from these observations are usually placed on the school system's formal appraisal form. It is important that this form be structured as objectively as possible.

Documentation

Teachers traditionally have had a negative view of the documentation of personnel, but this should not be the case since the process protects their rights. If it becomes evident that the nonrenewal or dismissal of a teacher may be necessary, documentation of problem areas or concerns must be initiated. The following guidelines may be helpful:

1. Observation of teaching
   a. Start as early in the year as possible;
   b. Identify problems;
   c. Inform teacher of your findings and expectations through conferences;
   d. Specify
      (1) acceptable performance level
      (2) corrective program
      (3) line of performance review;
2. The results of points 1b and 1d should be supplied to the teacher in writing, with the ad-

ministrator retaining a copy;

3. Utilize supervisory help through routine visits and special referrals to assist teacher in overcoming identified deficiencies;
4. Review performance (see 1d above);
5. Make written record of observation;
6. In conference, summarize observation of performance with teacher;
7. Make a written record of the conference; make note of dates of such meetings;
8. If satisfactory, retain record at school;
9. If unsatisfactory
   a. inform and schedule appropriate personnel into future meetings, and
   b. forward data to appropriate personnel with recommendation.

The acceptable performance level must be stated concretely; phrases such as "slight bit of improvement" should be avoided. An acceptable anecdotal report should always accompany documentation material. The teacher may or may not agree with the administrator's findings; therefore, there should be an established appeal procedure.

The observational schedule should be acceptable to all personnel involved, with the first observation coming early in the school year. Prior notice of specific deficiencies and assistance in improvement are important aspects of due process. Constant feedback is essential to the professional health of the teacher and supervisor. Neither can be comfortable without timely appraisal of "how we are doing." The "we" is very important.

Through a set of carefully documented records and continued observations, a teacher can be helped with increased attention and suggestion. But if there are no anecdotal reports to support the findings, as well as specific suggestions for improvement, the teacher's due process rights will be violated. Please note Appendix C carefully, as it is an example of carefully documented anecdotal teacher observational records.

Conclusion

Advocates of accountability and courts of law are demanding an appraisal system that utilizes objective criteria in judgment. In this is the assumption that the teacher is capable of making improvements or will continue to exhibit a high level of performance. The chances that the teacher will improve or continue at an expected level are enhanced if appraisal is carried out systematically in accordance with good planning, conscientious follow-through, and careful assessment of results. It is essential that all parties involved in the appraisal process accept and understand their responsibilities.

APPENDIX A

Teacher Evaluation Models

Teacher
  |
Principal

1. This is the most common model. In it only the teacher and principal are involved in the appraisal process. Its inherent weakness is the lack of involvement of the school district's support personnel.

Teacher
  |———— Supervisor
  |
Principal

2. This model is an expansion of the above and views the supervisor as appraiser. He is required to identify the the strengths and weaknesses of the teacher, and he is asked to suggest a corrective program for overcoming any deficiencies the teacher may have.

Teacher
  |– – – Supervisor
  |
Principal

3. This model views the supervisor as a support to both the principal and teacher. The supervisor's role is to do nothing which would detract from his relationship with the teacher. Therefore, the supervisor only assists the teacher in improving and does not submit any written reports containing negative statements about the teacher's performance.

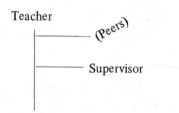

Teacher

(Peers)

Supervisor

Principal

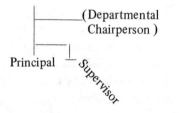

Teacher

(Departmental
Chairperson)

Principal   Supervisor

4.   This model utilizes the expertise of the supervisor and
     encourages the teacher's peers to give positive assistance
     to the teacher in overcoming any difficulties he may be
     having. This model is especially useful in team-teaching,
     differentiated staffing, and nongraded situations, where
     all of the teachers engage in a self-critiquing cycle.
     Teachers observe one another (similar to the supervision)
     and suggest how each teacher can improve, but they do
     not write anything which would destroy their working
     relationship. This model requires that an extremely high
     level of trust exist between teachers.

5.   This model utilizes the expertise of the department
     chairperson. The chairperson, however, should assist
     only in the improvement of performance by posi-
     tively assisting teachers in eliminating deficiencies they
     may have.

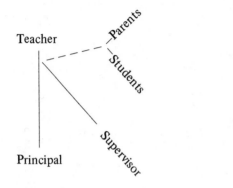

6.   This model is in its embryonic stage and is utilized by only a few school districts because of the questions it raises.

Unless there are clear guidelines which specify the role of parents and students in the appraisal process, a school district should be very cautious. This system can have a negative effect on the teachers' morale. (Virginia Department of Education, 1972, p. 57-58).

– – – – – –   dotted line indicates consultative role for both the teacher and principal

——————   solid line indicates total involvement in the appraisal process

Reprinted from the Tentative Report Evaluation of Personnel, State Department of Education, Richmond, Va., 1972, pp. 57-58.

APPENDIX B

Evaluating Classroom Teaching

Teacher _____ School _____ Date _____

Observer_____ Position _____ Date _____

Title of Lesson _____

Objective _____

_____

_____

Directions: Evaluate items according to the teacher's degree of accomplishment. Use space for comments to support your appraisal of the teacher.

Rating:	VG	-	Very good performance
	G	-	Good performance
	F	-	Fair performance
	P	-	Poor performance
	VP	-	Very poor performance

1.   Preparation of Lesson

   a.   Objectives stated in measurable terms

VP	P	F	G	VG

   b.   Individualization

VP	P	F	G	VG

   c.   Appropriateness of subject

VP	P	F	G	VG

   Comments:

2.   Classroom Organization

   a.   Learning centers in classroom

VP	P	F	G	VG

   b.   Clarity of presentation

VP	P	F	G	VG

   c.   Attractiveness of class

VP	P	F	G	VG

   Comments:

3.   Management of Classroom

    a.   Position of reinforcement of student behavior

VP	P	F	G	VG

    b.   Democratic class environment

VP	P	F	G	VG

    Comments:

4.   Level of Questioning

    a.   Pupil participation

VP	P	F	G	VG

    b.   Rapport between teacher and student

VP	P	F	G	VG

    Comments:

5.   Utilization of Instructional Materials

VP	P	F	G	VG

Reprinted from "Evaluating Classroom Teaching," The Department of Agriculture (Columbus, Ohio: Ohio State University).

APPENDIX C

The following illustrates an unacceptable teaching situation and the principal's subsequent notification of the Personnel Department. This report was based on several detailed observations made by each of five qualified observers:

The following statement pertains to the teaching performance of Mr. _____ _____ , Special Education teacher, _____ School.

During the first four weeks of the 1969-70 school year, as principal I observed Mr. _____ and his classwork on an informal basis. I did not make any extended observations; rather they were of a short unannounced "drop in" type. Each time I visited the classroom I noticed a lack of discipline and educational structure. I commented several times to Mr. _____ that he would have to exercise more control over his students and that he would have to try to individualize his instruction to provide for the wide range of individual differences which existed among his children. Mr. _____ had a habit of referring to the children in such a manner as to imply that they were unable to learn. I reminded Mr. _____ that slow learning children were usually normal in every respect except they learned at a slower rate. I also told Mr. _____ that he perhaps empathized with the children to such an extent that he excused behavior that would not normally have been tolerated.

During the month of October I began to become quite concerned with the learning situation which existed in Mr. _____'s classroom. I began to visit the classroom for longer periods of time. I observed the class on two separate occasions for thirty minutes or longer, once on 14 October, and again on 29 October.

On 14 October I saw basically the same lack of structure and control that I had witnessed before. There was no individualized instruction, and children were permitted to wander about the room at will. After the observation I informed Mr. _____ that he must take firm control of the children so that a learning situation could be established.

On 29 October I again observed Mr. _____'s class for about forty-five minutes. I saw the same situation which had been present at every other visitation. Children were given a lecture type of presentation, and many were wandering about the room at will. Several children made insulting comments to Mr. _____ which he ignored.

During the month of October Mr. _____'s teaching performance was observed twice by Miss _____. Miss _____ stated after each observation that the situation was impossible and that little, if any, learning was taking place in Mr. _____'s class. Miss _____ had made many suggestions to Mr. _____ concerning curriculum and discipline. To this date, I have seen no evidence of any significant improvement.

On 23 October, Mr. _____, Miss _____ and I had a conference concerning Mr. _____'s teaching performance. It was stated that Mr. _____ must show immediate progress or he should consider not teaching at all. Again, the focus of criticism was the lack of class control and the lack of a structured learning situation. After the conference Mr. _____ asked me to be patient with him and allow him time to get everything organized. I told him that there was no more time, that he had had two months to get organized, and now he would have to show immediate progress.

During the month of October Mr. _____ _____, Supervising Principal, also visited

Mr. _____'s class. Mr. _____ also stated that the teaching was unsatisfactory and that the situation within the classroom was not conducive to an effective learning process.

Mrs. _____ _____, a psychologist with the Board of Education, has visited Mr. _____'s classroom on several occasions. Mrs. _____ has made suggestions to Mr. _____ regarding his class and his methods of dealing with the children's behavior. Mrs. _____ has stated that she can see only a slight bit of improvement.

I feel, on the basis of what I have observed and many futile attempts that have been made to improve Mr. _____'s teaching performance, that he should not be allowed to continue teaching at _____ .

_____
Principal

_____
School

Immediately after this report was made, a meeting was set, to which the teacher invited his representative. A report of that meeting was filed:

17 November 1969

On 13 November 1969, a conference was held concerning the teaching performance of Mr. _____ _____, Special Education Teacher, _____ School. Representative; Dr. _____ _____ , Assistant Superintendent for Personnel; Miss _____ , Supervisor; and Mr.

_____ _____, Principal, _____ School were present.

    Mr. _____ was informed that his teaching was generally unsatisfactory and the following specific deficiences were noted:

    (A)   a lack of meaningful educational structure in the classroom

    (B)   poor discipline

    (C)   poor control of children

    (D)   lack of individualized instruction and small group work

    It was also noted that five persons had observed Mr. _____'s teaching and all five persons had mentioned the same deficiencies as noted above.

Mr. _____ asked for help in the following forms:

    (A)   consultant help

    (B)   suggestions for curriculum and class management

    (C)   additional materials

    (D)   permission to visit professional persons who might demonstrate additional help

    (E)   any other help necessary

It was agreed that additional consultant help would be made available. Mr. _____ will be permitted to visit other classes and consult with other teachers in an attempt to gain useful ideas. Each week Mr. _____ will discuss his lesson plans for the week with the principal. Additional materials will be procured as soon as possible, and every effort will be made to upgrade Mr. _____'s teaching performance.

It was made clear to Mr. _____ that a meaningful educational structure must be in evidence. Discipline and control of the children must be initiated and maintained at all times. Weekly lesson plans will be drawn up and maintained. These improvements must take place immediately or more drastic steps will be taken.

_____

Principal

I have read the foregoing statement and have been given a copy.

_____

Date _____ 11/18/69 _____

Part 3:
A Simplified Evaluation Process for Classroom Teachers
Robert F. Algozzine, Sandra K. Alper, David A. Sabatino

Introduction

Increasing pressure is being placed on special educators to provide evidence that efforts with exceptional children are beneficial (Lessenger, 1971). If charged to communicate the effectiveness of their programs, they must (1) state precisely what outcomes the program is designed to facilitate and (2) present evidence that the outcomes have, in fact, been produced. These demands on classroom teachers for accountability necessitate the use of an evaluation process; but the principles of evaluation may well be one area where pre-service academic preparation was limited or nonexistent for most teachers.

The special educator in the classroom or resource room, faced with the day-to-day reality of teaching children, does not need to learn another obtuse theoretical model or be overwhelmed by the academic prose in which most evaluation articles are written. Nor does he need what Ohrtman (1972) has aptly described: the "in and out researcher . . . gets two sets of kids, do A to one group and B to another, compare them and one group does better at the .01 level—then off to the next project" (p. 377). Vergason (1973) and Jones (1973) have delineated many of the problems associated with the evaluation process. All too often there has been more effort required than value provided. Jones (1973) writes that before any school district should presume to devise a system of accountability for special education, the following questions should be answered:

1. What are the common and specific goals to which the teacher and school are striving?
2. What student, community, or societal need inventories are available, on paper, to indicate change strategies that should be undertaken?
3. What specific and measurable performance objectives have been written down that would enable parents, students, and teachers to understand the minimum expectations of the unstructured programs?
4. What analysis of the existing delivery system is available to indicate that the current educational input approach is manageable as compared to the alternatives?

Vergason (1973) states that one area in which special educators can be more definitive about their program is that of standardized terminology.

Evaluation Terminology Used in This Model

Goals refer to the major aims to be accomplished during a specified period. In order to achieve an overall goal, objectives are necessary.

Behavioral Objectives are measurable, and generally contain three aspects: (1) what target behavior is to be modified; (2) to what degree; and (3) in what length of time. In all decision-making processes, a hierarchical structure of sequential objectives increases the probability of successfully achieving the goals. A clear distinction between goals and objectives must always be made. Goals are met by the achievement of appropriate objectives, which means that the process for determining goals and objectives might take several forms. The method used should be appropriate for the scope of the project and the facilities available. It is important to note that goals and objectives may be appropriate for one situation and not for another, and that they may have to be revised as the evaluation procedure continues through time.

Goals and objectives are always determined in the final analysis by teacher judgment. It is that judgment which distinguishes a teacher and a professional from a technician, who merely works from a set of given rules. While the model presented here can provide information regarding the appropriateness of the objectives, often it is feasible only after the evaluation process has begun. The objectives are appropriate only if they enable the proposed goals to be achieved.

Instructional Strategies call for the specification of a teaching method or materials to achieve a desired goal or objective. Frequently the term "strategy" can be used interchangeably with "technique" or "task." In other words, a well-defined teaching approach will be used as an enabling step to achieve a desired objective. Generally speaking instructional strategies are a specified teaching procedure (method and material) developed to obtain a desired objective.

Criterion is the standard by which the objective is successfully satisfied. Objectives are usually written to include (1) level of achievement statement and (2) time of achievement statement for the (3) specified target behavior to be modified. Criterion-referenced measurement specifies the absolute level or quality of performance of a student on some assessment task (Jones, 1973).

Feedback is the information obtained on daily performance, or the child's learning efficiency and effectiveness at specified periods. It is judgmental to the instructional progress, providing a green light to continue the same objective, or a red light to stop and examine the objective and/or strategy being used.

Judgment is the professional opinion that is rendered that successful progress is being made or that changes in instructional objectives and/or strategies are warranted.

A Simplistic Evaluation Process

The evaluation process presented here can be viewed as a simplistic means of understanding what is happening. It contains three major stages: the presituational, the situational, and the postsituational. During the first stage (presituational) the goals and objectives of the program are defined.

During the situational stage, data is collected which allows judgments (valuations) to be made (for example, statements about particular behavioral objectives which demonstrate attainment of the desired goals). This step is essential if the evaluation is to provide any information regarding objectives, goals, and their attainment. Such information may be collected by questionnaires, interviews, observations, etc. The information collected during this stage must be descriptively prepared so that its meaning and utility will be apparent. This involves representing graphically or otherwise the results of the "valuations" and defines the next step of the model. If the goals are not being met, the teacher can relate this information back to the first stage, and either new objectives can be formulated or new goals can be agreed upon. If, however, the goals are being met, the teacher then proceeds to the postsituational stage.

The postsituational stage involves determining which parts of the program are effective for obtaining the objectives and goals. The major function of this stage is to establish the relationship between the program goals and the successful achievement of objectives that lead to these goals.

Figure 27
Evaluation Process

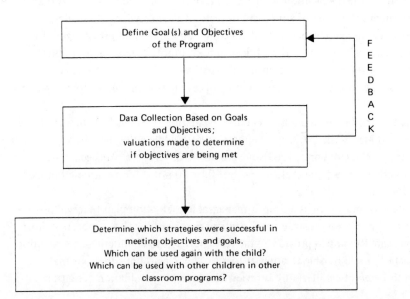

To summarize, the presituational stage involves defining the goals and objectives of the program to be evaluated. In the situational stage, information is collected, described, and related to the desired objectives and goals. In the postsituational stage, the obtained information is compared to what is intended.

Stufflebeam (1972) has recently assumed a position similar to that of Scriven (1967), who says that the fundamental goal of evaluation determines the value of a program or instructional activity. Originally, Stufflebeam (1969) saw evaluation as a systematic process of "delineating, obtaining, and providing useful information for judging decision alternatives" (p. 129). The CIPP (Context, Input, Process, and Product) Model he developed represents a frame of reference for presenting alternatives to decision makers and can provide a classroom teacher with information about the program; but this evaluation model is too complex for daily use in the classroom.

Other evaluators have discussed plans for curriculum and course evaluation (Cronbach, 1963; Krathwohl, 1965; Lindvall et al., 1964; Michael and Metfessel, 1967; and Popham, 1969), while still others have presented theoretical evaluation models (Aikin, 1969; Hammond, 1969; and Provus, 1969). These plans generally represent similar processes for conducting educational evaluations, but they do not offer a simplified procedure for the already overburdened classroom teacher to use.

What the practicing special educator must have is a simple, manageable evaluation plan that will provide information and feedback for determining whether instructional strategies are working and, if not, why not. The model presented in this section is an attempt to provide a practical approach to conducting an evaluation which follows a logical plan. A teacher should be able to apply it to everyday classroom situations that require evaluative decisions. When the theoretical literature is reviewed concerning evaluation designs, it becomes evident that there are not as yet any models which provide practical evaluation devices for teachers.

A Practical Evaluation Design

The following example illustrates how the proposed evaluation design might be implemented by a special educator to evaluate a unit on word-recognition skills for a learning-disabled child. While we are not recommending that a phonics approach be used to teach word-recognition skills in all situations, we merely use it here as an illustrative example. The steps within each stage are not all-inclusive but represent some possible choices in a sequenced flow of instructional activities. It remains for the teacher to determine those strategies which will be most effective for the individual child.

I.   *Presituational Stage*
The purpose of this stage is to state clearly the goals and objectives.
— Gather assessment information on the child from other personnel (for example, check school records, test results, other teachers' reports, etc., to gather any information which might pertain to the overall goal).
— Administer teacher-made informal tests to determine child's level of functioning (response to previous instruction). (For example, the child can recognize letter combinations but does not recognize words.)
— Specify behaviors in need of remediation (recognizing initial consonant blends, for example).
— Specify instructional strategies (methods and materials) to be used in achieving the behavioral objectives

(task analysis, behavior modification principles to be used, types of remedial materials to be used).
- Develop a hierarchy of sequential behavioral objectives based on the above information regarding the child's strengths and weaknesses. (For example, the child will recognize that *th, sh,* and *ch* represent different sounds and will then be able to identify these sounds orally from a series of words, i.e., shoe, choose, thick, etc.). At this point the teacher will have defined goal(s) within an instructional area and specified a sequence of behavioral objectives which should lead the child toward the mastery of the major aims of the instructional program.

II.   *Situational Stage*

The purpose of this stage is to collect and describe data based on the goals and objectives defined in Stage 1.
- Administer teacher-made, criterion-referenced tests to determine if the child has mastered the behavioral objectives being taught currently. For example, the teacher presents a list of words. The child has to orally identify all the *sh* words with 80 percent accuracy.
- Gather information from the child, parents, other teachers, etc. This could be attitudinal information on study habits at home, etc.
- If necessary, consult with others, e.g. resource teacher, supervisor, school psychologist. Self-determination of the classroom climate (child-teacher-curriculum interaction) may be helpful at this point.
- Feed back this information to the original objectives in order to determine the student's performance in interacting with the curriculum according to the standards specified.

At this point the teacher may want to ask questions, such as, "Are the objectives being met? Are the behavioral objectives, teaching materials, and instructional strategies appropriate for the child?" This information can be used to determine if continuation, modification, or termination of the original objectives is warranted. It might be determined, for example, that the parents need to work with the child more at home, that behavior modification is effective in maintaining the child's attention, that the child prefers free time as reinforcement rather than candy, that the child is not yet able to combine letter blends into meaningful words. This type of information leads to the next stage of the model.

III.   *Postsituational Stage*

The purpose of this stage is to make comparisons, predictions, and generalizations based on the data obtained in the situational stage as it relates to achieving the desired goals.

— Administer criterion-referenced tests to determine where the child is functioning now in relation to the hierarchy of behavioral objectives. How do strengths and weaknesses change as remediation is applied, and what new goals and behavioral objectives seem appropriate? (For example, the child can now discriminate between *sh* and *ch* sounds within words but cannot generalize this skill to reading orally words that contain the *sh* and *ch* blends.

— Determine which instructional strategies were successful with the child and which were not. Which ones, totally or in part, can be used again as work is initiated on new goals and objectives? (For example, the child likes to work in small groups or with one other child and has more success here than when left to work alone.)

— Determine which techniques might be successful for use with other children in the class (the teacher decides that task analysis, for example, can be used in many other instructional areas).

The answers to these questions provide the classroom teacher with evaluative information about the program. They tell which aspects of the teaching plan were effective, and they allow record keeping of the child's progress.

The following is an example of an evaluation worksheet which may be used by the teacher in order to carry out the instructional objectives proposed.

Evaluation Worksheet

I.   Presituational Information
     —   What do you want the child to learn? (goal or objectives)

     _____

     —   What does the child do now with regard to what s(he) is to learn?

     _____

     —   What should you do to teach or enable the child's learning the stated goal or objective?

     _____

II. Situational Information
     —   What is the effect of teaching on the stated goal or objective (as determined by the child's
          performance)?

     _____

—   Are modifications necessary at this point?

    ____ Yes. Is the strategy appropriate ____? Is your assessment of the child's skills appropriate ____?
Are your goals and objectives appropriate ____?

    ____ No. Go to the next stage.

III.   Postsituational Information

—   What was the reason for the success?

_____

—   Which strategies were most successful with the child?

_____

—   Can this be generalized? _____

—   Which strategies can be used again with the same child or with other children to teach other skills?

_____

Conclusion

If special educators are to increase their instructional accountability, they must be provided with the necessary tools and an environment that enables them to evaluate their programs. Too frequently teachers have been faulted in scapegoat fashion for the failure of difficult-to-teach children to interact successfully with curriculum when they were without materials, stimulation, and any assistance from other disciplines. The model presented here is, of course, not a panacea. Evaluation is a process; it is not in itself curriculum content. An evaluation model such as this should, however, enable special educators to carry out a simple evaluation process in the classroom and to generate accountable records of instructional efforts with children. Such a plan means that more precise use of curriculum can be stated—what is needed, how to use it, and when it works best.

LEARNING   OBJECTIVES
Chapter 10

Part I

Cognitive Objectives

After carefully reading Part I, you will be able to:
1) Define the term "evaluation."
2) Identify the factors involved in sound policy decision-making.
3) Classify the major steps in evaluating an educational program (Stufflebeam, 1969).
4) State the four types of evaluation as set down by Stufflebeam.
5) Select criteria (standards) for judging the evaluation activity.
6) Restate the functions of "context evaluation."
7) Identify the functions of "input evaluation."
8) Determine the functions of "process evaluation."
9) Identify the functions of "product evaluation."
10) Analyze the basic structures of Stakes and Scriven's models for evaluation.

LEARNING   OBJECTIVES
Chapter 10

Affective Objectives

After carefully reading Part I, the author intends that you will:

1)   Recognize the unique set of problems to the evaluation in the area of Learning Disabilities.
2)   Become aware of critically analyzing sources within the program, in order to clearly understand the program's problem.
3)   Distinguish the factors that should be kept in mind when developing the goods objectives in accordance with the identified problems.
4)   Value the principle of programatic evaluation.

READER'S NOTES

[Refer to p. _____ in manual.]

[Refer to p. _____ .]

[Refer to p. _____ .]

PROGRAMMATIC EVALUATION PRIMER

Learning disabilities present a unique set of problems to the evaluation dilemma. Learning-disabled children are:

1. _____

_____

2. _____

_____

The purpose of this part of the chapter is to emphasize program evaluation. Evaluation has been defined as: _____

_____

_____

_____

Programatic evaluation gives the educational decision maker a foundation on which to base policy and decisions.

Some factors involved in sound policy decision-making are:

1. _____

2. _____

PROGRAMMATIC EVALUATION PRIMER

3. _____

4. _____

Stufflebeam offers a plan for evaluating educational programs. The following block offers the major steps in the evaluation process. The reader should fill in the important functions under each step.

[Refer to p. _____ .]

_____
A.   Focusing the Evaluation
_____

_____
B.   Collection of Information
_____

_____
C.   Organization of Information
_____

READER'S NOTES

PROGRAMMATIC EVALUATION PRIMER

D.   Analysis of Information

E.   Reporting of Information

F.   Administration of the Evaluation

The supervisor's first task is to develop criteria (standards) for judging the evaluation activity. These could include:

1. _____
2. _____
3. _____
4. _____
5. _____
6. _____

[Refer to p. _____ .]

READER'S NOTES

PROGRAMMATIC EVALUATION PRIMER

7. _____
8. _____
9. _____
10. _____
11. _____

CONTENT EVALUATION

Once the criteria are developed, the supervisor should determine needed changes in the program, unmet needs of the learners, and causes for these. These causes can be found by analyzing the following sources:

1. _____
2. _____
3. _____
4. _____
5. _____
6. _____

[Refer to p. _____ .]

READER'S NOTES

PROGRAMMATIC EVALUATION PRIMER

7. _____
8. _____

At this point the supervisor should begin to establish goals and objectives with a clear understanding of the program's present problems.

INPUT EVALUATION

The supervisor's next task is to determine how to utilize available resources to meet the stated goals and objectives. This involves the supervisor identifying and assessing:

1. _____
2. _____
3. _____

In essence the supervisor collects information in order to decide whether additional resources will be needed to reach the goals and objectives. A great many decisions reached in

[Refer to p. _____ .]

PROGRAMMATIC EVALUATION PRIMER

this stage involve such things as scheduling, staffing, and budget allocation.

PROCESS   EVALUATION

After a strategy has been selected, the next step is to begin *continuous feedback* of the program's effectiveness. The supervisor's responsibility is to take corrective steps that will eliminate sources of potential failure so that the resources, staff, time, etc. continue toward stated objectives.

PRODUCT   EVALUATION

The last phase determines whether the objectives were met. If the objectives were not satisfied, product evaluation should provide the supervisor with insight into the reasons for failure. Once the *information is collected,* it is compared with that obtained from context and process evaluation in order to determine the changes which have been made by the program and the factors probably responsible for those changes.

[Refer to p. _____ .]

READER'S NOTES

PROGRAMMATIC EVALUATION PRIMER

Two other models were discussed by the authors. Below describe the major components of each.

[Refer to p. _____ .]

STAKES MODEL

Sources of information: _____

Antecedents: _____

Transaction: _____

Outcomes: _____

EVALUATION ACTS

Judgmental: _____

Descriptive: _____

PROGRAMMATIC EVALUATION PRIMER

Intents _____

Observations _____

SCRIVEN'S MODEL
Formative: _____

Summative: _____

Intrinsic: _____

Pay-off: _____

DEFINITIONS:
1. Congruence: _____

2. Logical Contingencies (LC): _____

3. Observation Contingencies (OC): _____

LEARNING OBJECTIVES
Chapter 10

Part II

Cognitive Objectives

After carefully reading this part, you will be able to:

1) Analyze the various models for teacher appraisal.
2) Restate the rationale for using the special education supervisor in assisting the LD teacher in the assessment process.
3) Identify the suggested criteria for comparing your teacher appraisal process.
4) Justify the need for "precise and measurable" criteria for "good teaching" before beginning a teacher appraisal program.
5) Identify the purposes and functions of "informal appraisal."
6) Identify the purpose and functions of "formal appraisal."
7) Justify the utilization of the "documentation process" in protecting the rights of all parties involved in formal appraisal.

LEARNING   OBJECTIVES
Chapter 10

Affective Objectives

After carefully reading this part, the author intends that you will:

1)   Be aware of the guidelines suggested for building principals and other supervisory personnel involved in the teacher appraisal.

2)   Determine what a teacher appraisal program should accomplish for both teacher and supervisor.

3)   Recognize that complicated procedures and voluminous paperwork do not help facilitate a teacher appraisal program.

4)   Value the principle of involving all parties concerned (teacher, principal, supervisor) in the teacher appraisal program.

5)   Value the principle of teacher appraisal.

READER'S NOTES

TEACHER   APPRAISAL   PRIMER

One of the recurring issues in the performance appraisal of special education teachers is to whom and in what chain of command are they responsible. Traditionally, special education teachers are hired through a Special Education Department in a school district or a regional administrative structure. Then they are assigned to a building. The "who" they are responsible to usually is an odd arrangement and generally is an unwritten rule.

The MLDS proposes the following organizational structure of the different personnel who might be involved in the performance appraisal of special eduation teachers:

[Refer to p. _____ in manual.]

READER'S NOTES

[Refer to p. _____ .]

[Refer to p. _____ .]

[Refer to p. _____ .]

TEACHER APPRAISAL PRIMER

Within this structure, the special education supervisor is
primarily responsible for _____
_____
_____

In this model the basic education supervisor and building
principal follow several guidelines suggested by the author.
Among these are: _____
_____
_____
_____

Redfern (1972) has also suggested some general guidelines
for principals, which are also applicable to supervisors or any
personnel involved in teacher appraisal. Please list some of the
more important guidelines as you perceive them:
_____
_____
_____

READER'S NOTES   **TEACHER APPRAISAL PRIMER**

_____
_____
_____
_____
_____
_____

The reasons for appraisal programs are many, but evaluative efforts should be viewed as a cooperative endeavor. For this reason, all parties should benefit from an appraisal program. The program should assist the teacher and supervisor to:

[Refer to p. _____ .]

1. _____
2. _____
3. _____
4. _____

Koontz (1971) suggests that all appraisal programs should meet some basic requirements. He suggests that the evaluator

TEACHER APPRAISAL PRIMER

of an appraisal program would do well to compare his program
with the following criteria:

[Refer to p. _____ .]

1. _____
2. _____
3. _____
4. _____
5. _____

The need for school officials to set a standard for "good
teaching" is vital. The criteria should be recorded in writing
and:

[Refer to p. _____ .]

1. _____
2. _____
3. _____

These serve in aiding the supervisor to find effective teaching
behaviors. Teachers should not only be familiar with the district
criteria for "good teaching," but also know the procedures to

READER'S NOTES

[Refer to p. _____ .]

[Refer to p. _____ .]

TEACHER APPRAISAL PRIMER

be followed in judging their performance. Procedural statements should identify the _____ , _____ , and _____ of the process.

In the following activity, the two phases of appraisal will be presented. (Informal/Formal Appraisal). Listed under each is a set of topics discussed by the author. The reader should fill in the definitions and/or explanations to each topic listed.

INFORMAL APPRAISAL

OBSERVATIONS _____
_____

STAFF ORIENTATION _____
_____

INITIAL OBSERVATION _____
_____

READER'S NOTES

TEACHER APPRAISAL PRIMER

INITIAL CONFERENCE _____
_____

OBSERVATIONAL TECHNIQUES _____
_____

FOLLOW-UP ACTIVITIES _____
_____

FORMAL APPRAISAL

FORMAL APPRAISAL FORM _____
_____

DOCUMENTATION _____
_____

DEFINITIONS:

[Refer to p. _____ .]

1.   "Good teaching criteria": _____
_____

READER'S NOTES

[Refer to p. _____ .]

[Refer to p. _____ .]

[Refer to p. _____ .]

[Refer to p. _____ .]

TEACHER APPRAISAL PRIMER

2. Observational Techniques: _____
    _____

3. Microteaching: _____
    _____

4. Interaction-Analysis: _____
    _____

5. Appeal Procedure: _____
    _____

L E A R N I N G   O B J E C T I V E S
Chapter 10

Part III

Cognitive Objectives

After carefully reading this part of the chapter, you will be able to:

1)   Identify the different phases of the evaluation model utilized by classroom teachers.
2)   Define the terminology used in the evaluation model.
3)   Demonstrate the use of this evaluation model by creating an illustrative example based on your instructional experience.

LEARNING OBJECTIVES
Chapter 10

Affective Objectives

After reading this part of the chapter, the author intends that you will:

1) Be aware of the questions that should be answered before creating a system of accountability for special education.

2) Value the principle of stated outcomes and evidence of fulfilling those outcomes in the daily instructional program.

EVALUATION PRIMER

A trend in educational accountability is taking place in our public school systems. Increasing pressure is being placed on special educators to provide evidence that their efforts with exceptional children are beneficial (Lessenger, 1971). As stated in the chapter, special educators may communicate the effectiveness of their programs by:

1. _____

_____

[Refer to p. _____ in manual.]

2. _____

_____

A basic reality in this infant movement of accountability is the appearance of obtuse theoretical models which are impractical for the everyday functions of the already overburdened classroom teacher. Several questions must be answered before considering the implementation of a program of accountability. The author considers four questions to be vital before considering devising a system of accountability:

READER'S NOTES

[Refer to p. _____ .]

[Refer to p. _____ .]

EVALUATION PRIMER

1. _____
_____
2. _____
_____
3. _____
_____
4. _____
_____

When discussing this simplified evaluation model for classroom teachers' usage, it is of the utmost importance to understand its terminology. The reader should define the following terms:

Goals: _____
_____

Behavioral Objectives: _____
_____
_____

READER'S NOTES

EVALUATION   PRIMER

Instructional Strategies: _____

_____

_____

_____

Criteria: _____

_____

_____

Feedback: _____

_____

Judgment: _____

_____

The evaluation model presented in this chapter can be viewed
as a simple means of understanding what is happening in the
classroom. It contains three major stages:

1. _____
2. _____
3. _____

[Refer to p. _____ .]

READER'S NOTES

[Refer to p. _____ .]

[Refer to p. _____ .]

[Refer to p. _____ .]

EVALUATION PRIMER

Each of these stages serves a specific task the classroom teacher is to perform in order to evaluate the instructional program. For instance, during the first stage, _____ _____ , goals and objectives of the program are defined.

During the second stage, _____ _____ data is collected and prepared in descriptive form. As the data is graphically or otherwise formulated, professional judgments are arrived at concerning the attainment of goals and objectives. Based on these professional judgments, the process returns to the original stage in order to move into the third stage if the goals and objectives have been judged not to have been fulfilled. The third stage is known as the _____ stage. This stage involves comparing the actual outcomes with what was intended. Distinguishing successful objectives from those that were not fulfilled is a prime example of this stage.

EVALUATION PRIMER

The reader, at this point, should review the section entitled "A Practical Evaluation Design." This section gives an illustrative example of the evaluation model in actual process. After reviewing this section, set up your own example based on experience in teaching a particular skill, concept, or unit. Use the block below for setting up your model.

PRESITUATIONAL PHASE:
GOAL(S) _____

_____

_____

_____

OBJECTIVE(S) _____

_____

_____

_____

READER'S NOTES

EVALUATION PRIMER

SITUATIONAL PHASE:
DATA COLLECTION _____

_____
_____
_____
_____
_____
_____
_____
_____

POSTSITUATIONAL PHASE:
GENERALIZATIONS, COMPARISONS, PREDICTIONS (you
will have to use a certain amount of speculation for this
activity). _____

_____
_____
_____

Bibliography

Abrams, J., & Belmont, H. Different approaches to the remediation of severe reading disability in children. *Journal of Learning Disabilities,* 1969, *2,* 136-141.

Ackerman, Walter I. Teacher competence and pupil change. *Harvard Educational Review,* 1954, *24,* 273-289.

Adelman, Howard S. Remedial classroom instruction revisited. *Journal of Special Education,* 1971, *5,* 311-322.

_____ . The resource room concept: Bigger than a room! *Journal of Special Education,* 1972, *6,* 361-367.

Agranowitz, A., & McKeown, M. *Aphasia handbook for adults and children.* Springfield, Ill.: Charles C. Thomas, 1964.

Aikin, M. C. Evaluation theory development. *Evaluation Comment,* 1969, *2,* 2-7.

Alsop, M. *Programming for reading disabilities in juvenile delinquents.* Paper presented at the Convention for the Association for Children with Learning Disabilities, Detroit, Mich., March 1973.

Anandam, Kamala, & Williams, Robert L. A model for consultation with the classroom teacher on behavior management. *The School Counselor,* 1971, *18,* 253-259.

Ariel, A. Behavior therapy for self-direction. (Doctoral dissertation, University of Southern California, 1971) *Dissertation Abstracts International,* 1972, *32,* 4408-A.

Atthowe, J., & Krasner, L. *The systematic application of contingent reinforcement procedures (token economy) in a large social setting: A psychiatric ward.* Paper read at the American Psychiatric Association Meeting, Chicago, Illinois, 1965.

Ausubel, David Paul. *Theory and problems of child development.* New York: Grune and Stratton, 1957.

Ayres, A. J. *Effect of sensorimotor activity on perception and learning in the neurologically handicapped child.* Los Angeles: University of Southern California Press, 1968.

Baer, D. M. Laboratory control of thumbsucking by withdrawal and reinstatement of reinforcement. *Journal of Experimental Analysis of Behavior,* 1962, *5,* 525-528.

Balow, B. The long term effect of remedial reading instruction. *Reading Teacher,* 1965, *18,* 581-586.

Banantyne, A. Diagnosing learning disabilities and writing remedial prescriptions. *Journal of Learning Disabilities,* 1969, *1,* 242-249.

Bandura, Albert. *Principles of behavior modification.* New York: Holt, Rinehart and Winston, 1969.

Banghart, Frank W. *Educational Systems Analysis.* London: The Macmillan Co., 1969.

Bangs, J. Preschool language education for the brain-damaged child. *The Volta Review,* 1957, *59,* 19-29, 39.

Barry, H. *The young aphasic child: Evaluation and training.* Washington, D.C.: Alexander Graham Bell Association for the Deaf, Inc., 1961.

Barsch, R. Counseling the parents of the brain-damaged child. *Journal of Rehabilitation,* 1961, *27,* 26-27, 40-42.

_____ . *A movigenic curriculum.* Madison, Wisc.: Bureau for Handicapped Children, 1965.

_____ . *A perceptual-motor curriculum.* (Vol. 1). Seattle: Special Child Publications, 1967.

Bateman, B. An educator's view of a diagnostic approach to learning disorders. In J. Hellmuth (Ed.), *Learning Disorders.* (Vol. 1). Seattle: Special Child Publications, 1965.

_____ . *The essentials of teaching.* San Rafael, Calif.: Dimensions Publishing Co., 1971.

Bates, L. Children with perceptual problems may also lag developmentally. *Journal of Learning Disabilities,* 1969, *2,* 205-208.

Beck, G. R. et al. Educational aspects of cognitive-perceptual-motor deficits in emotionally disturbed children. *Psychology in the Schools,* 1965, *2,* 233-238.

Beck, R., & Talkington, L. Frostig training with Headstart children. *Perceptual and Motor Skills,* 1970, *30,* 521-522.

Becker, W. *An empirical basis for change in education: Selections on behavior psychology for teachers.* Palo Alto, Calif.: SRA, 1971.

Becker W., Englemann, S., & Thomas, D. *Teaching: A course in applied psychology.* Chicago: Science Research Associates, 1971.

Bellack, A. A. History of curriculum thought and practice. *Review of Educational Research,* 1969, *39,* 283-292.

Bennett, Mildred E. et al. Prescriptive teaching workshop resource manual. ERIC Clearing House, 1972, ED 072598.

Bereiter, C., & Engelmann, S. *Teaching disadvantaged children in the preschool.* Englewood Cliffs, N.J.: Prentice-Hall, 1966.

Best, H. *The effect of structured physical activity on the motor skill development of children with learning disabilities (minimal brain dysfunction).* Memphis: Memphis State University Press, 1967.

Biddle, Bruce J., and Ellena, William J., (Eds.). *Contemporary research on teacher effectiveness.* Sponsored by the American Association of School Administrators, National School Boards Association, and Department of Classroom Teachers of the National Education Association. New York: Holt, Rinehart and Winston, 1964.

Bijou, S. W. What psychology has to offer education—now. *Journal of Applied Behavior Analysis,* 1970, *3,* 65-71.

Binet, A., & Simon, T. La mesure de developpement de l'intelligence chez les jeunes enfants. *Bull. Soc. Libre Pour L'Etude Psychol. de L'Enfant,* 1911.

Birch, Herbert G., & Belmont, Lillian. Auditory-visual integration in normal retarded readers. *American Journal of Orthopsychiatry*, 1964, *34*, 852-861.

Bloomer, H. A needle's eye view of language disturbance. *Education*, 1959, *79*, 395-398.

Bluestein, V. W. Factors related to and predictive of improvement in reading. *Psychology in the Schools*, 1967, *4*, 272-276.

Boeck, D. G. A study in the effectiveness of a learning disabilities inservice program for elementary classroom teachers. Unpublished master's thesis, Pennsylvania State University, 1975.

Borg, Walter R. Comparison between a performance test and criteria of teacher effectiveness. *Psychological Reports*, 1956, *2*, 11-16.

Bricklin, P. Counseling parents of children with learning disabilities. *Reading Teacher*, 1970, *23*, 331-338.

Brodie, R., & Winterbottom, M. Failure in elementary school boys as a function of traumata, secrecy, and derogation. *Child Development*, 1967.

Brolin, Donn. Career education needs of secondary students. *Exceptional Children*, 1973, *39*, 619-624.

Brolin, Donn, & Thomas, Barbara. *Preparing teachers of secondary level educable mentally retarded. Project report no. 1*. Menomenie, Wisc.: Stout State University, 1971. (ERIC Document Reproduction Service No. ED 050500.)

Browning, R. M. Behavior therapy for stuttering in a schizophrenic child. *Behavior Research & Therapy*, 1967, *5*, 27-35.

Bruner, Jerome Seymour. *Toward a theory of instruction*. Cambridge, Mass.: Harvard University Press, Belknap Press, 1966.

Brutten, M., Richardson, S., & Mangel, C. *Something's wrong with my child: A parents' book about children with learning disabilities*. New York: Harcourt, Brace, Jovanovich, Inc., 1973.

Bryen, D. N. Implementing the resource room. In D. Hammill and J. Wiederholt, *The resource room: rationale and implementation*. Philadelphia: Buttonwood Farms, Inc., 1972.

Buckner, R. *An experiment to study the effectiveness of school directed parental assistance to elementary school pupils with reading problems.* Unpublished doctoral dissertation, University of Nebraska, 1972.

Budoff, M. Providing special education without special classes. *Journal of School Psychology,* 1972, *10,* 199-200.

Cartwright, G. Phillip, Cartwright, Carol A., & Ysseldyke, James E. Two decision models: Identification and diagnostic teaching of handicapped children in the regular classroom. *Psychology in the Schools,* 1973, *10,* 4-11.

Cassidy, V., & Stanton, J. *An investigation of factors involved in the educational placements of mentally retarded children: A study of differences between children in special and regular classes in Ohio.* Columbus, Ohio: Ohio State University Press, 1959.

Chalfant, J., & Schefflin, M. Central processing dysfunctions in children: A review of research. U.S. Department of Health, Education and Welfare, (NINDS Monograph No. 9, U.S. Public Health Service). Washington, D.C.: U.S. Government Printing Office, 1969.

Chichester, J. B. Who is the good teacher? *Phi Delta Kappan,* 1956, *37,* 245-247.

Clark, A., & Richards, C. Learning disabilities: A national survey of existing public school programs. *Journal of Special Education,* 1968, *2,* 223.

Clarke, Jeanne, & Waters, Henrietta. Counseling the culturally deprived. *The School Counselor,* 1972, *19,* 201-209.

Clements, S. D. Minimal brain dysfunction in children. *National Institute of Neurological Diseases and Blindness Monographs,* 1966, No. 3.

Closson, Fred I. Delinquency: Its prevention rests upon the academic community. *Clearing House,* 1971, *45,* 290-293.

Cohen, H. C., Filipczak, J. A., Bix, J. S., & Cohen, J. E. *Contingencies applicable to special education of delinquents.* Silver Springs, Md.: Publication of the Institute for Behavioral Research, Inc., 1966.

Cohen, R. The role of immaturity in reading disabilities. *Journal of Learning Disabilities,* 1969, *3,* 73-74.

Cohen, S. A. Studies in visual perception and reading in disadvantaged children. *Journal of Learning Disabilities,* 1969, *2,* 6-14.

Cole, E., & Walker, L. Reading and speech problems as expressions of a specific language disability. In D. Rioch & E. Weinstein (Eds.), *Disorders of Communications.* Baltimore, Md.: Williams and Wilkins, 1964.

Cook, Martha A., and Richards, Herbert C. Dimensions of principal and supervisor ratings of teacher behavior. *Journal of Experimental Education,* 1972, *4,* 11-14.

Council for Exceptional Children. *First annual report,* National Advisory Committee on Handicapped Children, 31 January 1968.

———————————————— . *Basic responsibilities to exceptional children.* Extracts from a position paper adopted by the CEC at its Miami Convention, April 1971.

Counteracting school dropouts. *Illinois Curriculum Program.* Office of the Superintendent of Public Instruction, 1967.

Cox, L. S. Diagnosing and remediating systematic errors in addition and subtraction computation. *The Arithmetic Teacher,* 1975, *22,* 151-157.

Coyle, P. J. The systematic desensitization of reading anxiety, a case study. *Psychology in the Schools,* 1968, *5,* 140-141.

Craig, W. N., & Collins, J. L. Communication patterns in classes for deaf students. *Exceptional Children,* 1970, *37,* 283-289.

Cronbach, L. J. Course improvement through evaluation. *Teachers College Record,* 1963, *64,* 674-683.

Cruickshank, W. A. *A teaching method for brain-injured and hyperactive children.* Syracuse, N.Y.: Syracuse University Press, 1961.

Davis, John C. Teacher dismissal on grounds of immorality. *The Clearing House,* 1972, *46,* 418.

Dimitz, S. et al. Delinquency proneness and school achievement. *Educational Research Bulletin,* 1957, *36,* 131-136.

Domas, S. J., & Tiedeman, D. Teacher competence: An annotated bibliography. *Journal of Experimental Education,* 1950, *19,* 101-218.

Dorney, W. P. Effectiveness of reading instruction in the modification of attitudes of adolescent delinquent boys. *Journal of Educational Research,* 1967, *60,* 438-443.

Drass, S., & Jones, R. Learing disabled children as behavior modifiers. *Journal of Learning Disabilities,* 1971, *4,* 16-23.

Edgerly, R. Parent counseling in Norwell Junior High School. *Journal of Education,* 1971, *54,* 54-59.

Eisenson, J. Perceptual disturbances in children with central nervous system dysfunctions and implications for language development. *The British Journal of Disorders of Communication,* 1966, *1,* 21-32.

_____ . *Aphasia in children.* New York: Harper & Row, 1972.

Elenbogen, M. A. *A comparative study of some aspects of academic and social adjustment of two groups of mentally retarded children in special and regular grades.* Unpublished doctoral dissertation, Northwestern University, 1957.

Elkind, D. & Deblinger, J. Perceptual training and reading achievement in disadvantaged children. *Child Development,* 1969, *40,* 11-19.

Erikson, E. H. *Identity: Youth and Crisis.* New York: W. W. Norton & Co., 1968.

Fahlik, L. H. The effects of special perceptual-motor training in kindergarten on reading readiness and on second grade performance. *Journal of Learning Disabilities,* 1969, *2,* 395-402.

Fendrick, P., & Bond, H. Delinquency and reading. *Pedagogical Seminary and Journal of Genetic Psychology,* 1936, *48,* 236-243.

Ferinden, W. E., VanHandel, D., & Kovalinsky, T. A supplemental instructional program for children with learning disabilities. *Journal of Learning Disabilities,* 1971, *4,* 193-203.

Fernald, G. M. *Remedial techniques in basic school subjects.* New York: McGraw-Hill, 1943.

Ferster, C. B., & DeMyer, M. K. A method for the experimental analysis of the behavior of autistic children. In S. Bijou & D. Baer (Eds.), *Child development: Readings in experimental analysis.* New York: Appleton-Century-Crofts, 1967.

Fink, A. H. *An analysis of teacher-pupil interaction in classes for the emotionally handicapped.* Unpublished doctoral dissertation. University of Michigan, 1970.

Fitzhugh, L., & Fitzhugh, K. *The Fitzhugh plus program.* Galien, Mich.: Allied Education Council, 1966.

Flanders, N. A. *Teacher influence, public attitudes and achievement.* Washington, D.C.: United States Government Printing Office, 1965.

Foster, G., & Sabatino, D. *Examiner's manual: Test of visual perceptual discrimination and memory.* State College, Pa.: Model Learning Disabilities Systems, 1974.

Foster, G., Ysseldyke, J., & Reese, J. I never would have seen it if I hadn't believed it. *Exceptional Children,* 1974, in press.

Frank, M., & Frank, L. *How to help your child in school.* New York: Viking Press, 1950.

Frease, D. E. The schools, self-concept and juvenile delinquency. *British Journal of Criminology,* 1971, *12,* 133-146.

Freund, Janet W. The application of a flowchart process to learning difficulties in secondary schools. *Educational Technology,* 1972, *12,* 58-60.

Frierson, E. Clinical education procedures in the treatment of learning disabilities. In E. Frierson & W. Barbe (Eds.), *Educating children with learning disabilities: Selected readings.* New York: Appleton-Century-Crofts, 1967, 478-488.

Frostig, M. Education of children with learning disabilities. In E. C. Frierson & W. B. Barbe (Eds.), *Educating children with learning disabilities.* New York: Appleton-Century-Crofts, 1967.

Fygetakis, L., & Ingram, D. Language rehabilitation and programmed conditioning. *Journal of Learning Disabilities,* 1973, *6,* 5-9.

Gage, N. L., & Ingram, D. Guiding principles in the study of teacher effectiveness. *Journal of Teacher Education,* 1952, *2,* 294-298.

Gagne, R. M. (Ed.). *Psychological principles in system development.* New York: Holt, Rinehart and Winston, Inc., 1962.

Gerlach, V., & Ely, D. *Teaching and media: A systematic approach.* Englewood Cliffs, N. J.: Prentice-Hall, Inc., 1971.

Getman, G. N. The visuomotor complex in the acquisition of learning skills. In J. Hellmuth (Ed.), *Learning disorders.* (Vol. 1). Seattle: Special Child Publications, 1965.

Gibson, E. J. A developmental comparison of the perception of words, pronounceable trigrams and unpronounceable trigrams. Unpublished research memorandum, Cornell University, 1962.

Gibson, J., & Gibson, E. Perceptual learning: Differentiation or enrichment? *Psychological Review,* 1955, *62,* 32-41.

Gillingham, A., & Stillman, G. *Remedial work for reading, spelling and penmanship.* New York: Hackett & Wilhelms, 1936.

Gillingham, A., & Stillman, B. *Remedial training for children with specific disability in reading, spelling and penmanship.* (6th ed.) Cambridge, Mass.: Educators Publishing Service, 1960.

Glaser, R., & Nitko, A. Measurement in learning and instruction. In R. Thorndike (Ed.), *Educational measurement.* Washington, D.C.: American Council on Education, 1971.

Glueck, E., & Glueck, S. *One thousand juvenile delinquents—their treatment by court and clinic.* Cambridge: Harvard University Press, 1934.

Glueck, S. S. Home, the school, and delinquency. *Harvard Educational Review,* 1953, *23,* 17-32.

Glueck, S., & Glueck, Eleanor T. *Unraveling juvenile delinquency.* New York: Commonwealth Fund, 1950.

Goins, J. T. Visual and auditory perception in reading. *The Reading Teacher,* 1959, *13,* 9-13.

Gold, M. W. Preworkshop skills for the trainable: A sequential technique. *Education and Training of the Mentally Retarded,* 1968, *3,* 31-37.

Goldstein, William. An enlightened approach to supervising teachings. *The Clearing House,* 1972, *46,* 391-394.

Goodlad, J. I. *The changing school curriculum.* New York: Fund for the Advancement of Education, 1966.

Gordon, T. *PET—Parent effectiveness training.* New York: Peter H. Wyden, Inc., 1970.

Gorelick, J. C. The effectiveness of visual form training in a pre-reading program. *Journal of Educational Research,* 1965, *58,* 315-318.

Gorth, W., & Hambleton, R. Measurement considerations for criterion-referenced testing and special education. *Journal of Special Education,* 1972, *6,* 303-314.

Grant, E. *Parents and teachers as partners.* Chicago: Science Research Associates, 1952.

Grauhard, Paul S. Psycholinguistic correlates of reading disabilities in disturbed children. *Journal of Special Education,* 1967, *1,* 363-368.

Guba, E. G., & Stufflebeam, D. L. *Evaluating: The process of stimulating, aiding and abetting insightful action.* Paper delivered at the Second National Symposium for Professors of Educational Research, Boulder, Colorado, November 1968.

Guerney, B. Filial therapy: Description and rationale. *Journal of Consulting Psychology,* 1964, *28,* 304-310.

Guerney, B., & Guerney, L. Filial therapy. *Yale Scientific Magazine,* 1966, *40,* 6.

Hambleton, R., & Novick, M. Toward an integration of theory and method for criterion-referenced tests. *Journal of Educational Measurement,* 1973, *10,* 159-170.

Hammill, D. D. Evaluating Children for Instructional Purposes. *Academic Therapy,* 1971, *6,* 341-353.

——————— . A Problem in Definition. *Prise Reporter,* Regional Resource Center, King of Prussia, Pa., October 1972.

Hammill, D. D., & Wiederholt, J. L. *The resource room: Rationale and implementation.* Philadelphia: Buttonwood Farms, Inc., 1972.

Hammill, D., & Wiederholt, J. Review of the Frostig visual perception test and the related training program. In L. Mann & D. Sabatino (Eds.), *The First Review of Special Education.* (Vol. I). Philadelphia: JSE Press, 1973.

Hammond, R. Context evaluation of instruction in local school districts. *Educational Technology,* 1969, *9,* 13-18.

——————— . Evaluation at the local level. Project EPIC Report. Tucson, Arizona: Project EPIC, August 1967.

Haring, N., & Hauck, M. Improving learning conditions in the establishment of reading skills with disabled readers. *Exceptional Children,* 1969, *38,* 33-42.

Harris, Albert Josiah, & Sipay, Edward R. *Effective teaching of reading.* New York: D. McKay Company, 1971.

Hartshook, E. A. Merit rating—key to better pay and better teaching. *Phi Delta Kappan,* 1961, *42,* 157-160.

Hartup, W. Friendship status and the effectiveness of peers as reinforcing agents. *Journal of Experimental Child Psychology,* 1964, *1,* 154-162.

Heckerl, J., & Webb, S. An educational approach to the treatment of children with learning disabilities. *Journal of Learning Disabilities,* 1969, *2,* 199-204.

Heine, L., & Rahaim, B. *Prescriptive education: Diagnosis and implementation.* Marianna, Fla.: Jackson County Public Schools, 1973.

Helmer, D. *Social technology.* New York: Basic Books, 1966.

Hewett, Frank M. *The emotionally disturbed child in the classroom.* Boston: Allyn & Bacon, Inc., 1968.

Hewett, F., Taylor, F., & Artuso, A. The Santa Monica project: Evaluation of an engineered classroom design with emotionally disturbed children. *Exceptional Children,* 1969, *35,* 523-529.

Hickey, M. E., & Hoffman, D. Diagnosis and Prescription in Education. *Educational Technology,* 1973, *13,* 35-37.

Hobbs, N. Sources of gain in psychological therapy. *American Psychologist,* 1962, *17,* 741-747.

Jacobs, J. An evaluation of the Frostig visual-perceptual training program. *Educational Leadership Research Supplement,* 1968, *1,* 332-340.

Jenkins, J., Mayhall, W., Peschka, C., & Jenkins, L. Comparing small group and tutorial instruction in resource rooms. *Exceptional Children,* 1974, *40,* 245-250.

Jersild, Arthur T. *The psychology of adolescence.* New York: Macmillan Inc., 1957.

Johnson, D. Educational principles for children with learning disabilities. *Rehabilitation Literature,* 1967, *28,* 317-322.

Johnson, D., & Myklebust, H. *Learning disabilities: Educational principles and practices.* New York: Grune and Stratton, 1967.

Johnson, G. O. Special education for mentally handicapped—A paradox. *Exceptional Children,* 1962, *19,* 62-69.

Johnson, Marjorie Seddon. Factors related to disability in reading. *Journal of Experimental Education,* 1957, *26,* 1-26.

Jones, Anthony S. A realistic approach to teacher evaluation. *The Clearing House,* 1972, *46,* 474.

Jones, R. L. Accountability in special education: Some problems. *Exceptional Children,* 1973, *39,* 631-642.

Kagan, J. Inadequate evidence and illogical conclusions. *Harvard Educational Review,* 1969, *39,* 274-277.

Kaufmann, M. *Perceptual and language reading programs.* Newark, Del.: International Reading Association, 1973.

Keele, R., & Harrison, G. *The effect of parents using structured tutoring techniques in teaching their children to read.* Paper presented at the meeting of the Educational Research Association, New York City, 4-7 February 1971.

Keim, R. P. Visual-motor training, readiness, and intelligence of kindergarten children. *Journal of Learning Disabilities,* 1970, *3,* 256-260.

Kelgard, R. Brain damage and delinquency: A question and a challenge. *Academic Therapy,* 1968-69, *4,* 93-99.

Kelly, E. J. *Philosophical perspectives in special education.* Columbus, Ohio: Charles E. Merrill Publishing Co., 1971.

Keough, B. *Diagnosis of learning disabilities.* Paper presented at the meeting of the National Regional Resource Center of Pennsylvania, King of Prussia, Pennsylvania, June 1971.

Kephart, N. C. *The slow learner in the classroom.* Columbus, Ohio: Charles E. Merrill, Inc., 1960.

King, E. M. Effects of different kinds of visual discrimination training in learning to read words. *Journal of
Educational Psychology, 1964, 55,* 325-333.

Kingsley, R. F., & Spies, C. J. The relationship of interests to social acceptance of educable mentally
retarded in a school camping program. *Training School Bulletin, 1969, 66,* 93-99.

Kipfer, Bernice. Conceptualizing an administrative/management system for special education. *Educational
Technology, 1973, 13,* 16-21.

Kirk, S. Behavioral diagnosis and remediation of learning disabilities. Proceedings of Annual Meeting of
the Conference on Exploration into the Problems of the Perceptually Handicapped Child. (Vol. 1),
1963.

Klahn, R. P., (Ed.) *Evaluation of Teacher Competency.* Milwaukee, Wisc.: Franklin Publishers, Inc., 1965.

Klein, I., & Marsh, H. *Identification and remediation of perceptual handicaps in learning to read.* Glen Cove,
N.Y.: Glen Cove School District, 1969.

Koontz, H. *Appraising Managers As Managers.* New York: McGraw-Hill Co., 1971.

Koppitz, E. *The Bender gestalt test for young children.* New York: Grune & Stratton, 1971.

Krathwohl, D. R. Stating objectives appropriately for program, for curriculum, and for instructional materials
development. *Journal of Teacher Education, 1965, 12,* 83-92.

Krumboltz, J., & Krumboltz, H. *Changing children's behavior.* Englewood Cliffs, N.J.: Prentice-Hall, Inc.,
1972.

Kult, Lawrence. Alternatives to teacher evaluations. *The Clearing House*, 1973, *47*, 277-279.

Kunzelman, Harold P. et al. *Precision teaching: An initial training sequence.* Seattle: Special Child Publications, 1970.

Kvaraceus, W. C. *Juvenile deliquency: A problem for the modern world.* Paris: UNESCO, 1964.

LaCrosse, E. et al. Meyer children's rehabilitation institute teaching program for young children (prescriptive teaching program for multiply handicapped nursery school children). *Council for Exceptional Children.* Reston, Virginia; Head Start Information Project, Nebraska University Medical Center, Omaha, Nebraska, 1973.

Lazarus, Arnold A. *Behavior therapy and beyond.* New York: McGraw-Hill Co., 1971.

Lea, J. A language scheme for children suffering from receptive aphasia. *Speech Pathology and Therapy,* 1965, *8,* 58-68.

Lerner, J. *Children with learning disabilities: Theories, diagnosis and teaching strategies.* Boston: Houghton Mifflin Company, 1971.

Lessenger, L. Accountability: Its implications for the teacher. In D. W. Allen (Ed.), *The teacher's handbook.* Glenview, Ill.: Scott, Foresman and Company, 1971.

Letson, J. W. Inservice training. In L. C. Deighton (Ed.), *The encyclopedia of education* (Vol. 9). The Macmillan Company and The Free Press, 1971.

Lewis, Gertrude M. *The Evaluation of Teaching.* Washington, D.C.: Department of Elementary-Kindergarten-Nursery Education, National Education Association, 1966.

Lindvall, C. M., Nardozza, S., & Felton, M. The importance of specific objectives in curriculum development. In C. M. Lindvall (Ed.), *Defining educational objectives.* Pittsburgh, Pa.: University of Pittsburgh Press, 1964.

Litchfield, T. B. *A program of visual-motor-perceptual training to determine its effects upon primary level children with reading and learning deficiences.* Suffern, N.Y.: Romapo Central School District 1, 1970.

Lobb, H. Vision versus touch in form discrimination. *Canadian Journal of Psychology,* 1965, *19,* 175-187.

Lovaas, O. I. Some studies on the treatment of childhood schizophrenia. In J. M. Sclier (Ed.), *Research in psychotherapy.* Washington, D. C.: American Psychological Association, 1968.

Lovaas, O., Berberich, J., Perloff, B., & Schaffer, B. Acquisition of imitative speech in schizophrenic children. *Science,* 1966, *51,* 705-707.

Lovaas, O., Freitag, G., Gold, V., & Kassovia, J. Experimental studies in childhood schizophrenia: Analysis of self destructive behavior. *Journal of Experimental Child Psychology.* 1965, *2,* 67-84.

Lovitt, T. C. Assessment of children with learning disabilities. *Exceptional Children,* 1967, *34,* 233-239.

Lundgren, Ulf P. *Frame factors and the teaching process.* Stockholm, Sweden: Almquist and Wiksell, 1972.

Madsen, C. H., Jr., Becker, W. C., & Thomas, D. R. Rules, praise, and ignoring: Elements of elementary classroom control. *Journal of Applied Behavior Analysis,* 1968, *1,* 139-150.

Maloney, M. P. Analysis of the generalizability of sensory motor training. *American Journal of Mental Deficiency,* 1967, *74,* 458-469.

Mann, L. Are we fractioning too much? *Academic Therapy,* 1970, *5,* 85-91.

————— . Perceptual training revisited: The training of nothing at all. *Rehabilitation Literature,* 1971, *32,* 322-327+.

Martin, Edwin W. Individualism and behaviorism as future trends in educating handicapped children. *Exceptional Children,* 1972, *38,* 517-525.

McCandless, Boyd R. *Adolescents—behavior and development.* Hinsdale: The Dryden Press, Inc., 1970.

McCarthy, J. Learning disabilities: Where have we been? Where are we going? In D. Hammill & N. Bartel (Eds.), *Educational perspectives in learning disabilities.* New York: John Wiley & Sons, 1971.

McGinnis, M. *Aphasic children.* Washington, D.C.: Alexander Graham Bell Association for the Deaf, Inc., 1963.

McKenzie, H., Clark, M., Wolf, M., Kothera, R., & Benson, C. Behavior modification of children with learning disabilities using grades as tokens and allowances as back up reinforcers. *Exceptional Children,* 1968, *34,* 745-752.

McNally, Harold J. Teacher evaluation that makes a difference. *Educational Leadership,* 1972, *29,* 353-355.

McNeil, D. *Toward accountable teachers.* New York: Holt, Rinehart and Winston, 1971.

Michael, W. B., & Metfessel, N. S. A paradigm for developing valid, measurable objectives in the evaluation of educational programs in colleges and universities. *Educational and Psychological Measurement,* 1967, *27,* 373-383.

Middendorf, L. *Mothers as mediators of change in the perceptual and learning abilities of inner city kindergarten children.* Unpublished doctoral dissertation, Rutgers University, 1970.

Meichenbaum, D. H., Bowers, K., & Ross, R. Modification of classroom behavior of institutionalized female adolescent offenders. *Behavior Research and Therapy,* 1968, *6,* 343-353.

Miller, S. *Visual remedial program effects on visual perceptual discrimination and academic and drawing behavior.* Unpublished doctoral dissertation, Pennsylvania State University, 1974.

Millman, J. Passing scores and test lengths for domain-reference measures. *Review of Educational Research,* 1973, *43,* 205-206.

Mok, P. *Pushbutton parents and the schools.* New York: Dell Publishing Co., 1964.

Morley, M., Court, D., Miller, H., & Garside, R. Delayed speech and developmental aphasia. *Speech,* 1956, *20,* 4-14.

Muehl, S. The effects of visual discrimination pre-training with word and letter stimuli on learning to read a word list in kindergarten children. *Journal of Educational Psychology,* 1961, *52,* 215-221.

Mussen, Paul Henry, Conger, John Janeway, & Kagan, Jerome. *Child development and personality.* New York: Harper & Row, 1969.

Myers, E. Counseling the parents of sixth grade underachievers. *Journal of Education,* 1971-72, *154,* 50-53.

Myers, P., & Hammill, D. *Methods for learning disorders.* New York: John Wiley & Sons, 1969.

Myklebust, H. Language training: A comparison between children with aphasia and those with deafness. *American Annals of the Deaf,* 1956, *101,* 240-244.

_____ (Ed.). *Progress in learning disabilities.* New York: Grune & Stratton, 1967.

_____ . *Progress in learning disabilities.* (Vol. 1). New York: Grune & Stratton, 1968.

Myklebust, H., & Johnson, D. *Learning disabilities: Educational principles and practice.* New York: Grune & Stratton, 1967.

Neifert, J., & Gayton, W. Parents and the home program approach in the remediation of learning disabilities. *Journal of Learning Disabilities,* 1973, *6,* 31-35.

Nunnally, J. *Psychometric theory.* New York: McGraw-Hill Co., 1967.

Oberst, B. A community approach to specific school learning disabilities: The Omaha STAAR project. *Journal of Learning Disabilities,* 1973, *6,* 22-29.

O'Donnell, P. A., & Eisenson, J. Delacato training for reading achievement and visual-motor integration. *Journal of Learning Disabilities,* 1969, *2,* 441-447.

Ohrtman, W. F. One more instant solution coming up. *Journal of Special Education,* 1972, *6,* 377-378.

O'Leary, K., & Becker, W. Behavior modification of an adjustment class: A token reinforcement program. *Exceptional Children,* 1967, *9,* 637-642.

O'Leary, K., & Drabman, R. Token reinforcement programs in the classroom: A review. *Psychological Bulletin*, 1971, *75*, 379-398.

Orlando, C. Review of the reading research in special education. In L. Mann & D. Sabatino (Eds.), *The first review of special education.* Philadelphia, Pa.: JSE Press, 1973.

Orton, J. Parents as participants in the team approach to their dyslexic children. *Journal of Learning Disabilities*, 1971, *4*, 47-49.

Orton, S. T. *Reading, writing, and speech problems in children.* New York: W. W. Norton and Co., 1937.

Overline, H. M. *An investigation into the effects of an inservice program in learning disabilities on elementary school teachers' attitudes and classroom instructional activities.* Unpublished doctoral dissertation, Temple University, 1972.

Owen, F., Adams, P., Forrest, T., Stoly, L., & Fisher, S. Learning disorders in children: Sibling studies. *Monograph of the Society for Research in Child Development*, 1971, *36*, (4, Serial No. 144).

Painter, G. The effect of a rhythmic and sensori-motor activity program on perceptual motor spatial abilities of kindergarten children. *Exceptional Children*, 1966, *33*, 113-116.

Palardy, J. What teachers believe, what children achieve. *Elementary School Journal*, 1969, *69*, 370-374.

Patterson, G., & Anderson, D. Peers as social reinforcers. *Child Development*, 1964, *35*, 951-960.

Patterson, G., Shaw, D., & Ebner, M. Teachers, peers and parents as agents of change in the classroom. In A. Bensen (Ed.), *Modifying deviant social behaviors in various classroom settings.* Monograph 1, 1969.

Patterson, N. *Multi-sensory approach to reading disabilities.* Lexington, Ky.: Fayette County Public Schools, Division of Instructional Services, 1968.

Pendrak, Michael. Performance contracting and the secondary reading lab. *Journal of Reading*, 1974, *17*, 453-457.

Perry, O. Philadelphia: Personal Communication, September 1974.

Peter, Lawrence J. *Prescriptive teaching.* New York: McGraw-Hill Co., 1965.

Piaget, Jean. *The mechanisms of perception.* (Translated by G. N. Sedgrim.) New York: Basic Books, 1969.

Pick, A. S. Improvement of visual and tactual form discrimination. *Journal of Experimental Psychology,* 1965, *69,* 331-339.

Popham, W. J. Objectives and instruction. In *Instructional objectives,* American Educational Research Association Monograph Series on Curriculum Evaluation, No. 3. Chicago: Rand McNally & Co., 1969.

Popham, W. J., & Baker, D. *Systematic instruction.* Englewood Cliffs, N.J.: Prentice-Hall, Inc., 1970.

Positive approaches to dropout prevention. U. S. Department of Health, Education and Welfare publication, DE 73/12300, 1973.

Prillaman, D. Diagnostic and prescriptive teaching: Rationale and model. *Council for Exceptional Children Newsletter,* Richmond, Va., 1968, *1,* 1-4.

Proger, Barton B., Carfioli, Joseph C., & Kalapos, Robert L. A neglected area of accountability: The failure of instructional materials evaluation and a solution. *The Journal of Special Education,* 1973, *3,* 269-279.

Prouty, R., & Prillaman, D. Educational diagnosis: In clinic or classroom? *Virginia Journal of Education,* 1967, *61,* 10-12.

Provus, N. M. *Teaching for relevance: An inservice training program.* Chicago: Whitehall, 1969.

Quay, H. C. *Juvenile delinquency.* Princeton, N.J.: D. Van Nostrand Company, Inc., 1965.

Rappaport, S. R., & McNary, S. R. Teacher effectiveness for children with learning disorders. *Journal of Learning Disabilities,* 1970, *3,* 75-83.

Raven, J. C. *The coloured progressive matrices.* Los Angeles: Western Psychological Services, 1965.

Raygor, Betty Ruth. Mental ability, school achievement and language arts achievement in the prediction of delinquency. *Journal of Educational Research,* 1970, *64,* 68-72.

Reagor, Pamela A. Delinquency, socialization and type of social reinforcement. *Adolescence,* 1973, *8,* 225-246.

Redfern, G. B. *How to evaluate teaching.* Worthington, Ohio: School Management Institute, 1972.

Reed, R. J. The community school board. *School Review,* 1973, *81,* 357-364.

Reger, R. What is a resource room program? *Journal of Learning Disabilities,* 1973, *6,* 609-614.

_____ (Ed.). Resource rooms: Change agents or guardians of the status quo? *The Journal of Special Education,* 1972, *6,* 355-359.

_____. What is a resource-room program? *Journal of Learning Disabilities,* 1973, *6,* 15-21.

Reger, R., Schroder, W., & Uschold, K. *Special education: Children with learning problems.* New York: Oxford University Press, 1968.

Revelle, D. Aiding children with specific language disability. *Academic Therapy,* 1971, *6,* 391-395.

Risdon, G. A. Remedy is suggested for math carelessness. *Clearinghouse,* 1956, *31,* 203-206.

Robbins, M. P. The Delacato interpretation of neurological organization. *Reading Research Quarterly,* Spring, 1966, *1,* 57-77.

Roman, Melvin. *Reaching delinquents through reading.* Springfield, Ill.: Thomas, 1957.

Rosenthal, R., & Jacobson, L. *Pygmalion in the classroom.* New York: Holt, Rinehart and Winston, 1968.

Roth, J. An intervention strategy for children with developmental problems. *Journal of School Psychology,* 1970, *8,* 311-314.

Ryback, D. et al. Sub-professional behavior modification and the development of token-reinforcement systems in increasing academic motivation and achievement. *Child Study Journal,* 1970-71, *1,* 52-67.

Sabatino, D. A. The information processing behaviors associated with learning disabilities. *Journal of Learning Disabilities,* 1968, *1,* 440-450.

_____ . An evaluation of resource rooms for children with learning disabilities. *Journal of Learning Disabilities,* 1971, *4,* 84-93.

_____ . Auditory perception: Development, assessment, and intervention. In L. Mann & D. Sabatino (Eds.), *First review of special education.* (Vol. 1). Philadelphia: JSE Press, 1973.

_____ . *Neglected and delinquent children.* EDC Report, Wilkes-Barre, Pa.: Wilkes College, 1974.

Sabatino, D., & Abbott, J. Home instruction utilizing teacher-moms with academic high-risk pre-school children. *Exceptional Children,* in press.

Sabatino, D. A., & Boeck, D. G. *A systems approach to provide educational services to children with learning disabilities.* University Park, Pa.: Model Learning Disabilities Systems, 1973.

Sabatino, D., & Foster, G. *Test of auditory perception.* State College, Pa.: Model Learning, 1974.

Sabatino, D. A., & Hayden, D. L. The information processing behaviors related to learning disability and educable mental retardation. *Journal of Exceptional Children,* 1970, *35,* 21-30.

_____ . Prescriptive teaching in a summer learning disabilities program. *Journal of Learning Disabilities,* 1970, *3,* 220-227.

Sabatino, D., Miller, S., & Sabatino, M. *Early childhood form constancy.* Philadelphia, Pa.: Buttonwood Farms, Inc., 1973.

Sabatino, D., & Streissguth, W. Word form configuration training of visual perceptual strengths with learning disabled children. *Journal of Learning Disabilities,* 1972, *5,* 435-441.

Sapir, S. G. *A pilot approach to the education of first grade public school children with problems in body schema, perceptual motor and/or language development.* New York: Columbia University Press, 1967.

_____ . *Learning disability and deficit centered classroom training.* New York: Columbia University Teachers College, 1969.

Scagliotta, Edward G. A Special Organization of Learning for the Exceptional Child. *Academic Therapy,* 1969, *5,* 5-10.

_____. Home language training program for dysacusic and aphasic children. *The Volta Review,* 1966, *60,* 554-559.

Schlicter, K. Jeffery, & Ratcliff, Richard G. Discrimination learning in juvenile delinquents. *Journal of Abnormal Psychology,* 1971, *77,* 46-48.

Schulman, B. R., and Trudwell, J. W. California's guidelines for teacher evaluation. *Community and Junior College Journal,* 1972, *42,* 32.

Scott, R., & Pahre, B. The application of audio-tutorial techniques to remediation of learning disabilities: A case study. *Psychology in the Schools,* 1968, *5,* 277-280.

Scriven, Michael. The method of evaluation. In R. E. Stake (Ed.), *Curriculum evaluation,* American Educational Research Association Monograph Series on Evaluation, No. 1. Chicago: Rand McNally & Co., 1967.

_____ . The Methodology of Evaluation. In Ralph Tyler, Robert Gagne, and Michael Scriven (Eds.), *Perspectives of curriculum evaluation.* Chicago: Rand McNally and Company, 1967, 39-83.

Shelquist, J., Breeze, B., & Jacquot, B. *Resource handbook for development of learning skills.* Rosebud, Ore.: Educational Programmers, 1970.

Shaw, B. (Pygmalion), *Pygmalion and Other Plays,* New York: Dodd Mead and Co., 1967.

Sherman, J., & Baer, D. Appraisal of operant therapy techniques with children and adults. In C. Franks (Ed.), *Behavior therapy: Appraisal and status.* New York: McGraw-Hill Co., 1969.

Shoemaker, D. Improving criterion-referenced measurement. *Journal of Special Education,* 1972, *6,* 315-323.

Skinner, B. F. *The technology of teaching.* New York: Appleton-Century-Crofts, 1968.

544

Slack, C. W., & Schwitzgebel, R. *A handbook: Reducing adolescent crime in your community.* Privately printed, 1960, in D. A. Sabatino, *Neglected and delinquent children.* EDC Report, Wilkes-Barre, Pa.: Wilkes College, 1974.

Slater, B. Parent involvement in perceptual training at the kindergarten level. *Academic Therapy Quarterly,* 1971-72, *7,* 149-154.

Slosson, R. *Slosson intelligence test for children and adults.* New York: Slosson Educational Publications Inc., 1973.

Sluyter, D., & Hawkins, R. Delayed reinforcement of classroom behavior by parents. *Journal of Learning Disabilities,* 1972, *5,* 20-28.

Smith, G. The mentally retarded: Is the public employment service prepared to serve them? *Mental Retardation,* 1970, *8,* 26-29.

Smith, L., & Lovith, T. Behavioral prescription guide manual (Social parent/child home stimulation). The Marshall Town Project, 1973, ERIC ED 079920.

Smith, Lawrence L., & Riebock, James. A middle school tries contractual reading. *The Clearing House,* 1971, *45,* 404-406.

Snapp, M. Study of individual instruction by using elementary school children as tutors. *Journal of School Psychology,* 1972, *10,* 1-8.

Sparks, H. L., & Blackman, L. S. What is special about education revisited: The mentally retarded. *Exceptional Children,* 1965, *5,* 242-249.

Staats, A. W., & Butterfield, W. H. Treatment of non-reading in a culturally deprived juvenile delinquent: An application of reinforcement principles. *Child Development,* 1965. In A. Bandura, *Principles of Behavior Modification.* New York: Holt, Rinehart and Winston, 1969.

Stander, A. *Peer tutoring and reading achievement of seventh and eighth grade students.* Unpublished doctoral dissertation, University of Michigan, 1972.

Stanford Research Institute. *Parent involvement in compensatory education programs.* Report No. EPRC-RM-2158-20, August 1973. Menlo Park, Calif.: Contract No. OEC -0-72-5016, Office of Education (Washington, D.C.).

Stark, J. *Programmed instruction for perceptually handicapped children with language difficulties.* Stanford, Calif.: Stanford University, 1967.

Stake, Robert E. The countenance of educational evaluation. *Teachers College Record,* 1967, *68,* 523-540.
_____. A layout of statements and data to be collected by the evaluation program. *Teachers College Record,* April 1967, 529.

Steffy, R. A treatment of schizophrenic patients by operant conditioning. Personal communication, 1966. In D. A. Sabatino, *Neglected and Delinquent Children.* EDC Report, Wilkes-Barre, Pa.: Wilkes College, 1974.

Sternberg, L., & Sedlak, R. Mathematical programming for delinquent youths. Wilkes-Barre, Pa.: Wilkes College, Educational Development, in press.

Steenburger, F. *A practical guide to writing goals and objectives.* San Rafael, Calif.: Academic Therapy Publications, 1973.

Strauss, A., & Kephart, N. *Psychopathology and education of the brain-injured child.* (Vol. III). New York: Grune & Stratton, 1967.

Strauss, A., & Lehtinen, L. *Psychopathology and education of the brain-injured child.* (Vol. I). New York: Grune & Stratton, 1947.

Strauss, A., & Werner, H. Disorders of conceptual thinking in the brain-injured child. *Journal of Nervous & Mental Diseases,* 1942, *96,* 153-172.

Stufflebeam, Daniel L. *Evaluation as enlightenment for decision-making.* Address at working conference on assessment theory, the Commission on Assessment of Educational Outcomes, the Association for Supervision and Curriculum Development, Sarasota, Fla., January 1969.

_____. The relevance of the CIPP evaluation model for educational accountability. Unpublished paper, Ohio State Evaluation Center, 1972.

Stufflebeam, Daniel L., Foley, Walter J., Gephar, William J., Guba, Egon G., Hammond, Robert L., Merriman, Howard O., & Provus, Malcolm M. *Educational evaluation & decision making.* Itasca, Ill.: F. E. Peacock Publishers, Inc., 1971.

Suchman, E. A. Action for What? A Critique of Evaluative Research. In C. H. Weiss (Ed.), *Evaluating action programs.* Boston: Allyn and Bacon, Inc., 1972, 54.

Taylor, E. M. *Psychological assessment of children with cerebral deficits.* Cambridge, Mass.: Harvard University Press, 1961.

Taylor, S. E. Sensation and perception: The complexity of word perception. *Journal of Developmental Reading,* 1963, *6,* 187, 206.

Thomas, D., Becker, W., & Armstrong, M. Production and elimination of disruptive classroom behavior by systematically varying teachers' behavior. *Journal of Applied Behavior Analysis,* 1968, *1,* 35-46.

Thurstone, T. *An evaluation of education of mentally retarded handicapped children in special classes and in regular grades.* Chapel Hill, N.C.: University of North Carolina Press, 1960.

Tyler, R. W. Considerations in selecting objectives. In David A. Payne (Ed.), *Curriculum evaluation.* Lexington, Mass.: D. C. Heath and Company, 1974.

Ullman, L., & Krasner, L. *Case studies in behavior modification.* New York: Holt, Rinehart and Winston, 1965.

Umans, S. *The Management of Education.* New York: Doubleday & Co., Inc. 1971.

Valett, R. E. A social reinforcement technique for the classroom management of behavior disorders. *Exceptional Children*, 1966, *33*, 185-189.

Vaughan, R., & Hodges, L. A statistical survey into a definition of learning disabilities: A search for acceptance. *Journal of Learning Disabilities*, 1973, *6*, 658-664.

Vergason, G. A. Accountability in special education. *Exceptional Children*, February 1973, 367-373.

Vernon, M. I. The perceptual process in reading. *Reading Teacher*, 1959, *13*, 2-8.

Wade, Arnold, & Shertzer, Bruce. Anxiety reduction through vocational counseling. *Vocational Guidance Quarterly*, 1970, *19*, 46-49.

Wadsworth, H. G. A motivational approach toward the remediation of learning disabled boys. *Exceptional Children*, 1971, *38*, 33-42.

Wagner, Hilman. Attitudes of and toward disadvantaged students. *Adolescence*, 1972, *7*, 435-446.

Walle, E. *Learning disabilities and juvenile delinquency.* Paper presented at the International Conference of the Association for Children with Learning Disabilities, Atlantic City, New Jersey, 1972.

Walters, Harvey Eugene, & Krenzler, Gerald D. Early identification of the school dropout. *The School Counselor*, 1970, *18*, 97-104.

Ward, M. & Baker, B. Reinforcement therapy in the classroom. *Journal of Applied Behavior Analysis*, 1968, *1*, 323-328.

Wedell, K. Diagnosing learning difficulties: A sequential strategy. *Journal of Learning Disabilities*, 1970, *3*, 311-317.

Wepman, J. Auditory discrimination, speech, and reading. *Elementary School Journal*, 1960, *60*, 325-333.

Wertheimer, W. Studies in the theory of Gestalt psychology. *Psychologische Forschung*, 1923, *4*.

Wetter, J. Parent attitudes toward learning disabilities. *Exceptional Children*, 1972, *38*, 490-491.

Wheelock, W., & Silvaroli, N. Visual discrimination training for beginning readers. *Reading Teacher*, 1967, *21*, 115-120.

Wiederholt, J. Lee. Historical perspectives on the education of the learning disabled. In L. Mann & D. Sabatino (Eds.), *Second review of special education*. Philadelphia: JSE Press, 1974.

——————————. Planning resource rooms for the mildly handicapped. *Focus on Exceptional Children*, 1974, *5*, 1-10.

Wilson, J. *An investigation of selected aspects of the familial background of learning disability pupils and the effects of a parent training program on selected variables*. Unpublished doctoral dissertation, University of Kansas, 1972.

Wiseman, D. A classroom procedure for identifying and remediating language problems. *Mental Retardation*, 1965, *2*, 21.

Wolf, M., Risley, T., & Mees, H. Application of operant conditioning procedures to the behavior problems of an autistic child. *Behavior Research and Therapy*, 1964, *1*, 305-312.

Wolfe, V. *Wolf's embedded figures test*. United States and International copyright No. A27793, October 1968.

Worden, D., & Snyder, R. Parental tutoring in childhood dyslexia. *Journal of Learning Disabilities*, 1971, *4*, 52.

Yates, J. R. Model for preparing regular classroom teachers for "mainstreaming." *Exceptional Children*, 1973, *39*, 471-472.

Younie, W. J., & Clark, G. M. Personnel training needs for cooperative secondary school programs for mentally retarded youth. *Education and Training of the Mentally Retarded*, 1969, *4*, 184-196.

Ysseldyke, J. E., & Sabatino, D. A. An alternative to self-contained special education classes. *Illinois Education Review,* 1972, *1,* 59-65.

Ysseldyke, J., & Salvia, J. Diagnostic-prescriptive teaching: Two models. *Journal of Exceptional Children,* November 1974, *41,* 181-185.

Zimpelmann, P. *The diagnostic-prescriptive-individualized primary reading program: An introduction.* Louisville, Ky.: Louisville Public Schools, 1974.